UNITED SIR ALE[X] AND ME

UNITED, SIR ALEX AND ME

René Meulensteen

Reach Sport
www.reachsport.com

Reach Sport

www.reachsport.com

Written with Wayne Barton.

Published in Great Britain and Ireland in 2023 by Reach Sport.

www.reachsport.com
@Reach_Sport

Reach Sport is a part of Reach PLC.

Hardback ISBN: 9781914197710
eBook ISBN: 9781914197727

Photographic acknowledgements:
René Meulensteen personal collection, Alamy, Reach Plc.

Cover Design: Rick Cooke
Editing and production: Christine Costello, Harri Aston

Printed and bound by CPI Group (UK) Ltd,
Croydon, CR0 4YY.

I dedicate this book to my wife Marieke and my kids Joppe, Pien, Melle. Their support and understanding has shaped my journey. And to all the passionate Manchester United fans all over the world.

Gratitude, I count my blessings every day.

CONTENTS

AIG

FOREWORD

By Sir Alex Ferguson

'René Meulensteen has his career forged around the one important factor in his life - the ability to influence footballers on their ability to learn, and to give them skills which will make them better'

IN the mid-nineties I received a call from an idol and good friend of mine, Dave Mackay, who was one of the finest footballers Scotland ever produced. Dave was working as a coach in the Middle East and was ready to come back home. As always, Dave was straight to the point and said, "If you're looking for a coach then there is one out here that would be perfect for you." René was the man he was referring to, and his recommendation by Dave meant a lot; so I got René's number and invited him to Old Trafford for an interview.

To give me an idea of the type of work he did, René suggested he could do a training session with our youth players. He did the session and he was impressive. They say timing is everything, and it was at the time when we were spreading our wings extending our youth programme. We had started with Development Centres of 7-12 year-olds which is a precursor before we invite them into our Academy. René fitted the bill perfectly for the role and the development of the kids was obvious within a year.

Our reserve coach at the time was Ricky Sbragia and he had an offer to be assistant manager at Bolton Wanderers. I always encouraged my staff, if they had an inkling to change, as I didn't want them to have any doubts in their mind if they turned a move down. It seemed the easy thing to do was to ask René to move up to the reserves, but in hindsight, I maybe should have kept him with the young kids where he had outstanding success. René did very well with the Reserves and of course he was noticed by other clubs. Brondby FC came hunting so I allowed him to go. It didn't work out for him, so after a few months, he came back – by which time my first-team coach Steve McClaren had left to go to Middlesborough which left an opening in the first team. René filled the position, sharing it with Mick Phelan until I retired in 2013. With my retirement, it cost René and Mick their jobs as David Moyes wanted to bring his own staff.

Since then, René has moved around a lot but wherever he has gone he has helped to improve players to be better, and that is his mantra.

INTRODUCTION

I ACCEPT that for many people, the story of how I worked with Cristiano Ronaldo in the late summer of 2007 will stand out as one of the most memorable highlights of my career as a coach. Personally though, I would say my greatest triumph was achieved over my six years as a first-team coach at Manchester United – we were able to create that sustainability of winning, while playing in an attractive way. We won four league titles in those six years – it could easily have been six. We lost one by one point and one on goal difference.

Of course, I am proud that my work with Cristiano played a part in that success – but so did my work with Rio Ferdinand when he was suspended, and we spent a lot of personal time together. We all had our own personal journeys. Players came from other clubs. Coaches came from all sorts of backgrounds. I began as a skills development coach before I became reserve team coach and then had the opportunity to work individually with senior players. I saw my role as adding the one per cent or two per cent of technical or tactical ability which would help the players make a bigger difference in the game. That role evolved over time where I worked with individuals and then smaller groups – so when the time came for me to become first-team coach, I'd worked with most of the players before, and we were able to create scenarios, plans and patterns in our big group.

When I was working with such a talented group of players, I felt an enormous responsibility to get those sessions right. I have seen other coaches complain that because there are so many games, there is a lack of training time – but I was always of the opinion that regardless of the amount of time we had, that time should be spent well.

Sir Alex Ferguson always used to say that everything we did in training would manifest itself in a game, good and bad. We required world-class performances from those players twice a week and those players needed to rely on world-class support from us. I pride myself on the fact that in six years as first-team coach, not one of those players came to me after a session and complained about it. To be able to constantly hit that level where the players understand the purpose of a session, still feel challenged, and show quality and intensity in a game-realistic way – this preparation was fundamental in feeding their passion and putting them in the best place for the next match.

I'm proud of my work with the individuals, with the group, and around the club as a whole. For example, the influence I had, together with Simon Wells, our video analyst at the time, incorporating video technology into our sessions as well as match preparations. It was an exceptional period of success in Manchester United's history, and it was certainly a period where the unique expertise and quality of different individuals played a significant part.

One of the most beautiful elements of football is that so many people have their own perception and their own preference. Possibly the biggest compliment you can receive as a coach is a sporting acknowledgement from the supporter of a rival team when they tell you they enjoyed watching your team play. So, it follows that you sometimes have to accept that outside point of view, an opinion about certain aspects of your work which are perceived in a certain way because of how successful they were. I accept that the work with Cristiano in 2007 falls into that category, partly because of how successful we were that season and then because of the simple fact that he became such a phenomenal goal scorer.

I have to say there is a bigger picture. It's not as simple as saying that a period in 2007 could just happen by itself. You need the backstory. The backstory with Cristiano went back all the way to the day he arrived at the club as an 18-year-old. I remember Sir Alex nudging me and saying, "We've got a player now. That's a great project for you."

I'd heard the stories – what happened in Lisbon during that pre-season friendly. First impressions don't lie, and he was young and incredible – but raw. At that time, I was doing individual work with Diego Forlan. I was keen to get to know our new young signing. I wanted to know what he was made of. When people have the intrinsic or inherent motivation to do things, they learn and progress much more quickly than someone who has merely been instructed. Diego and I were doing some work after training and Cristiano asked if he could come and join in. "This boy wants to learn," I thought to myself.

Four years later, the boy was a young man with experience playing in the Premier League. He was starting to get a clearer picture of what he wanted to achieve in his career, and he was being talked about as among the best in the world following a remarkable performance against Roma in the Champions League earlier that year. He was an important player for the United team who had just won the Premier League.

In the early part of the season, we played at Portsmouth; the game became a little bad-tempered towards the end and

Cristiano was sent off after getting involved with Richard Hughes. A three-match ban meant he would have to do extra individual training sessions with me on the weekend mornings when the first team was preparing for their game. So, while they were travelling across town to play Manchester City, Cristiano and I were at Carrington. I felt it was a convenient moment because I had wanted to spend some personal time with him to take him from awareness to understanding in certain aspects of his game.

I wanted to work with him specifically to make his skill-set more functional, and, more than anything, improve his finishing. I was keen to make him understand the importance of having aims and targets in life because that puts a greater purpose to what you're doing and, just as importantly, provides direction. He had spoken publicly about his desire to become the best in the world and I felt that goal was achievable with a little more focus.

Before the first session I asked him, "Cristiano, have you set your new targets for the season? How many did you score last season?"

"Twenty-three."

"I would assume you want to be better. So, what do you think?"

"About thirty?"

I asked him if he thought it was realistic. He asked what I thought.

"Well," I told him, "I think you should be finishing around the forty mark."

"That's nearly double," he replied, with a tone of disbelief.

"What are you going to do after training?" I asked. "Apart from showering and getting ready and all that."

"I'll go home."

"So, you're going home," I said. "That's your target. How are you going to get home?"

"By car."

"That's your strategy. Which way are you going to go?"

He explained the roads he would take.

"So, you know exactly the route to take and how to get there," I replied, "and this might sound stupid, but life and football are not that far apart. If you want to score forty goals, we now need to find ways to get there."

I explained to him that I didn't think he'd done any true work on his finishing. I had created a video that was maybe four minutes long and it featured Andy Cole, Dwight Yorke, Teddy Sheringham, Ruud van Nistelrooy and Ole Gunnar Solskjaer scoring goals.

"What did you see?" I asked him after I showed the video.

"A lot of goals."

"No, what did you see? I want you to specifically watch what is happening. How the goals are being scored. Where they are being scored from. Let's look at it again and I'll ask you the question again."

We sat through it again.

"I know what you mean now," he said, "most of them are scored in the box, most with one touch. There's a variety, headers, volleys, tap-ins."

"Perfect," I said, "those three things are what we're going to work on. In the box, one touch, variety. We're going to work to improve your awareness and understanding."

I marked out three zones in front of the goal on a diagram. Zone one gave him the biggest chance of scoring. The goal-keeper would be in the middle of the goal and that gave the chance of scoring in either corner, high or low. I drew lines to represent zone two, from the goal posts towards the corner of the 18-yard box, which represented the angles to goal – analysis showed that most goals are scored from these areas because teams naturally try to defend zone one.

"If you're in zone two," I said, "remember that the goal never moves, but the goalkeeper does." We discussed what would happen with a defender in front of him; how it would be smarter to move towards zone one instead of away from it, because it naturally increased the chances of scoring.

The sessions focused on the service and his positioning. Was it a first-touch finish? A two-touch finish? Is there a defender or no defender? Are you facing the goal or facing away from it? Inside or outside the box? We followed this process. We filmed the sessions and watched them together to analyse the execution.

I felt the journey of awareness to understanding was important for Cristiano because he had always seemed desperate to score the perfect goal. He wanted the moment that would get a 'wow' from the supporters. I told him those goals would come anyway. But it was about the quantity, not the quality.

"The more you score," I said, "the more likely Manchester United are to win. The more important you will be. The more likely it is we will win trophies. The more likely it is you will achieve your goal of becoming the best footballer in the world."

There's a word in Dutch: *bewonderenswaardig*. It means admiration; that you have respect for a certain attitude. To be so young and yet have the conviction and determination to have the clarity of what you want. He was very clear. He wanted to be the best player in the world. He was going to use everything in his power to get there and nothing would stop him.

I know I wasn't the only one to talk to Cristiano. Sir Alex,

Carlos Queiroz and Mick Phelan, for sure, had lengthy conversations with him about the mental aspects of the game. To focus on the right things. To remember that individuals could decide games, but it was teams that won trophies. One can't do it without the other. What happened in the period between 2007 and 2009 was a culmination of all the work done with Cristiano and the benefit was easy to see in the trophy return.

Cristiano started with us as a winger. Wingers are creative players who occasionally convert. Over time, and especially after these sessions, he became more of a converter as he developed an appetite for goals. We identified that he was such a threat and was becoming so difficult to defend against – especially when he was advancing into the second striker position that might be temporarily vacated by Wayne Rooney or Carlos Tevez – that it became necessary to employ this as a part of our strategy.

On occasions we would play him as an out-and-out striker – for example, against Arsenal. We knew he would be a threat running in behind the back four and have the freedom to attack from all areas. My opinion was that he was at his best, or most dangerous, when he was coming from the left and attacking the space in the middle.

For United the result was easy to see. Ronaldo's performances were a huge factor when we won the Premier League and Champions League. It also redefined the way modern forwards played. You might even say that Barcelona followed suit with how Lionel Messi was used from that point; and it had a similarly liberating effect on him, and a devastating impact on his opponents. United are not really credited with the invention of this trend and I'll be honest, it doesn't really bother me – I'm a creative coach, and for me the satisfaction is in the successful execution of an idea. It doesn't matter if we got the credit for it.

Many coaches are pragmatic and insist on the execution of a theory. For me, I liked to look at the individual qualities of whatever 11 players we were going to play, and then work on strategies that maximised their ability as players and as teammates.

In 2007, Cristiano finished second to Kaká of Milan in the Ballon d'Or. Milan, of course, won that year's Champions League. Cristiano won it in 2008 after scoring 42 goals and winning the double with the Premier League. I must admit I felt a personal satisfaction – and yet, still, I just saw it as doing my job.

I would like to think that having that mindset was what made me an effective coach for such a talented group of players. There was satisfaction and fulfilment in jobs well done – whether they be individual accolades or the trophies we won – but never a contentment that it was over or complete. We were making history and I still felt driven by disappointments. We won more often than we lost but I was still motivated by those defeats. If we were beaten to the league, or in Europe – why? How could we improve? These are the feelings when you are in that bubble.

Now, reflecting, I can explain how proud I am to have worked for such a great club under the greatest manager the Premier League has ever seen. To be a part of that success, to contribute to it, it counts for everybody involved in the club at that moment in time. I can accept that working with the players every single day made me an influential figure and I am proud of that also.

Cristiano went on to become the best goal scorer in the history of football. Before 2007 it's probably fair to say he had a scattergun approach to goalscoring.

"You have a counter in your head," I told him. "As soon as you score, that counter starts ticking. You can envision it. You score the first. Forty in a season. Hundred for your club. Two hundred. It keeps ticking. It never stops." I tried to use these metaphors and analogies to get the message through to him. He had it within him – my job as coach was to unlock it to help him realise.

I feel that coaching is nothing else if it is not the pursuit of making people better, or trying to improve them. And there are many aspects in which someone can still improve as long as he wants to.

Cristiano still learns today. He has maintained that attitude. That's how he became the greatest goal scorer in the history of the sport. He understands the need to adapt his game as he gets older and his body changes. He might still look 27, but he's not; and the game has changed slightly. You're not as explosive or as unpredictable as you once were. It's about employing your intelligence to maximise your impact on the game.

When we won the Champions League in 2008, my work was still mostly with the individual players, with Carlos Queiroz taking charge of the training sessions. He was applauded for the work he did on the successful semi-final against Barcelona; defensively we were well-organised. We nullified their threat, although it's fair to say that Barcelona's own game wasn't as fluid as it would be in the years to follow.

If you show teams like that too much respect, they'll take control of the game. It's necessary to cause them problems that they are not used to dealing with; keep asking questions, make them defend. There were some hairy moments in that second leg at Old Trafford – but it worked. It took a fantastic shot from Paul Scholes from outside the box to send us through with a tremendous boost into the final.

As a coach I was watching that tie with two mindsets; the first as someone close to the club, desperate for them to qualify for the final. The second as a coach, wondering what I might do differently if I was in control of the preparation of such a game. Easier said than done as the future would prove to me in the time to come.

That summer Carlos left to become Portugal national team manager. Mick Phelan was promoted to assistant manager, and I was moved into the role of first-team coach. This to me was a huge honour and I had a chat with Sir Alex talking about how we saw the best of Manchester United. We needed to be more on the front foot and have opponents worry about us – play with high energy, pace and pressure. Those were the ingredients that I wanted to implement straight away.

"Let's give that a go," he agreed.

Chapter One

GRASSROOTS FOOTBALL

I WAS 16 when I realised my love of football was about the philosophy of the game and the teaching of it as much as it was about playing. It's strange, isn't it? Sixteen, with your life and career ahead of you. Not least because coaching is a moment where you assume responsibility for the performance of players.

I suppose it's easier for me to set the scene. It was the 1970s in rural Holland. There were no mobile phones. I was at my local football club in my hometown village Beugen, VIOS'38, every day and it was the church tower clock that told me when it was 6pm and time to go home for food. I was a young player for my local team and I couldn't get enough of the game so in the evenings I'd help coach the young kids and watch the first team train.

In Holland, you have teams that go from A to F – A being the U18s and F being the U9s. I'd watch a lot of the teams train when I wasn't training or playing myself in the U18s. One day

I was asked by the coach of the F team if I wanted to help out as he needed an extra pair of hands.

"You're always here," he said, "you might as well."

I found it very enjoyable to engage with those sessions – to start teaching the young kids, and to see them improve as a result. Then, just three weeks after he brought me in to help, the coach left himself. He had full-time work commitments and had to give up football. I was happy to assume the responsibility – and the kids loved it. And honestly, I've been involved in coaching ever since.

I was about 21 when I discovered a book in a nearby village. There, as a new arrival in the shop window, was a book titled *Leerplan Voor De Ideale Voetballer* by Wiel Coerver (the translation is as you would expect). I was intrigued and had to go inside to read it. I flicked through pictures of the likes of Cruyff, Beckenbauer, Charlton, Best and Pele, and little segments with four pictures that would explain a particular technique, move or skill. Little diagrams that would show how to do, for example, the Cruyff turn.

I went back to the start of the book to read the preface and noticed the shop assistants giving me a funny look.

"Are you going to buy it or get out of the shop?"

I had to read it, so I took it with me and devoured it. Wiel's message was, in a nutshell, that all the coaching courses and all the messages from football federations that insisted the game had to be played a certain way were, in fact, a load of rubbish. You just need to look at the best teams and best players in the world.

He felt that he could organise teams defensively – to make them hard to score against – but that he didn't feel he could coach teams to create chances and score goals. He was making statements like this – Ajax were great because of Johan Cruyff,

Manchester United were great because of George Best and Bobby Charlton – and analysing those individual players. He looked at their skill level. He looked at their individual capability to get past players and create the sort of magic they were renowned for – and he wanted to try and articulate, in the most straightforward way he could, how this could be taught for youngsters to try and emulate the great players. He analysed what they did and tried to explain it. That was right up my street. I loved it – I couldn't get enough of it. That mentality stayed with me throughout my entire career, it shaped the way I developed my own philosophy and vision of how I coach players and teach coaches.

It also inspired me to think of things differently in my own coaching. I wanted to try and develop players from a young age in the vision Wiel Coerver had. But I wanted to try and do that in a team, a structure, that played football the way that Cruyff saw it. This was on show throughout the 1970s; the successful Ajax team and the Holland team of 1974 that should have won the World Cup redefined what football was and how it should be played.

It's a great thing that different nations have their own interpretations of the sport. Rinus Michels was an extremely influential coach but let there be no misunderstanding – his philosophy was taken by the Hungary team of 1953 and 1954. Cruyff, as a young pioneer, thought of things that were so innovative they were completely fresh to the game. Previously, right-backs were right-backs. Now they could be attackers. It was the birth of total football; the idea that players could play in multiple positions, that these positions were interchangeable, and the overarching philosophy of dominating the ball.

The early versions of this style were thrilling then, but in the modern game might look ridiculous. There was no real video analysis to study the disorganisation so sometimes it might look like six or seven players chasing for the same ball, 10 attacking all the time.

If opposition coaches had been wiser, it could actually have been quite simple to counter this strategy by just playing clever balls in behind; but for the moment, it was new, and so very impressive. In fact, one of the players who famously played in that system – Wim Suurbier, the right-back – spoke to me about that when he later became my assistant coach. Our objective was to refine that approach for the modern era.

A story, by the way, that you might not know about Wim – he had a contract dispute with Ajax in the mid-70s and for a couple of weeks he actually went to Manchester where he trained at the Cliff when United were managed by Tommy Docherty. Wim was keen to go – and United were keen to sign him – but the English FA had a rule that their clubs couldn't sign foreign players. Wim later went to Schalke. In the 90s, when we were both coaching in Qatar, Tommy came out and we spent some time with him. I really did indulge in the time I spent with Wim to get into the psyche of that great Ajax and Holland team. I wanted to know everything.

"Why were Ajax the best?" I'd ask.

Wim talked about Rinus taking Ajax from being semi-professional to full-time, and the importance that extra training made. Wim spoke of the Hungarian team, and of Johan's intelligence to read the game and contribute his own ideas. But the biggest thing I took from Wim was that the players were so confident in themselves, in their ability, in the strategies they had, that they weren't afraid of anybody. That attitude transferred into the Dutch national team which should have won the World Cup in 1974.

I was in my 30s when Wim and I had those conversations

so you can imagine the satisfaction and indulgence that finally fed that boy of 16 who had grown up watching this fantastic football. I couldn't say it was inevitable that I went into football. I grew up in Beugen, a tiny village with around 1,600 people situated between Venlo, Eindhoven and Nijmegen, and close to the German border.

My exposure to football was in the local amateur scene. My mother always used to tell me that as soon as I could walk, I had a ball at my feet. I was the youngest of seven – four sisters (the eldest two were twins) and two brothers. We lived in an old farmhouse that had plenty of space. We had a goal in the yard and often had friends over; it seemed like my entire youth revolved around playing football there with my brothers and friends.

I was a midfielder. I would say I was more like a Paul Scholes than a Roy Keane. I was quite a smart player. I understood the game. I was good on the ball; a good passer who liked to take a risk. And I could score a goal, most likely from distance. Defending wasn't really my thing, I admit. I would come alive when we had the ball. It became a topic of discussion in training.

"I'm a pro-active defender!" I would say, trying to explain my lack of defensive contribution.

"What does that mean?" was the confused reply.

"Well, when the ball has gone past me and I can't affect it in winning it back and while you guys try and solve the problems at the back, I'll take up a very good attacking position so you can find me in transition when you regain possession." It worked plenty of times at that level.

I was lucky. In our group of friends we had a lot of good players – seriously good. If we had lived closer to one of the bigger cities like Eindhoven, Utrecht or Amsterdam, I am certain that at least one or two would have made it professional. Today a player can advertise themselves online, but back then even traditional scouting was non-existent. If a scout did come to the area, it was to watch the district team, and if one of our players were lucky enough to make the district team, it would usually be one of those from the bigger local teams that would have their attention. It does present a bigger question however – how many great players were lost in this way?

I will say, my own experience was enriched by this because playing alongside those guys made me a much better player today. And I would never complain about the circumstances of my upbringing because I absolutely loved every bit of it.

Our parents were great. They were hardworking. Our father had his own driving school and we all learned to drive with him. We were only allowed lessons if someone had cancelled theirs. He worked in Nijmegen, so we'd get the train in.

"What are you doing here?" he'd ask before the penny dropped that we were there as a substitute student. He'd make us pass in the least possible lessons. I think I only had 10. I was lucky that I passed the first time. Whenever we had our last lesson Dad would tell us to drive home from Nijmegen, a journey of around 30km.

It was warm on that journey and he would end up with one white arm and one brown arm from always having it out the window when the sun was shining. I have very fond memories of those lessons. Dad would whistle as he smoked his cigarettes but could get angry quickly if you were doing something wrong.

I had a strong relationship with my siblings. They were all growing up and having their own lives while I was still the little lad playing football in the backyard. You grow older and the years between you disappear. My eldest sisters Leny and

Gerda, although they were twins, did not look like each other at all. Gerda was a very good volleyball player and a teacher with unbelievably neat handwriting. She unfortunately passed away when she was just 50. Leny, all her life, worked as a nurse in an elderly home. My brother Theo was a good amateur player – a left-footer with a good shot and vision. He made his career in accountancy and numbers. My sister Anita was a lovely girl, such a caring soul, but again, tragically she passed away when she was just 40, after a battle with breast cancer. To see our parents outlive one of their children was a strange and traumatic experience. My other sister, Elize, was also a great volleyball player, keeping that sporting theme running through the family. My brother Cor, who is a couple of years older than me, went into the police force and he's very passionate and determined about his vocation. He too was a great footballer, in the Roy Keane mould, and I always felt he could have been a professional if he'd wanted to.

In fact, I talk about being 16 at my local club as the moment where my love for coaching started. But I'm sure you can trace some of it back to being in that backyard with my brothers and friends, the love of building strong relationships on the pitch and understanding the game of another player to develop that connection. I had a telepathic bond with my brothers, and was always intrigued as to how that same bond could be cultivated with players through good coaching.

Dad was a local footballer too. He loved the sport. Unlike him, though, I'd always pictured that my life would involve football as my profession. I didn't really have any other ambitions that I felt I was studying towards. I was creative, I enjoyed art class, I was good at sports, I was good at languages and enjoyed studying history. Generally, I was academically okay. I knew it would be difficult to become a professional footballer, and I knew that without that, it would be near impossible to get on the UEFA Pro Licence courses for coaching in Holland. There was such a high demand and spaces for these courses generally went to people who were sportspeople at a high level or from a privileged background.

It forced me to try and find a solution. I looked at the modules on various courses. I wanted to further my study in physical education and the most relevant educational path available to me was to study to become a teacher in a primary school. I didn't want to do that, but I knew by doing the course, I could get the certificate that would stand me a better chance of getting into the sporting academies. At the same time, I was taking as many coaching badges as I could. That only got me so far and eventually I spent a year and a half on this teaching course that I was starting to feel was a complete waste of my time, as one of the ministers changed the modules and took the certificate of physical education away.

The instructors on the course tried to reassure me I'd be a good teacher – but that wasn't the point. I quit the course and started to work for my uncle who had a frozen dough product factory. It wasn't a great job, but I needed time and a little bit of money to consider my options and next step. I felt the best option was to try and get as far up the ladder as a player as I could. My team in Beugen was called VIOS'38 and if you would describe them as bottom of the footballing ladder, I felt I had enough quality to at least try to play for a team which would be the equivalent of League One or League Two in England.

I achieved some progress by joining RKVV Volharding, Vierlingsbeek, who played two divisions higher, for a few years. It was an important time for me, as it was at that club where I met Peter Jansen, the coach at the time. Peter was as convinced about Coerver and skill development as I was. And on certain days of the week, we would go out to a field close to his house to practise all those moves and turns.

After that I went back for a short spell to VIOS'38 before moving on to de Treffers in Groesbeek, which was effectively League Two level. It was a strong semi-professional standard – Jan Peters, ex-professional and ex-international, for AZ '67 Alkmaar, who won the Dutch league in 1980-1981, was also on my team. He scored two famous goals at Wembley in 1977. That year we ended up winning the Dutch National Amateur Championship for the Hoofdklasse, which was the name for the third tier of Dutch football.

Whilst at de Treffers, I hardly played in my preferred position in midfield. I was asked to play full-back or centre-back, next to Willy Willems, our captain, who was the Dutch equivalent of Steve Bruce! The strongholder and a no-nonsense defender of the first team.

Sure, I said, I'll do the job, although I saw myself more as a link player. But I did enjoy playing for de Treffers as we had plenty of other fantastic players in the team and we were always challenging for the championship. I imagine that my coaches felt I was a bit of a clever bugger; I never took anything for granted just because someone said something. I always wanted to question things. To understand why.

All the while I was taking courses and working. I applied for the course Trainer Coach One, which allows you to be an assistant coach at a professional level. I was knocked back by the KNVB.

I was given a number for Anton Brouwer by one of my fellow students. Anton was the Director at the Central Institute of Sports, (CIOS, Arnhem) and requested a meeting to explain my situation. I remember how determined I was in wanting to get that meeting as I said to him over the phone,

"Hi Anton, I know you're a very busy man, but you tell me the time and place and I'll be there, I only need thirty minutes of your time."

I discussed how I'd tried everything I could, and I'd taken all the necessary steps to help myself, but I was finding every door being locked.

"I will open that door for you," Anton told me simply..

To this day I am very grateful to Anton for giving me that opportunity. I also feel a lot of gratitude towards Ton de Hoop, who was the docent for Football and Coaching and Ben Halle, the Marketing and Management teacher, two people who supported me all the way through my time at the CIOS.

I was 27 on the course with 18 and 19-year-old boys and girls who wanted to pursue their careers in sport. The first year was a general introduction, one where you must do everything you're told. Gymnastics, athletics – everything, before you specialise in certain topics. Fortunately, I was told by Anton that because of my age and previous education that wouldn't be necessary for me. My subjects were football & coaching, strength and conditioning, sport and management, marketing, and management.

For my final assignment to finish the course, I had to create a project – it just so happened that the same project which would help me earn my certificate acted as my gateway into the professional game. I saw it as an opportunity to kill two birds with one stone. I wanted to create something that would guarantee that I would pass the course, but I wanted to also use that same moment to make something that I could use again for my overarching goal.

I decided to make a video showcasing training techniques using the Coerver method under my interpretation of it. At the time, while I was attending the CIOS, Arnhem, I was also coaching the U14s at NEC Nijmegen and I could use that group of boys, effectively recording the sessions we were doing anyway. I borrowed 10,000 Dutch guilder from my brother Theo (which I am still grateful for), the equivalent of £3,500, to hire a professional videographer; I constructed a storyboard of how I wanted it to go.

I talked about how the very top footballers have the skill level to dominate the 1v1 situations and influence games and how Coerver had picked up on it and created a strategy. I wanted to show it in practice with the sessions; ball manipulations, 1v1s, small-sided games and so on. The video was around twenty minutes in length, and I concluded it with a comparison to some of the top players of the time – for instance, Romario, who was at PSV Eindhoven. It took me hours to edit the video and get the right text for the voice over to go with it. But it was all worthwhile.

There is a saying – luck is what happens when preparation meets opportunity. After my team, the U14s at NEC, had played their game on a Saturday, I would go and watch the U18s. There was a game close to the end of the season – we'd won 9-3, and as I was watching the older boys, one of the parents of the boys I coached walked up to me on the sideline. He was enthusiastically praising me about the match, how the team played and how he'd noted a clear progression in his son over the season. I mentioned my frustration with the KNVB and how they didn't seem to adopt this approach through the national system, especially considering how complementary it was to Cruyff's vision.

Suddenly another man – a big, tall moustached man stood next to us – interrupted and said, "Excuse me, but who do you think you are to make such a statement?"

I introduced myself as the coach of U14s and explained it

wasn't really a statement, just a matter of what I believed in. He pushed further and at half-time we continued the conversation. I told him my entire story going back to seeing Wiel's book in the store.

"Well," he said, "I am Johan Derksen, and I wrote the preface to that book. I am fully behind his method and fully behind your statements." Johan was the chief editor of the most influential Dutch football magazine; *Voetbal International*. To this day he is a very well-known TV pundit in several talk shows in Holland.

I told him about my video, and he said once it was finished, I was to show it to him. I went to see him in Gouda, at the headquarter office of *Voetbal International*, with the tape and politely asked if he could either suggest improvements or send it to Wiel if he felt it was right to do so. He rang me the morning and told me he'd watched it three times.

"I am sure Wiel wants to do something with this," he said. A few years later, whilst I was managing Al-Ittihad in Qatar, Johan would help me to secure the services of Wim Suurbier, the ex-Ajax and Dutch National team player, as my assistant.

Within weeks of that initial conversation, I was contacted by the secretary at NEC. She said that Wiel had telephoned them to ask for me. She passed on his number.

Towards the end of a season and during the summer, I would often go to America to coach young boys and girls for the Midwest Soccer Academy owned by a Dutch guy, Klaas de Boer, who emigrated there in the 50s. One day I was travelling together with Klaas to another camp location in one of those yellow hire vans with all the equipment. He knew that I was big on skill development as I was implementing it during his camps and the progression of the kids I was working with was clear to see.

It was during that trip I said to Klaas, "Believe me Klaas, one day I will be working for a big club."

Klaas laughed out loud, but years later when he saw me on television when I was working alongside Sir Alex Ferguson as the first-team coach for Manchester United, he was dead proud. I would also help him with coaching groups of young players who came over from the USA for Soccer Camps in Holland.

Coincidentally, those players were going to be based near Wiel this summer, so when I made that call to Wiel, I used that as an introduction. He sounded somewhat impressed with the tape and we arranged to meet at a small pub near a train station close to where he lived.

So there I was, finally having a conversation with the man whose philosophies I'd adopted as my own. Wiel was in his late 60s and the initial impression I got from him was that he was sceptical and apprehensive. It seemed to take a while to break the ice with him. We got there eventually. He asked what my intentions were and I told him I wanted to go to England and do a course there to continue my development as a coach.

"Why would you want to do that?" Wiel scolded, and this was the voice of experience. Here was a man who had been invited by the FA and Bobby Robson to undertake some courses but had found the process difficult for many reasons.

At the heart of it was the idea that Wiel believed so strongly in his methods that there was a conflict with the way other courses were taught. I tried to explain that I was a true disciple of his method but to influence other cultures, first you must understand where they are coming from. He could understand.

I would later meet Bobby Robson myself when I was coaching in Qatar. Alan Jones, who was the coach of Al Shamal in Qatar, knew that Bobby was going to join PSV for a second spell.

"He should take you with him," Alan said, and reached out to Bobby to see if he would meet me. Bobby agreed. It must have been somewhere in December in 1998 when I went to meet him at the PSV training ground, De Herdgang. When I walked into the clubhouse, Bobby was still engaged with someone and I politely waited until he was finished. I always had a lot of respect for Bobby as he was a true gentleman in every way he presented himself.

"Bloody mobile phone," he mumbled when he came to see me.

I asked what the problem was and he said this guy had been trying to explain how this mobile phone works, but he hadn't got a clue.

"It's actually quite simple Mr Robson," I replied. "You see that button with the little green phone?"

"Yes."

"Well if someone rings you, your mobile will make a sound and you press that button and say 'Hello Bobby here' and you will hear the person who is ringing you. When you're finished talking press the button with the red phone and that will end the conversation. Now if you have numbers you tend to ring regularly, then you save them with the button which has the icon of a phonebook. Job done."

"Bloody hell René, it took you five minutes to explain that, thanks."

Obviously, we spoke a lot about football. His career, my career and PSV but it proved to be difficult for him to bring me in as he had only signed a one year contract at PSV.

"But I am sure you will be an asset to every club you work for in the future," he said. He also spoke about how keen he was to one day manage his big love Newcastle United, which he did after PSV. Before I left I said: "There is another interesting thing about us, Mr Robson."

"Oh yes, what is it?"

"Well your date of birth is 18 February 1933. Nothing special that I know this as you can find it on the internet. However it's the same birthday as my mother! So, do you know the moral of this story?"

"No?"

"Well, you could've been my mother!" I said, smiling from ear to ear. Bobby laughed and wished me well. Years later when I was already working at Manchester United, I met him again, as he was one of the guest speakers at the Pro Licence at Warwick University. I bumped into him in the lobby and he remembered me vividly.

"Well it worked out nicely for you René, but I should have taken you to Newcastle."

"Too late now," I replied.

During his talk he referred to an incident he had to deal with whilst being the manager of Barcelona, when Ronaldo stayed away in Rio for the carnival for a few days longer than expected. The knives were out and every media outlet in Spain was looking at Bobby Robson, how he was going to deal with his star striker.

In a packed out press conference Bobby said, "Well it looked like Ronaldo really enjoyed himself in Rio according to the pictures I saw. Next year I will be giving him 10 days off and I will be going with him." It was so funny and a masterstroke from him as a manager.

Shortly after that meeting with Wiel in Sittard in the south of Holland, I took my American players to compete in a tournament in Groningen near the north of the country, where I spent time with the other Dutchman whose ideals of football I admired. I am of course talking about Johan Cruyff.

I knew Barcelona were in a training camp in the area, so

I arranged to go and watch one of their sessions. I got the attention of Johan's assistant, Tonny Bruins Slot. I had a chat with him and told him why I was there. I mentioned where we were staying, and he said they had been going in there for a drink after the evening training sometimes.

"Are you going in there tonight?" I asked. He said yes, so I asked if he would mind bringing a signed Barcelona shirt for the players.

Back at the hotel, I spoke to the other coaches about the exchange, and they didn't believe me. Sure enough, although it was quite late that evening, Johan, Tonny and Manuel, the kit man, arrived. I remember the bar quite vividly – it had a giant car wheel in the middle that was holding the lights. Tonny saw me, waved and came over. I had an incredible conversation with Johan.

There was a crazy atmosphere in the bar that evening – everyone was having a sing-song and Johan kept pulling the wheel back and letting it go, and each time it narrowly missed Manuel. It would have knocked him out. I was crying with laughter.

Naturally, I remember that conversation with Johan. He talked about football as a simple game, with the aim being to score goals and to not concede them. The essence of the game is where you place the emphasis and the intent. To score goals is exciting. To be defensive is boring. One makes the crowd excited; another turns them away.

At the time he was playing with a 3-4-3, the midfield as a diamond. Everything was geared towards creating situations where you can find an extra man in the build-up, breaking the lines, and getting the ball to the likes of Laudrup and Stoichkov.

I told him I was a student of Coerver and of his own philosophy, and how I felt combining the two could have an incredible result. If we could create youngsters who were technically proficient, the only thing they would need was Johan's philosophy to play the game.

Chapter Two

"NOW DO IT WITH SPEED!"

IT was a summer of indulgent education for me with two of my holistic idols before some actual further practical education. At the start of the following season, in the summer of 1993, I signed on to a course in Lilleshall, England. I stayed on the premises there and the first course was an international preliminary course with around 25 other coaches. I think there must have been 20 different nationalities – it was brilliant. I'd already done my youth level coaching at levels one, two and three in Holland, so this course was pretty straightforward for me – it was just the basics.

English football was still trying to get out of the Charles Hughes era. Hughes wrote *The Winning Formula*, a coaching book that we can say had some conflict with the Coerver method. English football had something of a reputation for being 4-4-2 and long-ball and there was a historical feeling of resistance to continental methods. I would say my experience was different.

I met people who were open to different ideas. There were some great people and great teachers among these coaches. David Burnside was one – a lovely guy and an excellent tutor with a great sense of humour. Dave Sexton, the former Manchester United manager, was a prominent figure. I was a young coach, whilst he had a lot of experience and it was interesting to talk to him. I didn't have too many conversations with him, but he was a very impressive person with great knowledge about the game and coaching.

The one thing about the English coaching methods I disagreed with was the preferred 'stop, stand still' approach where sessions would be stopped to analyse what was going wrong. I, on the other hand, was more used to highlighting what was going well in sessions. The problem with this was that you had to coach in this 'stop, stand still' way to pass the course, and to show you understood. Even if you didn't believe in the same methods, you always stood to benefit from the experience of learning more about different approaches.

It became clear that ideology was one side of it and personality was another. You must be able to use different styles. It became apparent to me that part of coaching is to be versatile, to almost be like an actor where you must present yourself in a certain way during training to achieve your goals and to maximise the outcome of a session. For example, if you want to coach a high-pressing game, your voice and demeanour has to reflect that in the way you coach and instruct the players. In this case, I would be quite aggressive and loud. Whereas if you want to coach calmness on the ball in possession, my approach would be reflecting that; calm and reassuring.

To make sure I always got the best from my sessions, I always used a roadmap for training. The question I would ask myself after every session was: "Have I given the players the opportunity to become better players or have I given the team the opportunity to become a better team?"

So what does that roadmap for training look like?

When I am coaching young players, let's say between the ages of six and 12, I would always let them play at the start of the session. Any small-sided game where the kids can release their energy and excitement. This would only be around eight to 10 minutes. Thereafter, they are more receptive and responsive to what you want to do in training. Plus, whilst you observe these free-flowing, small-sided games, you might see something that you're planning to focus on in training anyway.

For me, as a coach, it is important that you have a clear objective to what you want to achieve during a session. That objective stems from your analysis in relation to the long, medium and short term. Then you must be able to facilitate the correct drill, exercise or game in the right area and with the right number of players whereby repetition is key, otherwise players will not be able to learn and implement what you want them to.

To deliver the key coaching messages you have the tools to tell (audio) the players what to do. To show (visual) them what to do and of course let them try it themselves (kinaesthetic). At the start of every exercise or game I would stand back for a few minutes and observe to see if the players understood what to do. If they don't, I would stop the drill and explain again exactly the drill is about. If the players understand what to do, it's important to highlight and praise good play. Positive coaching and reinforcement has by far a bigger impact than telling the players constantly what is going wrong.

As Sir Alex would say to me: "'Well done' are the two most important coaching words during training." The better the players and the higher the level, the more I would challenge them by making sure there was a clear progression in the session.

Some players turn up every morning not knowing what the training would be about. Wayne Rooney, however, would always walk up to me before training and ask, “What are we doing today René?” He was always keen to know. I also made sure that there was no time lost before or during training by letting one exercise or game flow into the next with the least possible disruption of setting up the next organisation.

Back to Lilleshall. I hadn't been there long when my girlfriend, now wife, Marieke, telephoned me, as there were no mobile phones then, to say Wiel had been in touch. I contacted him and he said he had been offered a position in Qatar and he wanted me to go with him as his assistant.

My course ended in August and before long I was on a plane to join him. The video had proven to be a wise investment. I did return to Lilleshall to do my other badges in the following years, such as the UEFA A course and the Pro Licence, but by then I was at Manchester United.

A natural question for you to ask at this point, as I discuss the historical approaches British football took to its own development, is why, if Wiel's methods were so convincing, did the KNVB not adopt them? Why did he have to go out to the Middle East?

The first thing to tell you about Wiel is that he was a very strong-minded individual. He was not the easiest person to deal with. He talked to people at the KNVB and tried to convince them that his philosophy would transform Dutch football if we developed more technical coaches. Sometimes it's all about how you convey the message; if you don't deliver it in the most diplomatic way, or even a way that's receptive to the person you're talking to, you can run into strong resistance. That's what happened with Wiel and we found ourselves as outcasts. He was bitter about it and I could understand why. He resolved to go to a country where football was effectively non-existent and prove himself in that environment.

It was an interesting time. Obviously, it wasn't the first time I'd left my homeland, but the first time I'd done so to work for any extended period, and of course the prospect of working closely with Wiel was an added bonus. It was September 1993, two years before the coup d'état. Qatar was not what it is now. As my flight approached the runway, the only thing I could see was sand. Everything felt so unfamiliar as I disembarked the plane and saw all the natives wearing their traditional clothing – until suddenly, I heard a voice I recognised.

"René, René."

Wiel was sticking his head out of a little window and telling people to get me through and fill all the visa forms. We stayed at the Ramada Hotel; Wiel had me up at 6am for the half-hour walk to the Al Arabi stadium. It was already 25 degrees.

When we finally got there, everything was locked up – but these were open build stadiums, and the walls were not so high, so Wiel had the smart idea to get a leg up over the wall. He had two balls in a bag and threw them over, then instructed me to lift this almost 70-year-old man up and over the wall. Great – now what about me? I had to walk all the way around until I found a railing, I was just about able to squeeze through.

Training was just him and me. Wiel also wanted to film some more videos of different sessions. We filmed sequences of exercises and made a video called *The Creative Dribbler*, which was based on skill development and functionality. But this first morning, he was testing to see if I really and truly understood what he wanted. Could I do the various moves and turns? The step-overs? I had to sweat my arse off every morning doing this – and then after doing that for 30 minutes he'd say, "Okay, great, now do it with speed!"

Mornings were spent doing this routine and afternoon sessions would be spent with the local youngsters. He put me through terror – but I convinced him. He told me I had to try and invent new moves, which I did, and he seemed somewhat surprised, as he thought that it was impossible. At breakfast he would take seeds from a melon and arrange them on the table into formations.

"Let's say we've got eight players," he'd start and then he'd create these structured patterns that we would organise and repeat. We'd set up players in pairs or in groups of three, four, five or six and arrange triangles, diamonds, squares and think about different skill and passing exercises whereby it all revolved around repetition whilst creating and filling spaces. Some exercises were so complicated, but we managed to get them all working into practice, and I admit sometimes I would think to myself, "How the hell did that work?"

We were creating situations where these kids constantly needed to think and find solutions for themselves and subconsciously, we were developing pro-active players. All those skills and passing drills would then lead into 1v1s, 2v2s, 3v3s and 4v4s. We would also have them playing a lot of 2v1, 3v2 and 4v3 whereby the players automatically had a decision to make whether to dribble or pass to a free player.

It was an indulgence for me. What I was most impressed with from working so closely with Wiel was the uniqueness of his new ideas and I knew that understanding where he was coming from was the key to unlocking even more new ideas.

I wrote down all these challenging exercises and sessions and even developed a specific way in doing that, so other coaches could understand them as well. He had been a successful manager in his time even though he confessed to me that he felt he had been blessed with top players – and that he couldn't give his star attacking talent anything more in terms of weaponry. It was in acknowledging this and looking at similar patterns with the top coaches across Europe that led him to conduct and build his strategy.

He looked at the elite attackers and how they moved; how the top defenders would try to stop them. He would write these moves down and teach them to kids and try to find new ways to attack or defend. To perfect the talent, he emphasised the importance of repetition. You have two choices – do you go with a structured approach, or do you favour the free-flowing nature of a game, knowing that in a match, it's all about the kids trying to do the skills they've learned in game situations? Nothing is right or wrong, good or bad, it's a matter of creating the right training environment, whereby kids learn new skills and have opportunities to implement them into various small-sided games.

Our way was to go from our structured environment with repetition, into small-sided matches, expecting this would improve and assist those instinctive moments in a bigger game. The objective was to make a player competent and confident in his approach to dominating a 1v1 situation. Making the right decision and being unpredictable whilst doing so.

To achieve that they need to be smart in their passing – when to hold and when to release – or when to go on the dribble. If you don't have the tools to do that then your opponent knows you're going to have to pass it. We wanted to equip as many players as possible with the power of this unpredictability. The fundamental principles of our development plan stem from the analysis of the key qualities in 11v11 games of the best teams in the world, which I will come back to later in this book. One of those key qualities is that those teams have the best players and players who are world class.

I analysed the best players past and present. Defenders like Franz Beckenbauer, Baresi, Maldini, Stam, midfield players such as Bobby Charlton, Platini, Xavi, Modric and forwards like Pele, Maradona, Cruyff, Best, van Basten. They're all exceptional players who are tactically very good. Physically, very well-equipped. Mentally, very strong, and technically they have high ability levels both in their basic skills such as passing, receiving, shooting, and heading, as well as the ability to dominate the 1v1 situation. To enhance this player profile overview, I colour-coded them; tactic has the colour yellow, physicality is red, mentality is blue and technicality is green. Now we know why those players were so good, we also know what to develop in young players. The key is to emphasise the right things in the different ages and stages to maximise player development.

I call them 'Windows of Development'. In each window the players add to their development but it's crucial the kids get exposed to the right things at the right time.

The first window is at home, whereby the parents play an important role to introduce the young kid to a ball. Like kids learn a letter first, then to read a sentence and thereafter a story, after which they learn to understand what they read. It's the same with skill development.

The road I follow is from technique into skill into strategy. Firstly, it all starts for young kids with ball familiarisation, through ball manipulation and fast feet drills. These are drills where the kids are touching the ball in a small space by tippy-tappy touches where different moves are combined.

This type of drill should be introduced at home as it is a

great way to make young children fall in love with the ball. It's important that the coaches can demonstrate and teach the kids all those different techniques in an environment where the kids have lots of fun, learn new things and try them in small-sided games.

Then you get the entry window from about six to nine where kids join a football club and receive their first coaching. Ideally all focused on skill development during these early years.

This is followed by the third window, the so-called 'golden age' window from 10 to 13-year-olds. This is the best age and stage for kids to become excellent at certain moves and turns and use them in all the different small-sided games. A technique becomes a skill if a player can execute it under game-realistic pressures such as time and space. But also when he or she gets challenged by an opponent. In this phase the coaches must encourage the players to take initiative and be creative and confident in the various small-sided and bigger games. Around the age of 12, the identity of the player will become clear, as well as the preference of what position they like to play.

The fourth window, for 14 to 16-year-olds, marks a period where a lot of players are unsettled. Here is where you see early and late developers and a lot of differences between the maturity of players. When they start to become more familiar with their position in 11v11 games, it's important that they have coaches who can turn that skill into strategy. In other words, can they help the players – do they know when to pass, or when, how and what type of skill to use in any 1v1 situation on the pitch?

In the fifth window, players are becoming young men, and everything is geared around player development in a team setting.

In the last and sixth window the players make the transition from junior to senior players, an important time whereby players follow different paths to fulfil their potential.

Some players are ready at 18 or 19 years of age. Other ones get there at 22 or 23. At any age level, coaches must understand that the development of players is key rather than winning at all costs. It saddens me to say, but this misunderstanding unfortunately still happens a lot.

We had some success and I could see instant improvement in the players. It was an immediate vindication in the decision to move away from the KNVB and the reasons for why it was necessary; in many established football associations there are regimented and established ways of doing things and decisions for change can quickly become political.

For example – professional players will always be given preference to get on the Pro License as opposed to someone who never played at pro level. But being a player and being a coach are two completely different things; it's like a horse and a jockey. You might be the best player in the world but the worst coach in the world. The number of elite coaches who weren't great players and vice versa proves that.

I have to say – and it does not please me to say it, but it is a fact nonetheless – that everything I achieved on my own path in the sport owed nothing to Dutch football and the KNVB, aside from possibly the reputation Dutch football had in the world.

The Qatari FA had a very ambitious president – Mohammed bin Hammam. His vision was good, and he wanted to strengthen grassroots football in the region as it was practically non-existent at U14 level. In Qatar, things were quite easy to organise as it was a small country with only about eight professional clubs, and everything revolved around Doha.

We worked with different age levels – U11, U10, U9 and U8 and organised a festival every month where we'd have the younger players play in 4v4 games and the older ones in 6v6 and 8v8 games. We would invite coaches from the clubs to observe – but we'd also be working with them on a regular basis as well to try and improve skills development at their clubs. Of course, not everyone was proficient with picking up skills, from the players to the coaches, but just about everybody embraced it because they saw the progression and the enjoyment. It was clear that our structure was working.

Wiel and I took some of the best players back to Holland to film our videos. We played against local professional clubs and our boys blew them out of the water. The scores were embarrassing. The only thing we told our players was to express themselves and enjoy the game. "If the pass is on, fine, but go at them – we know you can beat them." Before we'd taken them to Europe, we'd split the boys into two groups at our local festivals.

We wanted them to be prepared to compete against different approaches so I said I'd ask my group of players to concentrate more on passing the ball and Wiel would place the emphasis on attacking in 1v1s and passing when players were in better positions. It was a successful strategy that we deployed back home whilst playing games against Dutch opposition.

Wiel and I worked together for over three years before he was invited back to the UAE. He became a little frustrated in Qatar and asked me if I would go with him – the idea was that we would work for different clubs. It didn't sit right with me. I felt we were letting the Qatari FA down and eventually I convinced Wiel that it was better for me to stay there, otherwise we were effectively throwing away all that work we had done. He agreed that was a good idea.

It was around this time I had the fortune to meet the

legendary Dave Mackay. Dave proved to play a very important role in my life. Dave was the manager of the Qatar national U17 team and had an assistant, George Blues. George was a nice guy and a great chef. He learned that trait whilst playing in Australia where there was a big Italian influence in the club. In all honesty, George made the best lasagna in the world! We all lived in apartments close to one another. Every night we'd have a meal and a game of dominoes together. Dave would lock the door and say jokingly, "Nobody is leaving until I have won." Dave's stories were unbelievable. He would entertain with his tales of winning with Spurs and managing Derby County. Dave offered me the chance to do some work with him with the U17s and I agreed.

Sometime later, I was given the opportunity to coach Al-Ittihad (now Al-Gharafa), and that was the first opportunity for me to see how I could transfer my coaching ideals into senior football. I took over as head coach maybe three or four weeks before the Arab Cup – this is a tournament that doesn't exist anymore but was effectively the same as the Europa League. It was a big trophy and took place over two weeks in Kuwait. Against all odds and against all expectations we did very well.

The job offer at Al-Ittihad had come around because their coach, Džemal Hadžiabdić, had been hired as the Qatar national team coach after he enjoyed success at club level. Džemal, though, had the demeanour of someone carrying the weight of the world on his shoulders – and his team played with this personality too. They were a little dour, defensive, but well capable of winning games 1-0. The squad had all the ingredients necessary to play a more progressive style of football and the message I told them straight away is that I wanted them to play 25 metres higher up the pitch and play a more expansive type of football. The players really bought into it.

We had a hell of a tournament. Before a ball had been kicked, at the first-team meeting after we landed in Kuwait, I asked the players to put their hand up if they believed they could win. I put my hand up and I was the only one.

"If I didn't believe I could win, I should not be here," I told them. "My job is to make you guys believe, to make you convinced, that we can win."

We won our first two group matches comfortably, 4-1 and 3-1, meaning we could afford to draw the last game to qualify for the semi-final. In the run-up to that we included some focus on the added factors of a knock-out game. What do we do if it gets to extra time?

At the time the golden goal rule was still in effect and this increased jeopardy would significantly impact the game as a spectacle. It could become too cautious with neither side wanting to lose. I instructed my players that if we were in that position – as, it turned out, we were, against Al-Masry – that we must go for the throat. We also prepared for penalties, making sure we had a sequence prepared and that there would be no doubt about how we would approach it. I wanted to make sure the players knew I was taking that responsibility and I told them that if they did miss, it was not a problem. I wanted to remove the burden.

As we went into extra time, I told the players to look over at the Al-Masry lads. Their coach was remonstrating. We were calm. I reminded my boys of the plan. Going for it meant a slight change of shape. The wingers would push higher and wider. Two strikers. Put balls into the box. Push players high, so that when the balls come out, they're there to pick up the pieces. Get the ball wide as quick as we can. In the first 10 minutes of extra-time, we had seven balls in the box. Seven. The seventh was met by the head of Akwa, one of our forwards

– he cushioned it down for Mujeeb to fire into the top corner from the edge of the box. That was it. Boom. Golden goal and game over.

I felt a strong sense of vindication that I had painted a picture of what might happen for these players if we tried these strategies. They clearly felt it was going well. In the meeting before the final, I asked them the same question.

"Who believes we can win the cup?"

Every hand went up. Except for mine. I told the players that everything that had already happened was now unimportant. What we had to concentrate on was our organisation and our discipline. Prepare to take advantage of the key moments and opportunities. I told them that I felt the team who wanted it more, and showed that through the quality of their play, would win the trophy.

We were 1-0 up at half-time against the Syrian side Al-Jaish.

We were playing at the Mohammed Al-Hamad Stadium, the home of Al Qadsiah, the most successful club in Kuwait. As you walk to and from the changing rooms you have to pass through the trophy rooms; so as we were walking back in for our half-time talk, the players walked through this room to get to our dressing room. It was full of people who I had never seen and presumed were from the director's box. There was a bubbly atmosphere and to be fair, my players were feeling that way too. But it was too much, and I asked Majed Al Khelaifi, our team manager, if they could clear the room.

Majed was very important to me as he had a clear understanding about the game, how I wanted to play and of course the Qatari players. We worked very well together. Time was ticking. I stayed out until the coast was clear so there might be enough time for the players to wonder where I was. I picked one of the trophies up and walked into the dressing room, which was now quiet. I approached our captain and asked him to take the trophy. He did.

"How does it feel?"

"Great."

"What do you think they're talking about? They'll be saying how we have the momentum, but if we lose focus for just a moment, they can get an equaliser. Then who has it?"

I snatched the trophy from his hands.

"That's how quickly it can go," I told the group, "If we're not on the ball for the next forty-five minutes plus."

I told him to hold the trophy and to not let go of it. I made a play about trying to pull it off him – and the point was made. I told the players now their responsibility was to defend that trophy because it was theirs. I told them we had two objectives: keep a clean sheet and score another goal. I ended up with only six minutes to talk to them – but within that six minutes I had them right back in the headspace I needed them.

Our second goal was unbelievable. If Ronaldo or Messi had scored it, they'd talk about it today – there was a long ball over the top, our player Frank Sitora controlled it beautifully and finished it with the same level of finesse. That was just after the hour mark, and of course, we were able to hold on – it was one of the first major Qatari club achievements in foreign competition, so it was a major moment for us, and for me.

The Qatari FA was good to me as they allowed me to do both jobs. I was still in charge of the U17s and coordinating the strategy in the lower age groups. But the success I was feeling with that structure, and then the instant success I'd enjoyed with Al-Ittihad, immediately gave me a strong curiosity about how these same methods would translate with better players at both junior and senior level.

I discovered that Franz Beckenbauer was coming over to Qatar to lobby for votes to host the 2006 World Cup. I was keen to meet up with him, so I found out what hotel he was staying in. When I went to the Doha Sheraton in the morning, he was sat having a coffee. I felt confident enough to introduce myself as I spoke fluent German. I started to talk to him and he stopped me.

"The Sheikh will be here in five minutes," he said.

I joked that it must be his first time there, as people in Qatar don't tend to be very punctual. I asked if it would be okay if I talked to him while he waited and had his coffee, and if the Sheikh was five minutes or 50 minutes then I'd be out of his hair. I talked to him about what we were doing – we talked for an hour. He seemed interested. I explained we were holding a session in the afternoon and invited him to come and see, as I was of the belief that these were the sort of sessions we should be holding at academy level, at the big clubs back in Europe. I felt there was an opportunity to utilise a link there – Coerver Coaching was always sponsored by Adidas, who also had close links with Bayern Munich.

Franz agreed to come. I still have the picture of us standing on the pitch in the old Doha stadium. I made sure the session consisted of three parts; skills development, 1v1 scenarios and small-sided games, and then finally into an 8v8, so he could see the difference in touch, repetition, intent and success. Franz was only supposed to stay for 15 minutes but he stayed for the full hour and was engaged as I walked him through what I was doing and why I was doing it.

At the end of it all, Franz invited me and Wiel to Germany where I would have presumed the intention would have been to implement this sort of system at Bayern Munich. Before this, I reached out to the guy I knew from Adidas and for some reason, he completely shut the door on the whole thing. Franz came back to Qatar a few months later and I went to the hotel again to see him. This time Wim Suurbier, my assistant, who played against Beckenbauer in the 1974 final, was with me.

"Do you remember me?" I asked.

"You were supposed to ring me!" was his reply.

I told him how I'd tried. An opportunity missed, but I was not to be deterred. By the time of his return, I was coaching at Al-Ittihad, and Wim and I would speak at length about how these methods could succeed and hypothesise about the different countries where the national characteristics could complement and be enhanced by our work. I thought about English football's passion, drive, and energy – but what was missing was that high level of skill, creativity and therefore unpredictability.

Wiel and I were not the first to leave our country to try and impress our footballing ideologies on another team. I felt we had achieved a great deal in the years we spent in the Middle East but with every further success – Al-Ittihad also won the equivalent of the FA Cup – the idea of what I might be able to bring to a bigger stage lingered and grew in my head.

I would say that I was more of an explorer of opportunities than I was a direct opportunist – I did have intentions of staying on but I became frustrated with some of the regulations and politics. We were only able to field three foreign professional players. I intended to move one of our foreign professionals on to free up a space, only to find out he'd been given a new contract by the Sheikh who owned the club. Realising I wouldn't be able to have control like a normal head coach, I left that post to concentrate on my role with the FA.

Soon after, the coach of Al-Sadd, Rabah Madjer – the Algerian who famously scored against France in the 1982

World Cup and of course his famous backheel flick during the 1987 European Cup final v Bayern Munich – got the sack. I was offered that position and we were also successful, winning the Emir Cup.

Sheikh Tamim, the owner, offered to sign me a star player before this prestigious cup competition. The man he had in mind was George Weah. Weah was a legendary striker, but too old. What I needed was a link player. The Sheikh suggested Ali Benarbia and we signed him for only three or four games, but he did exactly what was needed, and helped us win the cup against Qatar SC. Ali was a great player and named French player of the year whilst playing for Bordeaux during the 1998-1999 season. During the final in the second half, when the score was still 0-0, Ali came over to the sideline and said, "Coach, if we make the right substitutions now we can win this."

I replied, "Ali look over my shoulder and tell me what you see."

"I see players on the bench, coach."

"Correct," I said, "however, none of them will improve our current team on the pitch." Ali looked at me, smiled and carried on. Eventually we won the Emir Cup 6-5 through a penalty shootout.

The next day both teams were invited to the Emir's palace. The showcase of wealth was extravagant. The Emir Cup was there – it was pure gold and looked a bit like the World Cup trophy. I asked if it would be okay to take it home and show the family. The kids were only five and six! Even in football circles – and I had the fortune to travel the world with the most popular team on the planet – this was not the sort of experience that came every day. Everything you see is gold, it feels overdone; they have special parties with swords and dances. It was a magnificent and indulgent experience.

I wouldn't say that I had a difficult relationship with the owners of Al-Sadd, but there was a lot of moving going on in the boardroom at that time, and it was clear that it was not going to be a long-term role.

These talks coincided with another return to England as I continued to travel to pick up my different coaching badges. I bumped into Dave Richardson at Lilleshall – he had been put in place when Howard Wilkinson was in charge of setting up the national academies. Dave was part of a three-man group, along with Len Ashurst and Dave Buxton, who would visit academies across the country and evaluate their criteria and so on.

On this particular visit I'd taken the national U17s to Keele – purely by coincidence – where Dave was holding a coaching course with around 60 coaches. We'd had many conversations in the past but now he was able to see the by-product of what I was talking about.

"What you're doing is what we need in England," he told me. "Would you like to do a presentation and a training session to show us how it works?"

I was able to talk through the process of a group of players that I'd looked after since the age of eight or nine. I talked about how we did things when they progressed through the age groups, the different emphasis that we placed upon each stage of development.

The proof of how far we had come showed when the Qatar U16 boys took on England juniors in a tournament at Newcastle-under-Lyme. We lost 1-0 – but we played them off the park. After the match the entire team was crying. They thought they'd let us down – I told them how proud they should be of themselves. I told them to forget the result and remember the standing ovation they'd got from everyone who watched them as they walked off the pitch.

In other games we were defeated by Sweden 3-2, but we beat Norway and Iceland – we did okay.

I was still in touch with Dave Mackay, who was now based back in the UK in Nottingham. I knew he was trying to exercise his contacts to see if I could get set up at a club. Dave Richardson also spoke to Sunderland, Coventry and other clubs – in fact four or five clubs – but none of them had any interest. I had flown back to Qatar by this point, but I had a telephone conversation with someone at Sunderland and I knew from the tone of his voice that it was not going to go anywhere.

I planned to go back to the UK and stay with Dave Mackay whilst I was attending a coaching seminar in the area. I also contacted Dave Richardson and explained that I would be available if any clubs wanted me to put on any sessions in the area. Three days before I was due to go to England, I received a call. It was Dave Richardson.

"I've got something even better for you," he said. "Les Kershaw's been on the phone. They're struggling. They've got all the access to U9 players but they're looking for a technical coach and they can't find one in England. I suggested you to them. Would you be available to have a chat with Les?"

Les was the academy director at Manchester United. I told Dave that it would be no problem – go ahead and organise it. So a few days later I met with Les and Geoff Watson, one of the academy scouts, at a Little Chef somewhere in Staffordshire. I prepared documentation to go over my philosophy and I brought the video Wiel and I made in Qatar, called *The Creative Dribbler*.

Les was enthusiastic but informed me that United was like an oil tanker. They didn't make decisions quickly. I told him not to worry as I was still the manager of Al-Sadd. It seemed to be positive, and I went away feeling optimistic about what their response might be.

I hadn't told Dave Mackay of the meeting with Les before it happened, but I did so when I returned, as he had been trying to find a place for me to work and I didn't want him hearing something that wasn't from me. A couple of weeks later I was back in Qatar when he called me.

"Has Alex Ferguson contacted you?" he asked.

Dave always loved to joke and take the Mickey.

"No," I said, "but I just got off the phone with Prince Charles."

He insisted that he'd just spoken to Sir Alex and that he was going to call me. I reminded Dave, if he was being serious, that phone numbers in Qatar had recently added an extra 5 and that's where he might have been going wrong.

Ten minutes later the phone goes.

"Hello René, Sir Alex here," that familiar Scottish tone says to me down the line.

Sir Alex Ferguson told me how he'd spoken to Les Kershaw and how highly Dave Mackay was speaking about me. He asked if there was any time I was planning to come over to England again – it was currently October, and I informed him we had a break in January.

Fast-forward to January, and Les Kershaw is picking me up at Manchester Airport. Les was brilliant from start to finish and I must take the time to mention him here because he's one of those that barely gets the credit he deserves. He was a man crucial and integral to the smooth running of the entire operation at Manchester United. He was highly intelligent and could give you a detailed analysis in conversation about why United were scouting in the way they were and who they were looking for. He was a brilliant professional and a fantastic person.

I spent five days in Manchester and those days were very well organised. First of all, I was introduced to Sir Alex Ferguson. Well – that's not true. The first person I met was the first person just about everyone at Carrington meets – Kath on reception. Then I saw some of the first team players hanging around, the players I'd only seen on television. I wasn't one to get starstruck – I'd kept company with great players before. But I was nonetheless feeling excited about my possible new environment.

The first thing that struck me when entering Sir Alex's office was the giant replica European Cup he had in there, sitting beside his desk. Spreading for acres behind Sir Alex in the windows surrounding his office was the immaculate, new Carrington complex. There was the famous image of *Lunch Atop A Skyscraper* hanging on the wall.

I was given a warm welcome. Sir Alex reiterated the kind things Dave had said about me, told me he was looking forward to seeing what I could do, and he also invited me to watch the first team train in the morning.

We walked out of the office; Sir Alex and Les were very clever with what happened next. Les took me to the academy office, where I was introduced to Tony Whelan, the U16 and U12 coordinator (later assistant academy director) and Paul McGuinness, the U18 coach. I was left with them for a while on an individual basis, alongside first-team coach Steve McClaren, and Bill Beswick, the sports psychologist. It was completely informal and gave me a comfortable start. I had met Steve and Bill on previous coaching courses in England. I was completely at ease. I can't recall why, and I can't explain it, but I was nerveless. I just had a conviction that what I had to deliver was the right thing.

The plan was to do different sessions throughout the week.

A couple of sessions at the Cliff, with the younger age groups, maybe eight or nine-year-olds. I'd work up to the U16s and then do a couple with the U18s. Different coaches were there at different sessions, observing my work and reporting back to Sir Alex when he wasn't able to watch. I was asked to work as I would normally – to show the technical training, into skill development, into how that worked in small-sided games, and how that all worked into a complete strategy.

It's difficult to tell in the space of a week because obviously any strategy of this nature bears full fruit with patience and time, but I was pleased to see the boys in Manchester were just as receptive as the boys in Qatar had been. You show them something new, they take it on board, and you've immediately contributed towards their development.

I met Sir Alex on a Thursday morning and did my first session that evening. I did another on Friday and on the weekend I watched a youth game and then the first team against Everton. They won a narrow game 1-0 – but it was their fifth in a row and the club were well on their way to winning a third consecutive Premier League title. I watched some more academy games on the Sunday before a couple more sessions on Monday. On the Tuesday I was leaving I went into Carrington in the morning to say my goodbyes.

I was with Les in Sir Alex's office.

"Well, I've heard a lot of good things and the reports are positive," Sir Alex says. "Les, how long have you been with me now?"

Les has a think. He says something like, "Twelve years, I think, boss?"

"Well, you've been useless," he jokes, "so give this man a job!"

He was in a light-hearted mood. "You speak better English

than I do," he said. "Half the players can't understand what I'm saying."

"Well boss," I took a chance, "that might be why you're so successful."

"Scandalous!" he roared.

I had a new job.

I was at a decent salary in Qatar and had to take quite a significant pay cut to join United. I felt, in a way, that I was starting again, as I'd risen through the ranks in Qatar to get more established and senior jobs throughout my years in the country. Obviously, I would have to return to Qatar to wrap up everything there. I travelled through Holland to see my family and tell my parents.

"Dad," I said. "I'm going to leave Qatar at the end of the season."

"Where are you going to go?"

"In England, with a club in the Premier League."

"Oh, wow," he replied. "But it won't be United."

"Well, who do you think it is?" I let him name every club he could come up with. He went, basically, from bottom to top. He mentioned Arsenal and Liverpool. "Who is it?"

"It's the first club you mentioned!"

He couldn't believe it.

"I've just spent five days with them, and Sir Alex Ferguson has offered me a job."

He still couldn't believe it. I eventually took him to Manchester to give him a tour around the stadium and to meet Sir Alex at Carrington. Maybe that's when the penny dropped for him. He was so proud. His reaction was a genuine reflection of how unreachable and how unattainable such a thing was supposed to be. He was only supposed to watch Manchester United on the television. And he did – it was always a family event. Dad and his brother would go to Theo, my brother's house, and watch the games. Not only for the matches, but also to see if I was on the bench. "There he is!"

I was proud of myself too. I reflect now on what an enormous privilege it was – the footsteps I was following. Sir Alex. Sir Matt Busby. Jimmy Murphy. Eric Harrison. I've named four but, like Les Kershaw, there are dozens more who worked tirelessly at creating and recreating an identity at the club that was recognised worldwide.

It was one of the few elite clubs in the world that had a strong history of developing its own talent and nurturing it into the first team. Manchester United's best periods in history came with a strong core of players they had developed themselves. I was not only following that lineage, but I was also given a free rein to implement my own ideas at a level that was even new to Manchester United; this development region between the age of six and 16 that few had ever truly concentrated on before.

In the moment, though, I was more driven to succeed than I was proud. I told Dave Richardson the news.

"I don't want you to go to Manchester United," he complained. "It's not that I don't want you to go, or that you shouldn't be there. But I know United will be leaps ahead of everybody else because you're bringing something that nobody has."

That was my conviction.

Don't get me wrong – if you talk about what you want from life then there are clichés that I adhere to; health, friendship, contentment. But what do you have to drive you, what gets you out of bed in the morning? It's about the experiences in life. The achievements you can celebrate. And the people you can share it with. That to me is a representation of what life is supposed to be about. I knew immediately that at Manchester

United I was connecting with like-minded people who spoke the same language. Especially Sir Alex – as much as he might joke otherwise.

I knew that Manchester United had people there who lived and breathed the club. Tony Whelan and Paul McGuinness, whose father Wilf had served United as a Busby Babe, a coach and then manager. Paul was affected by the fabric of the club and grew up almost indoctrinated in the United way of doing things as the right way to do it – and when I say that, I say it as the deepest compliment I could give. I knew I was coming in as an outsider – someone with a tremendous respect for the club's history – and I was keen to add something. I knew exactly what I wanted to add. I couldn't wait to get started.

Chapter Three

EARLY DAYS AT CARRINGTON

MY arrival at Manchester United coincided with the era in British football where professional clubs were looking towards the development of young footballers before they left school for the first time. Previously, clubs could only take players after they left school, then sign them to professional terms on their 17th birthday. The latter part of that process remained the same, but now clubs had the ability to scout players and place them into academies from a very young age. It was a huge evolution for the British game.

As someone who worked with U10s in my first coaching roles, it will come as no surprise that I was an advocate for this change. I believe it's still an ongoing process and I feel there's a lot of unexplored territory, so to speak. A good friend of mine, Tom Byer, did a lot of research on how early you can engage children within football. He started a project called 'Football Starts at Home', where the parents are encouraged to make an introduction to skills development. It's a simple process and starts with the different sizes of balls. It has remarkable benefits for young kids, not only in their ball manipulation education but also in other areas – it also helps to develop focus which is conducive to an overall aptitude for learning.

The ages between six and nine, nine and 12 are crucial for skills development. These are the golden years for kids to learn and to develop a subconscious level of creativity – they become so good at skills, they don't have to think about executing them. You can still technically improve as you get older, but it must be more position-specific because at an older age, a player has developed more personal traits within the comfort zone they operate in. If players are not good enough in terms of skill to dominate a 1v1, they can find a solution in passing to somebody else. But if a player has the capabilities and confidence to show their skill, it can make all the difference in the unpredictability of a player and a team.

One of the exercises we did with the kids was to play 4v4s in four different small-sided games. These games challenged them in terms of the skills they would use.

The first type of game would have a big goal with goalkeepers on either side of the pitch to challenge the players to outplay their opponents and encourage them to shoot. In another game we had one small goal on each side of the pitch. In this game the players were asked to be patient, keep the ball and find the right skill or pass to find a way through and score.

Then there was the four-goal game where we placed two small goals in the wide areas of the pitch. Each team had to defend two of them and score in two of them. It was all about changing the angle of attack and beating defenders through unpredictability. Sometimes we'd have 4v4 with 'line ball', a challenge where the players must be direct – if a player can dribble past an opponent and get over the touchline, they score.

This is just one example of the way we would get the kids to develop their skills. It was, in my opinion, very beneficial with an instant and obvious impact. Over the course of one season, we asked Rick Fenoglio from Manchester University to do research regarding the benefits of playing 4v4s at a young age in comparison to playing 8v8. The feedback of coaches and parents alike were very positive, and the stats backed up that this was the ideal playing environment for young kids, as there were more 1v1 encounters. Players were doing more passes and skills in a shorter period and there were more opportunities to score.

Ask me now, more than 20 years later, if these approaches have evolved to their maximum potential? To me, the answer is no. There is still more work to be done. I still feel the number of one-directional and one-dimensional players in the game is a reflection on the lack of technical development at a grassroots level.

The very first thing we discussed during a course I took in Holland to be a youth football trainer was the psychology of young children. They live in a different world and therefore your entire method of communication must adapt to that. Training is all about repetition and gaining success through that repetition. When kids experience success, they become confident. Through confidence, they develop their personalities.

With increased confidence to show their personality comes an increase in their tendency to take initiative. This is beneficial in everyday life – there are many positive psychological by-products that children experience in an environment where they can experiment with failure and success and see how they react to it. It's important for them to develop these reactions in an environment where the coaches and parents aren't constantly criticising the negative; shouting when things go wrong. You are there to support and help them through these processes in the best way you can, encouraging them to find their own way.

If you'll forgive the lengthy introduction, what I'm trying to say is, firstly, that I was brought into Manchester United to implement this philosophy. I knew I wouldn't be given the remit to look after one team or age group.

The second point is that there is a consequential reward that extends beyond football, both for the young players and me, because it was of course immensely rewarding to see young children become more confident simply through playing a game.

I was fortunate that I had these experiences from Holland. I had seen the enjoyment and progress of young children playing the game and it had left a significant impression on me. I won't say they were all world beaters – let's say from the outfield players I had five average players, three good ones and two excellent ones for that level. The average ones became good, the good ones became very good, and the excellent players became outstanding.

You can't just tell kids to dribble freely and expect it to go well in the game at the weekend. You must make them understand what skill-set is required for the area of the pitch they might be playing in. You must keep possession, create the build-up, and change the angle of attack in your own half. In the opposition half, you must try and break lines. Can you take players on in the final third? Can you get a shot away or a cross in? The players knew they were permitted to use their skills without any reprimand if things went wrong.

We created a traffic light system with regards to skill implementation in the game. Guiding the kids through from awareness to understanding. First the kids must be aware of their position, their situation on the pitch, and the skills they possess to solve a 1v1. This will help their decision-making in the game. There are many 1v1 moments in a game, however there are only four key 1v1 situations. This all depends on the position of the opposing player and in what way he challenges the player on the ball.

There are four key 1v1 situations in the game. A lot of times players are challenged side on. For instance, if Ryan Giggs or Antonio Valencia were running down the line ready to put a cross in, they would often be challenged by a defender beside them trying to stop the cross. To solve that problem, they could pretend to cross the ball, but turn the opposite way by using a Cruyff turn, step-over-turn or any other effective turn. This would give them the time and space to find another pass to one of their teammates.

In midfield, players are often challenged from an angle. So, if Scholes, Fletcher or Carrick were carrying the ball forward into space, an opposing player would try to stop them. The most efficient way to deal with this situation is to turn away from the opponent whilst shielding the ball and change the angle of attack. Then there's the situation where a midfield player or forward gets challenged from behind when the ball is played into their feet. So players like Rooney and Berbatov could set the ball back with one touch to a teammate or they could turn away from the defender by letting the ball run over the outside of the foot and get away with a quick and sharp turn.

There are various skills they could use to achieve this. The advantage of this turn being used is that not only would they lose their direct defender, but they would also break the line of the other midfielders and, or, defenders. 1v1 is often associated with just an opponent in front of you, which will most likely happen for wingers and forwards.

Any successful team will have players who can take opponents head on. For us, those players were Giggs, Rooney, Nani and, of course, Cristiano Ronaldo. If they were to pass an opponent in one of the wide areas, they would cause all sorts of problems for the opposition. A lot of times, however, this type of 1v1 situation turns into a side-on challenge because the defender has forced the attacking player in or outside. That's why it is so important that players have all the necessary skills to deal with any given situation. In 2003 I made a DVD *Play Like Champions* with a number of young academy players who featured alongside first-team players. Each first-team player explains a certain skill and how it can be used in a game situation.

So, when we're playing out from the back, the traffic light is on red, because this is obviously the area of the pitch with the highest danger – if we try the wrong skill in the wrong area, we might lose the ball and lose a goal. In the middle part, it's yellow – cautious and responsible. We still want to use skills to change the angle of attack or to play ourselves free when under pressure. However, there needs to be good cover and rest defence if things were to break down. In the attacking third, the light turns green, as it's all about taking a risk. Being creative and unpredictable in forward play to create chances and score goals.

When I moved to Qatar I maintained this same philosophy. This was with kids from different backgrounds, a different culture, and a different language – I had to learn Arabic to communicate with those kids as not many spoke English. The common thread I found with the Dutch and Qatari kids was that the appreciation, enjoyment, and progression was the same. The more time you put in, the quicker that progression comes on. Working with the kids in Holland, training was twice a week with a game on Saturday. In Qatar it was six days a week. In England I would have four sessions a week – three training sessions and the 4x4 programme. Wiel Coerver was right – he said no matter where you work in the world, youth is pure gold, they just need people to create the right environment to encourage the best to come from them.

Manchester United had as strong a tradition and as strong a commitment to the development of young footballers as anyone in the world. That tradition started in the 1940s with Sir Matt Busby, Jimmy Murphy and others. The quality of the system they put in place was measured by the success in the Youth Cup, how many of those players graduated to the first team, and how beloved that team was. It was clear, though, that the development of a player was favoured over winning at junior level.

Les Kershaw didn't want me to spread myself too thin. He wanted my impact to be broader, so the title they gave me was skills development coach. I loved that title. My remit was to look at the development centres and what was happening with the players before they got through the filter to possibly getting signed. Of course, only part of my job was with the players – the other part was with the coaches, many of them established with plenty of experience, and I have to say they were all very receptive. I had to get them on board and educate them on the way I wanted to do things.

The first person I sat down with was Mike Glennie, the parent liaison officer. "If you can believe in what I believe in," I said, "our messages will be very, very strong."

I talked about how we needed to educate the parents for them to support what we were doing and to understand why we are doing it. Mike was a very important piece of the jigsaw for me as he fully understood what I wanted to achieve over time. He was very good at communicating this to the parents. I told them they would be seeing something completely different. They had to abandon the idea of watching a child's game through the eyes of an adult. I gave them a quick example. If a six-year-old shows promise at volleyball – are you going to hang the net as high as in the adult game? No. Children needed to develop in an environment designed that was conducive to development.

I remember one game at the start of my first season with the U9s. This was the group that included Jesse Lingard, Ravel Morrison, Zeki Fryers, Ryan Tunnicliffe, Michael and Will Keane. We lost at Leeds and it was a heavy scoreline – I think they won 7-3.

The parents were in uproar. I asked some of them what they were upset about. Were they embarrassed that they might have to tell neighbours or relatives that we lost? I said it was a process.

We had to play them again at the end of the season. I asked them to evaluate where we were then. I told them that they were going to have to expect, and accept, that these kids were going to make some wrong decisions. They were going to do a step over at the wrong time in the wrong place and it was going to cost them. All of that would be part of the learning process. When you fail, knowing how to do it better next time is all part of the journey to be successful.

To know what you want to achieve, you must start with the final picture and break it down. You want them to develop, to be proficient in the technical, tactical, physical and mental aspects of the game.

I had been in the job for maybe three or four years when Les, impressed by how things were going, invited Henry Winter of the *Telegraph* to have a look. I showed him some of our sessions and made a prediction that when the group of Jesse, Ravel and company were of age, they'd be the next United team to win the FA Youth Cup.

It's not an easy thing to predict because players can stagnate for whatever reason. And from the age of six to 16 there are at least two major culls where you lose a lot of players. The system is responsible for this. You always want as many fish swimming in the pond as possible, but the system forces you to let go of several players when they get to the age of nine where you evaluate their progression. Because they are so young you don't look at the tactical side – you have no way of truly knowing what their specific position will be in seven or eight years. They all attack. They all defend.

I've always been sceptical of the system – why can we only sign so many players after investing three years or so in their progress? Is there any way we can keep track of the ones we lose? You have players and children who develop at very different paces. That number of roughly 30 which you are allowed to keep on falls again when it's time to give apprenticeships. I just couldn't understand it. You've spent around eight years developing a young Manchester United player, you've helped shape them as a player and a person with their character, and suddenly they're deemed not good enough. I feel it's the worst exit moment imaginable. When they hit 15 or 16, only the do you know what sort of player you're looking at. From 16 to 18 you have an enormously important part of development. That's where everything falls into place, where the wrapping comes off.

My own son Melle is a great example. He was at United through that entire system and was released at 15 because he was too small! He plays in Holland now as a 6'2 centre-back. The system is the problem, and I couldn't understand why the process for young players provided such a significant obstacle.

I was part of the decision-making team – I'd give my opinion, weighted of course with my feelings on the process. The final decision, however, would be made by the academy manager at the time, as well as coaches working with specific teams. I made it clear how I not only didn't support the system, but it was also against everything I stood for.

Soon after I joined the club, the manager did me a great favour when he called a meeting for all full-time and part-time staff who were working in the academy to introduce me and how much he valued the new ideas regarding skill development that I was going to bring to the club. This support was vital for me. It made it a lot easier for me to get my messages across to other coaches as they all knew I had the support from the boss.

Earlier that season I invited him to the training grounds on Littleton Road to have a look and get a feel for what we are trying to put in place at grassroots level. He loved it. In all, Sir Alex visited Littleton Road and the Cliff, our other training ground, about three times that season and saw the progression these young players were making.

In May, at the end of the season, I had a three-hour meeting with the boss about my ideas and how I saw things developing in the future. I told him that it was important that we developed players who could meet the future demands of the game. Players would get physically stronger, faster and fitter. The strategies and tactics to nullify opposition attacks would get better and the mental demands of player performances would increase.

I said, "We must develop players that, on top of the above-mentioned qualities, have the ability to technically dominate any given 1v1 situation in the game. To do this they need the best possible skill levels as this will make the difference."

It was also during this conversation that I first mentioned to the boss and planted the seed, that there was room for improvement for reserve and first-team players if technically coached in the right way. The improvement would probably range from one to five per cent but those margins would be the difference in winning more games and possibly more trophies.

In my second year at the club there was major speculation surrounding the future of the manager when Sir Alex announced his intention to retire. I'll be honest, I was so busy in the early stages of my own job and working around the clock to make sure all the people were familiar with the message I wanted to deliver, that it wasn't something I paid too much attention to. I spent much of those first months working with Mike Glennie. He understood what we were trying to put in place. There were many staff who did the same – too many for me to mention off the top of my head. Eddie Leach was one of them – he was very important in bringing young kids to the club and was an excellent skills coach. Phil Brogan, Ken Baggaley and Louis Garvey were also helping me at Cliff and Littleton Road at the time. These were good guys who worked very hard and were very receptive to my ideas.

We had something like 20 development centres in and around Manchester because we were still hampered by the rule that said you could only develop players who lived within 90 minutes of the club. In that same pond we have Manchester City, Liverpool and Everton, not to mention Blackburn, Bolton, Stoke, Wigan – so many clubs in the same locality fighting for the same players.

To get us in the best shape I held courses with all our coaches to make sure everyone knew what we were looking for. When it came to young players, I told the coaches not to concern themselves too much with tactical awareness or physical development. What you can see is how technically skilled they are for their age, and you can also make an assessment on their motor skills – how agile they are, if they have natural pace.

The most important thing is learning about their character. Are they open? Are they upfront? Are they shy? Are they competitive? You can only do the best you can to supply and create the healthiest framework for a young player to develop. There are some elements you cannot control. A child's home situation. Their friends. The environment they grow up in. The personality and character.

One of the most fundamental issues with youth development was how the calendar was viewed. The FA used the school year – from August to July. Many countries around the world used January to December. I conducted my own research and the evidence suggested that, in England, most kids were scouted between August and January.

I discussed it with the coaches and scouts because I found it impossible to believe that no players could be found in the other half of the year – in fact, I had my own suspicions about it, so I set up an event at the Cliff, our academy training centre, where I divided the pitch and had players play in 4v4 games.

I ran different rounds of games. The first would have all age groups mixed. The next saw those born August to January playing those born between February and July. The last round featured players born within three months of each other. We played eight-minute games and I invited scouts to watch and present their observations. I asked each scout to watch each game for two minutes and to write down one, two or three players who stood out. After the games finished, I asked them to select two or three players from each game.

The conclusion was that in the first round, not one player was picked who was born from February to July. In the second round, there were one or two picks from the latter half of the year. In the third round, four players were identified from the May to July group – half!

I explained to the coaches that we had a situation where you would have players who might not be picked up because they were always competing against older children. I wanted the coaches and scouts to not make the mistake of missing a player because of how much younger the kids were, that even an age gap of a few months could play a significant role in competition.

Someone born in August would have a natural physical advantage over someone born in July, even though it's the same school year, and you would expect this difference to remain obvious right through until a child is eight or nine. As they get older, the difference becomes more marginal.

I wanted everyone on the same page throughout all the development centres. Before I arrived, the departments tended to do their own thing before a kid moved through, and I was keen to ensure that everyone did the same thing. In fact, what I really wanted was to try and encourage this kind of thinking at a national level. I talked it over with Dave Richardson and we held a festival down in Birmingham – afterwards, we held a Q&A where it became clear that many people were resistant to change. One participant summed it all up for me:

"I just like to watch 11v11 on a Sunday morning and have a nice cup of tea." No justification or motivation why that would be the best thing for an eight to 10-year-old on a Sunday morning. It was just about him rather than the kids. Fine – but

I was convinced that what we were doing at United was the right thing for the kids and it was working.

Game by game you could see the levels improving. When you saw the kids do something in a match that they'd worked on in training, you could see their confidence take another step. It felt wonderful seeing these kids accomplish things, to observe them every Sunday and see it all come out on the pitch. I felt sheer joy – regardless of the result of the match on the day.

The parents started to appreciate it more and as coaches we started to embrace them more when it came to explaining the philosophy. We wanted to maintain the environment of encouragement, which meant not going away in the car and confronting or criticising their boy which contradicted what we were trying to achieve. If we had encouraged him to go on a run, we didn't want a parent saying to them in private that they should have passed the ball. Parents started to understand that winning wasn't necessarily about winning the game. Success came in different ways. Every kid was a winner if he enjoyed playing that day. If he had learned something in training and implemented it on the day – that was success.

It just so happened that what we were doing did start to have a positive impact on the results and the quality of the players. One day I invited some of the first-team players to come to one of the 4v4 festivals we were holding – Forlan, Van Nistelrooy and Ferdinand came along and were all surprised by how talented the boys were. It comes as no surprise then, that I was so disappointed by the system that forced us to abandon some of this development with many talented young boys before they had gone through their own natural stages of maturity.

When you are at a club like Manchester United, even if you are a coach like me who had the fortune of being able to implement a structure and philosophy, you still have a responsibility to respect the history of the club. In some respects, the history is so famous that most people in football are aware of it, but in the six months between being told I would be hired to the moment I started work I made sure I educated myself in whatever spare time I had. That meant reading, watching documentaries on the Busby Babes, studying how they rose from that to win the European Cup.

I looked at the process Alex Ferguson went through when he took the job. I personally reached out to Eric Harrison because it was clear what an influential figure he was in United's history and I cannot speak highly enough of him. He gave me so much of his time and I loved every minute of it – he discussed the way he did things and his ideas about player development. He was a person who typified the club's DNA. I knew the history of Jimmy Murphy; but he had died in 1989 and was almost mythical in a sense. Eric was there, he was present, and he would often come to Carrington to watch me work. I explained my long-term vision and he would always support it. In fact, it was Eric who provided my first real link into the first team, when he asked if I would like to work with Ryan Giggs. He felt Ryan, one of his most famous protégés, had lost his way a little bit.

I felt a responsibility to educate myself about the history of the club so that I could better understand the culture of it. Maybe my willingness to do that made the likes of Eric – and Paul McGuinness who would take control of the players after me – so open and accepting of my own vision.

In 2006 I took our young kids over to play in the Dallas Cup. We had a really good group which included Giuseppe Rossi, Gerard Pique and Jonny Evans to name just three. It was great to get exposure to facing teams from different nations – I think we played against teams from North America and Mexico. Our opening match was against Real Madrid in front of a full stadium. We won 3-2 on an incredible afternoon. Afterwards, the players – who had given everything and left their heart and soul out on the pitch – were too exhausted to even properly acknowledge the congratulations of the legendary Sir Bobby Charlton who had accompanied us on the trip.

"Just remember," he said, "it's not every game you play against the likes of Real Madrid. You treasure those moments. To come out of that moment on top is something that will live with you forever. I hope you'll be able to relive it when you go and play for United's first team."

Initially, Sir Bobby had been a little shy. He had been invited by Gordon Jago, the president of the tournament and a former manager of QPR, to be guest of honour and open the tournament. He travelled with us and on the first morning, when we were having breakfast, I noticed he was sitting alone. I approached him and asked how he was doing. I asked if he would join us for breakfast and the team meeting I was holding in 30 minutes' time. He said he really appreciated the invitation – can you believe that? One of the most legendary figures of the game didn't want to impose himself on us.

The reason for the team meeting is that we had a mixed group – some played for the U18s and some played for the reserves. I wanted to get three things out of the meeting. The first was that we get to know each other. The second was the roles and responsibilities, the expected conduct of a Manchester United player in an international tournament. Thirdly, what did the players wish to get out of the tournament? Most of them said, instantly, they were here to win.

I had a flip chart and put two categories on there. I asked what would stop us from winning and I wrote it down in red. They answered with the following: conceding silly goals, making individual mistakes, getting a red card, among a few other things. I then asked the players to replace the negative column with positive solutions. If we don't want to concede sloppy goals, what do we want to do?

In green I wrote their replies: strong defending, good organisation, keeping clean sheets, discipline, we play on the front foot, we play our attacking football, and we try to enjoy ourselves. I told the players that the right-hand side, the green side, was our navigation system for the upcoming games. It was important to me that within those green answers lay elements of the club's DNA, and that the players understood it.

Because we were part of the same family, but we hadn't spent much time all together, I spoke about this experience being an opportunity for the players to learn from each other as much as they would from the opponents they'd be facing. So, we started with a very simple exercise – getting them to know each other. I told them I was going to throw them a ball and when it was their turn, they'd have to say their name and say a little about themselves. How many brothers and sisters they had, where they grew up. I started. The ball went around the players and the staff.

"There's only one person we haven't heard from," I said, "and that's Sir Bobby."

The ball was thrown to him.

Sir Bobby stood up – and honestly, he must have spoken for about 10 minutes. Maybe more. I couldn't have wished for more poignant, relevant, and powerful words. It was a speech from the heart and yet it felt as though he'd prepared it specially for the occasion. He spoke about his youth, his upbringing, how proud he was to become a Manchester United player, the first time he wore the shirt. The highs, the lows. The great players he played with. Winning the European Cup. He spoke about football bringing him everything he had in life through two things – hard work and commitment. He spoke about how he had always felt pride representing the club even all these years after retirement. He spoke about the rare opportunity of facing Real Madrid and told the boys to enjoy themselves.

The lads returned to their rooms while the staff and I stayed downstairs with Sir Bobby. I thanked him for what he had said. He said he really enjoyed being around it all.

The tournament lasted a week – during that time, Sir Bobby had a family emergency and wanted to return home. The organisers wanted to keep him there because he was supposed to do the final presentation and hand the trophy to the winners. I discussed a compromise where we could film a video message and allow Bobby to return to be with his family. I know he appreciated what I'd done – but I was the one grateful for the memories he'd given me during our time together.

After the opening game, he and I shared a car back to the hotel. I decided to ask what it was like when he was playing. I dared to ask him about Duncan Edwards, and he said very plainly that Duncan was, by light years, the best player he'd ever played with. He described him as the biggest loss not only for Manchester United and for England, but for the sport of football. This was Bobby Charlton, a World Cup winner, scorer of two goals in a European Cup final, and a Ballon d'Or winner, speaking about another player who was much better even than him. It really made me think and feel regretful that we never had the opportunity to see more footage of Duncan playing.

While I'm talking about the legends of the past, I want to go back to September 2002, when a statue of Denis Law was unveiled in the upper concourse of the Stretford end. Denis had invited a few old friends including Dave Mackay, so I, of course, took the opportunity to catch up with him. Joining the party was Bobby and the great George Best. There was some delay – I can't remember why – but I do remember Dave joking that they probably couldn't fit the statue in the van because of Denis's nose.

I was awe-struck in a way, by Dave's ability to just joke with three of the biggest legends of the game like old mates – which to him they were. George was someone I had a weakness for. He typified and personified what I wished I could develop in a young player. I wanted them to be free spirits but with the tools to prepare them for the game. George just seemed to have all that naturally. That was the only opportunity I really had to talk to him about what I was trying to do at the club, and it meant a lot to me that he seemed to think it was a great idea.

My childhood fascination with George had only increased as an adult following a conversation I'd had with Wim Suurbier. Wim was asked by Rinus Michels, the famous Dutch coach who changed Ajax fortunes in the early seventies, to look after George when all three were at Los Angeles Aztecs. They spent a lot of time together and Wim insisted that in smaller areas, George was even better than Cruyff as an individual. Cruyff was a more effective conductor – he had something to say about everyone in every position. George managed his own performance; but Wim was astonished to see just how good of a dribbler he was. He spoke of George's fitness in the three months they trained together before it was time to play.

On the day of the first game, George didn't show up and went to a bar instead – Wim later found him and asked what was going on. How could it be that he'd got himself into such incredible shape, and he was looking so good on the ball, and yet he had succumbed to his addiction right when it was time to go? Wim felt sure it was fear of failure – that George was afraid he couldn't be what he once was, even though everybody else felt sure he would be by far and away the best player in the league.

George passed away in 2005, so sadly there were to be no future conversations. I was luckier to spend more time with Denis, including on the way back from one of our League Cup wins. Just listening to his stories was an education and each conversation left me with a significant realisation of my own responsibility and opportunity. I could write my own place in the club's history and help others write theirs.

I always found with the likes of Denis and Bobby, that their achievements seemed to speak for themselves, and it created this atmosphere around them where they commanded respect – and yet, as people, they couldn't have more humility. They were men who were friendly, shared the same passion for the game and understood and represented the values and principles of the club. I was – and remain – fascinated to be in the company of such legendary figures.

We didn't win the Dallas Cup, but I was sure that we all – myself included – had benefited from the valuable experience. By that time, I had already been working for quite some time with senior players, starting with individual sessions. Around the same time as Eric recommended that I work with Ryan, I also had long conversations with Diego Forlan, who I found to be a lovely, friendly guy. He still seemed to be finding his feet at the club. Ruud van Nistelrooy was the main striker and Diego just took a while to settle – taking 27 games to score his first goal.

One morning we were talking and I invited him to come and watch one of the sessions I was doing with the kids at Littleton Road. He was enthused about how good the young lads were and I said to him that I felt he could benefit from doing some work following the same principles to improve his skill-set, if he was willing to do extra sessions.

So we spent time at Carrington. Ten minutes became 20. That became 30. I thought it was going well but I recognised it was time consuming and I didn't want to cause any issues with the first-team training schedule, so I talked to Sir Alex about it. I said Diego seemed to be benefitting from it and enjoying it, but I didn't want to continue if he and Carlos Quieroz were not happy with it. He told me it was fine to continue if it was done at the most appropriate times. Over time, some of the other players noticed – like Cristiano, as I mentioned right at the start of this book – and asked to join in.

With Ryan Giggs, I felt my role was to take him from awareness to understanding that he was no longer the explosive winger who had destroyed the football world as a teenager playing on his intuition. Now he had experience and was almost 30 with his fair share of injuries behind him. I was one of the few to suggest that he try yoga as it could help with injury prevention. It made a hell of a difference.

I told him that he was at the stage of his career where he needed to utilise his imagination in a different way. Clever movement, clever passes. Use the skill of changing angles. He was so good at that. Giggsy seemed to enjoy it, and I think that speaks volumes about the dedication of someone who was already well on his way to becoming the most decorated player in the history of British football.

My conviction of being able to deliver this message to a player of such experience was probably helped by the fact that I was able – as Wiel had insisted – to demonstrate the skills I was showing the players myself. It wasn't a case of me setting up a drill for Diego or Ruud and then tripping up over the ball. If they could see me doing it, and I was 10 years older than them, then they knew they could do it too. A player wants to see technical proof of skill development, so if I could do the things I was advocating and then explain where it would be useful in a game, they were much more convinced.

Later, as I became more familiar with the players, I would get footage of games and sit down with them – much like I did with Cristiano – to explain alternative moves that might have achieved more success. When I saw positive examples I would get those clips too, and pull the player aside before or after training to show them how well they'd done with something we'd worked on.

Two players I did not get much experience working with were David Beckham and Juan Sebastian Veron, which was a great shame as you are talking about two exceptional midfielders, two of the greatest even. David had unbelievable energy; a very dynamic player with reserves of stamina and a world-class technique for kicking the ball. David had specialised himself so well and had such a complete understanding of what his strengths and weaknesses were that I wondered if I could have added anything. He wasn't flashy as a player – he was efficient. His finishing was as exquisite as his delivery.

Veron too was a magnificent player. He wanted the ball all the time – often to the frustration of Roy Keane because the insatiability for the ball would see him regularly abandoning his defensive position. When you have a free spirit who is cavalier like that you have two options – you either try to manage him and restrict him, knowing that you might not be getting the best out of him, or you try and compensate for him by asking other players to assume that discipline. Keane was excellent in that regard.

David and Juan left in the summer of 2003. I'd spent two years at Old Trafford by then and I had developed a very deep, burning desire to prove that if the technical development was put into place in the right way from an early age all the way to the U18s and then continued at first-team level, where it was still possible to add between one and five per cent to the level of top players, you could achieve a great deal of success. I was seeing those percentages in players like Ruud and Diego.

Wiel had always wanted to get his foot in the door of a big club and do something like that. My gut feeling was that his personality and certain traits he possessed would always get in the way. He seemed very much an individual and wasn't a real team-worker. He was also a controversial man who would fight with others while trying to convince them about his ideas. But Wiel and his philosophy were important to me.

Wiel meant a lot for me in my early career; even though he was not involved in any of the process that resulted in me going to Manchester United, I still felt some sense of obligation to prove for Wiel and for the KNVB who kept him on the outside all the time, that the strategy could be very successful if implemented at a big club. Going from Qatar, a developing country, to Manchester United, arguably the biggest club in the world amid one of their most successful periods, you might think that I was overawed by the sense of the step up.

I really don't know how to explain it but the more time I spent at Carrington and the greater the conviction I had that things were working with the kids, the more convinced I was that it would work with the senior players too, and the more driven I was to embrace that. It wasn't a matter of ego – just a professional curiosity about the effectiveness when implemented all the way up to first-team level.

Chapter Four

HOW TO BUILD A WINNING TEAM

I ARRIVED at the club two years after the landmark achievement of winning the Treble. The team had won the following two Premier League titles and moved from the Cliff to Carrington. I think the biggest thing that struck me about Carrington was that it was an environment everyone wanted to be around. It was still work, and yet Carrington was a sort of magnet. You were compelled to be there. I often wondered if that was part of the reason Sir Alex reversed his decision to retire.

I would watch training, observe the competitiveness, and the high standards. You could see the expectations players held for themselves. Roy Keane was a standard bearer, of course. But there was also Ryan, Paul Scholes, the Neville brothers, and Nicky Butt. In the slipstream you had players like Darren Fletcher, John O'Shea and Wes Brown, players in the same mould raised in the same environment.

There was an enormous winning mentality at the club.

This was something I studied myself while evaluating the parameters of successful teams. I determined there were 10 key elements to success: Good Ownership, Organisation and Management (Manager/Head-Coach/Support Staff), Quality Players, Hard Work and Competitive Spirit, Teamwork and Team Spirit, Game Plan and Style, Strategies and Tactics, Winning Mentality, and finally, Don't Concede Goals… and Score Goals!

Let me try to explain this in a bit more detail as, in my opinion, these key factors function like a navigation for any successful team past or present. Of course, you must see those key elements in the context of signs of the time as obviously these things continue to evolve.

Good Ownership

With good ownership, I mean owners who understand the culture and identity of the club will have a clear vision and provide the support to develop successful strategies on and off the pitch, in the long, medium and short term. Like any well-run company, a football club must have a clear structure regarding organisation and management. To run a successful business you need people with experience and expertise. After Peter Kenyon left, it was a smart move from Manchester United to promote David Gill to CEO. Together with Sir Alex they were a very successful management team.

Organisation and Management

When David Gill and Sir Alex both left Manchester United at the end of the 2012-2013 season it had a huge impact on the club – and not in a positive way. David pursued other ambitions with the UEFA and Sir Alex retired. Both are still connected at the club as ambassadors. And of course, one must have an outstanding manager as we did for so many years in Sir Alex Ferguson; I got asked this question over time a lot: What made Sir Alex so special and successful as a manager? Because he was a person who had a clear vision of how he wanted Manchester United to be successful. Sir Alex was a true leader whose drive, experience, knowledge, communication, and management skills were exceptional.

He had the ability to adapt with the times as well as the skill-set to make tough decisions when it mattered. Nobody is bigger than Manchester United – that was Fergie's motto. He was good at surrounding himself with the right people – quality staff that would help him and Manchester United to achieve his ambitions. To illustrate the growth and development of the club he would often say, "When I started here back in 1986 I had eight staff, now I have more than Marks & Spencers."

Quality Players

One cannot be successful without top quality players. The boss knew what he wanted and needed to do to achieve success with Manchester United and he embarked on a journey with the likes of Brian Kidd, Eric Harrison and Les Kershaw alongside him to maximise the amount of quality players coming through the academy. He knew he had to invest in youth. It was part of the Manchester United DNA. We all now know the teams Sir Alex has created throughout the years and I was fortunate to be part of his staff during his last six years as manager. A time which turned out to be the most successful period in the history of Manchester United, not least because we had a fantastic squad at the time whereby experience and youthfulness was the perfect recipe for success. Every successful team has that balance including players who can make a difference. Players who are world class or who possess world-class qualities. We had them in abundance.

Hard Work and Competitive Spirit

If you take an X-ray of those players, you will see that it's made up of tactical, physical, mental and technical qualities. When players are tactically good, they show good awareness and understanding in their positions. Those players make the right decisions more often than not. For example, Ferdinand and Vidic must be aware of the dangers and threats the opposition team have and therefore understand when to step up and engage, slide or drop off when they are defending. Michael Carrick needs to know when to hold on to the ball, carry it, switch the play, or play one touch when in possession. The first thing the boss wanted those players to do was to work hard and compete – an integral part of Manchester United's DNA. You can have all the talent in the world, but if talent is not prepared to work hard, it will always be defeated by hard work.

Teamwork and Team Spirit

The next big thing is to make sure that those players are prepared to work together. Teamwork and team spirit are two other elements a successful team cannot do without. The boss felt it was crucial to have a good atmosphere in the dressing room as that meant a spirited 11 on the pitch. The road to the top is riddled with pitfalls, obstacles and disappointments and it can only be conquered by the team who possesses all of these traits.

Game Plan and Style

To make players click and play well together, successful teams must have the right game plan which utilises the strengths of its players. A good game plan has a distinctive style where strategies are supported by clever tactics to ensure the best possible chance of a good performance and result. We are in the results business and it's all about winning. But it was Sir Alex's and our conviction that the better you prepare, the better you play, the greater the chance of success, that gave us a critical advantage. He always used to remind me by saying, "René, remember everything you do in training will manifest itself in the game! Good and bad." As a result, I made every session the best I could. If we expect a world-class performance from the players, they should be able to count on us for world-class support and preparation.

Strategies and Tactics

In terms of systems we opted mostly for a 4-3-3 or 4-2-3-1 formation with flexibility in midfield and wide areas. When it came to our defending strategy, it was all about denying time and space for the opposition. Whether that was done by a high press or a well-organised defensive block depended on the opponent and competition. In possession, it's the opposite. It's all about creating time and space to break lines, getting in behind the back four, creating chances and scoring goals. One thing I always remember is that Sir Alex hated it when players passed the ball backwards instead of looking for a forward option. His idea about possession was; think forward, look forward, play forward. The key is that players are aware and understand their role and jobs when defending. There can be no excuses on this part. In possession, yes there are clear build-up patterns and rotations but players were free to express themselves when it came to offensive play to ensure the creativity would create unpredictability in attack which is hard to defend against. Players like Scholes, Giggs, Rooney, Ronaldo, Berbatov and Nani thrived on that element of freedom whilst playing for Manchester United – also a big part of the club's DNA under Sir Alex Ferguson.

Winning Mentality

The element that sets successful teams apart from the rest is a winning mentality. All those teams that have won numerous domestic and international trophies like Real Madrid, Barcelona, AC Milan, Juventus, Bayern Munich and Ajax have this in their DNA. It took Sir Alex Ferguson six years to win his first Premier League with the Class of '92 coming through from the youth system. By that time the winning mentality was very much implemented by Eric Harrison and, of course, Sir Alex himself. A winning mentality that drove those players on in the 90s and beyond to achieve sustained success for Manchester United Football Club. If that team did not hit all the right notes in a game, they would roll up their sleeves and outfight or outrun their opponent or wait patiently to outplay them at the end of a game. I'm paying tribute to the players, but it starts with the manager, and he was the driving force behind it. As mentioned before, he was never afraid to make a bold choice.

Don't Concede Goals and Score Goals!

Football games are won or lost by goals, so the two final key elements are keeping clean sheets – or limiting opposition goals and scoring goals. Sir Alex always reiterated the importance of defending well and where possible keeping a clean sheet.

He took enormous pride in not conceding too many goals throughout a season.

Equally, scoring goals is the other most important element as goals win you games. But on top of winning games, Sir Alex also made it very clear to the players how important goal difference could play out at the end of a season, so he always encouraged the players to score as many goals as possible. It's fair to say that during that period quite a few teams got battered whilst paying a visit to Old Trafford. Apart from the fact that goal difference could be important for the final standings in the league table, he also felt that we had an obligation to entertain the fans.

When you analyse those 10 key elements and you rate them in plusses and minuses you get a clear view of the status of Manchester United, or any other club for that matter. The more plusses, the better the chances the club is in a good place and in a good situation to be successful. Under the guidance of Sir Alex Ferguson and David Gill, Manchester United ticked all those boxes and therefore it's no surprise how successful they were during his 26 years at the club. When there were more minuses than plusses, the boss made sure that these got addressed and improved.

My introduction to working with the players on a closer basis didn't just come through the avenues I mentioned before. If a player was coming back to fitness, I would be asked by the medical department to run through four or five sessions with them before they moved back into group training. The physios would talk to me about the physical tests we needed to do and I would always try and incorporate it into practices that would be appropriate for a game setting whilst also trying to improve something about that player's game.

I was happy to see a few results quite early on from my work with the first team. Ryan was criticised for his form in the early stages of the 2002/3 campaign but had a major influence as the club won the league title at the end of the season. The same with Diego who scored some very important goals. In the late winter I had been watching Ruud van Nistelrooy and felt there was something I could add to his variety of goals. I spoke to him about the key moments. If he was receiving the ball from a cross, he would need to understand what sort of cross was coming in. Would it be at the front or back post? Drilled hard or floated in?

Inside the box there were few who could match him. The timing of his runs and the clinical quality of his finishing was world class. He was so dangerous at scoring first-time that opponents were now trying to smother him. We worked on the element of surprise – pretend to shoot, shift the angle, and make a one-touch finish a two-touch finish. The second thing we worked on was Ruud's movement. Ruud was good at link-up play but he would often shift the ball out wide when receiving it before making his run into the box. I noticed a trend where he would do this against opponents whose centre-backs were dropping deep while their full-backs bombed on. I showed him some examples and explained that if he moved on the half-turn and started moving with the ball, it would be almost impossible to defend.

We worked on some drills where I was the attacker and he was the defender. I said even though I was 15 years older than him I'd run past him every single time. I ran straight at him, forcing him to make one of two decisions. He had to commit immediately – at which point I could reach his body language, and feint past him. Or he would try to delay, pedalling backwards, whilst I kept the pace. The penny dropped.

We talked about the key moment in this scenario, and that was when the defender looked at the ball and not Ruud. That was the moment he could change direction and use a burst of speed to get away.

The following weekend we played Fulham at home. Ruud scored a penalty to give us the lead at half-time. Midway through the second half he received the ball on the halfway line – on the half-turn – and started to move. There was a directness the defenders couldn't cope with. He steamed through them to get into the box, shifted his feet and scored a magnificent goal. It was moments like that where I really felt that those specific 1v1 sessions were paying off and making a difference. A few weeks later he scored a similar goal against Arsenal where you could see the value of the correct judgement in the split-second.

As players reach their peak and then start to creep towards the end of their careers, it is often said that experience compensates for any physical changes – for example, in Ryan's case, not being as explosive with his pace as he was when he was a teenager. At the level United are playing at, you're looking to add an extra percent here or there and my work with individuals evolved as they went into the dressing room and talked about what they'd done. It was as simple as that.

We wanted the players to be the best they could be and to accomplish that meant I had to strive to be the best I could be as a coach.

Chapter Five

THE RESERVES

A REAL progression for me was when I started working with the reserve team more often. This happened gradually until one moment in 2005 when I was given the responsibility of becoming reserve team manager. In the academy I floated around the groups because we had different coaches running the team. I considered it my mandate to oversee that the philosophy was being delivered in the right way, and that the skill development of the players was improving as they went through the age groups and went from 4v4 to bigger-sided games. I wanted to see how the players were developing in their tactical intelligence – how they were moving from awareness to understanding.

The older the players were getting, and the bigger the pitches they were playing on, the more specific you wanted the skill element to be executed by a player in a particular position. For example, the full-backs. What situations do they normally find themselves in their own half? They might come under pressure from wingers. That's when we would talk about the importance of team-mates helping to provide solutions so that the play can remain progressive. The further you get down the line and the closer you get to full side games and to the first-team environment, the more closely involved I wanted to be – but still the final step to that involvement came about by chance, when Ricky Sbragia was given the opportunity to move to Bolton as a first-team coach. I felt it was a perfect scenario for me to show what I could do, and for Sir Alex to get an opportunity to experience what my vision was. I decided I was going to write him a letter.

"Dear boss," I wrote. "I know the club is looking for a replacement for Ricky Sbragia… but why look outside if the solution is already here? I've been thinking about this for some time, and I thought I would take a pen to paper and explain to you what I feel the benefits are. At this moment in time, I feel the reserve team is a group of lost individuals who need guidance and attention, but also, they are in such an important age group that we need to bridge the gap and provide direction and encouragement. I think that gives me a great opportunity to work with these talented players and show you how I can work with older players and introduce the skill element in a more senior environment, as I do feel strongly that this will be a difference maker for us in the coming years when it comes to winning trophies. I'd be delighted to discuss this further."

I got to Carrington even earlier than the boss the next morning to slide the letter under the door of his office. Later in the day he called me in.

"I got some mail this morning," he joked.

"Oh yeah?"

"Yeah, I received a letter from somebody. And, it makes a lot of sense. If you can prove that you can combine this with your work with the academy, then I quite like the idea."

I knew it would be increasing my workload, but I was happy

to do it. In fact, I enjoyed it. We had a very promising group of players, but this also gave me the opportunity to work with the likes of Gary Neville, Roy Keane and Paul Scholes, when they sometimes trained with the reserves after coming back from an injury, in a group setting and they could see me as a coach running full sessions. I always tried to make those players into player-coaches in this environment – for example, asking Paul what he expected of the full-back when he was receiving a pass from the opposite side, so that he could inform the younger players. I felt like they enjoyed that involvement.

I was pleased to do some work with Roy. When I tell you he was opinionated and had strong views and that he had very high values and expectations of everybody, I suppose it will come as no surprise. I explained what I was doing with the reserves and he seemed to think it was a good approach.

"Well, Roy," I said, "it's not rocket science – it's just common sense."

"René," he replied, "Common sense is not so common."

I never forgot that. It was such a simple and direct way of articulating the message, but it resonated with me. Roy was coming towards the final stage of his career so my involvement with him was minimal, but I did enjoy all our interactions and I felt he was a phenomenal player, person, and personality who seemed to rub off on everyone else around him. He typified winning – if you were to pick one football player who personified a winning attitude, it would be Roy Keane. When he did come and train with us, he was a fantastic influence, lifting the entire group. I would have brief discussions with him before the sessions if I intended to highlight something, because I felt that it might be a stronger message or make a stronger impact if the words came from Roy. He was always receptive to that.

In 2004, when Rio Ferdinand was out for a long period

with a suspension from the FA, I did one-on-one work with him. One of the most important things we worked on was his heading technique. He was 6'2 and there was little wrong with his defensive style of play, but I felt there could be an improvement when it came to his heading ability. We talked about when he went forward, and how he would need momentum, power, and direction, and in order to achieve that, we would need to improve that technique. I asked him to visualise what he felt a great attacking header was and to freeze the moment; to describe the body shape of the player. Look at the position of his arms and how high he is off the ground. How did that happen?

We went back to basics and did the simple drills you do with school kids. Sit down on the floor, straight legs, I throw the ball, he heads it back. This easy exercise already places an emphasis on the core and straining the neck muscles. Then you need to start using the arms; they act like grabbing two sticks to generate some momentum. Then you bend the knees whilst heading the ball to the left and right. This is all about turning. Then, you kneel and follow the same heading sequences. Once you're standing up, you've already increased your general understanding and capability to direct headers into the right areas. This informs your subconscious decision-making and as his confidence grew, his timing improved and so did his conviction and presence. We ran through similar processes with Cristiano. What I really liked about Rio was that he was never afraid to discuss or ask things. It was a tremendous quality of his. He knew, coming back from the ban, he had a lot to prove. He had the potential to become one of the all-time greats and, in my opinion, he firmly achieved that.

High achievers want to maintain that top level of performance for as long as they possibly can. Anything they can add that makes them stay at that level for longer, they will embrace, and when that comes to attitudes on the training pitch, it makes them more receptive to new ideas or suggestions.

When I had the opportunity to work with the reserve team, I felt that my priority was to get that team playing in the Manchester United way again. I considered that to be exciting football, aggressive and on the front foot, creating chances and a style that was great to watch. I felt the group was a lost assembly of individuals who had no idea what they were doing or where they were going.

There were some who felt that they were ready for a step up to the senior team – the likes of Gerard Pique and Giuseppe Rossi. There were others who had made a step up and now wanted to make themselves a fixture in reserve team football, and I'm thinking of Jonny Evans, a bright prospect in defence, Markus Neumayr, a very talented midfielder, and Phil Marsh, who had fought his way back to fitness after a car crash. Then there were those wanting to get just a chance in the reserves. I made time to try and make sure these players were appreciated as people – and it did take time, because first we needed to work on that identity of the reserve team.

I told them that when I saw them at Carrington, I saw a group of individuals who walked with their shoulders slouched and their heads down. There seemed to be no enjoyment coming from them. We needed to change that first and foremost.

I told them that I wanted that reserve team to be the buzz of the canteen – I wanted people to ask, 'Did you see them play last night?' Wes Brown played a few games for us. So did Alan Smith, Ole Gunnar Solskjaer and Gary Neville. Patrice Evra and Nemanja Vidic dropped in when they arrived in English football. Roy Keane trained with us. I'd invited some of the other senior players to Littleton Road to give the younger players a boost. Day by day, the atmosphere improved, and players were increasingly responsive. It helped that some of our early performances were fantastic – we got off to a fine start, winning 3-0 at Bolton, and then a couple of weeks later we won at Leeds. In the winter we went on a run where we scored 37 times in 11 games. I never rushed anything, but the players embraced everything pretty quickly and a natural chemistry developed organically.

The reserve team is possibly the most difficult team at any club to coach because your squad is always changing and always unpredictable. You want players to do so well they get called into the senior side. While you have a complete jumble of different aspirations and your job is to keep them motivated to perform as a collective.

I told the players that I could guarantee them, whether I was working with one, two, four, eight, 16 or 32 players, every training session would be of the highest calibre and there would always be a purpose and a challenge. Quality and intensity would always be there so the players could enjoy it and I wanted to make sure all these attributes were present in the way we played.

Their response was magnificent, particularly in the free-scoring run, and my proudest moment came as the season came close to the conclusion. We played Manchester City at Hyde – this was my team: Steele, Marsh, Evans, Pique, Rose, Gibson, Neumayr, Jones, Campbell, Rossi, Mullan. We were 4-0 up at half-time and we absolutely blew them away. We could have scored another four in the second half, but in the end we had to settle for 'just' a 6-0 win at full-time. Campbell had scored four of them. From start to finish we were fantastic.

To celebrate, me and a few friends went for a drink in a

pub called the Unicorn in Wilmslow. I was relaxing when my phone rang. The boss. He was in Milan watching a game.

"I believe you did well today."

"Boss, they were outstanding. Defensively they didn't give anything away. The build-up was slick, there was pace, lots of chances, lots of goals. I couldn't be prouder of the boys."

"Great. What are you doing now?"

"What do you think? I'm in the pub."

"Good for you lad!" he laughed.

You'll note that from the team I mentioned, three of them were foreign prospects. Regulations always seemed to change regarding the catchment areas and overseas recruitment and there were differences of opinion when it came to those who strongly believed that it was better to concentrate on the development of homegrown players at that level and those who felt it was a strong opportunity to bring in the most talented prospects on the continent. I could understand both sides of the argument. You do have an obligation to the domestic game to focus on the home players, but the level of competition is so high, and everyone is always attempting to find an advantage, that you can understand the logic in bringing in young lads from overseas.

The answer – as usual – lies in balance. You don't want to fill the pond and then end up with so many players that you ship so many out on loan. It defeats the objective, in my opinion. But if you can bring in a player nice and early and keep them around, they can grow and become accustomed to the identity of the club and the identity of the philosophy you're trying to put in place. It could be said that in my position as a foreign coach, and being multilingual, this placed me at an advantage with the squad I had.

One of the players we had brought in, from Germany, was

Markus Neumayr, a midfielder who had Beckham-esque qualities. He was a fantastic passer and had a complete range; short, crossing and diagonal. The boy was one of those who seemed to have low confidence because he hadn't had many opportunities so I wanted him to know he'd have a fair chance to show me what he could do. When he appeared to be receptive, I made him the captain of the team, wondering what that confidence boost might bring. A captain must take responsibility. I wanted Markus to seize that responsibility and dominate in the middle of the park and I felt he really thrived in the year under me.

Gerard Pique had all the talent but different factors stood in the way of him becoming a regular first-team player. Gerard certainly had a lot of character and wasn't afraid to be cheeky, even when he was with the first team. He'd often have a go at Rio or Nemanja. He made a few first-team appearances but when he eventually made the decision to go back to Barcelona I believe it was the correct one – obviously, in terms of trophies, but I also felt the Spanish league suited his style better.

We were spoiled with the talent we had – as back-ups we had Wes Brown and Jonny Evans, so we were well-covered. Ryan Shawcross – another example of a player in the wrong time at the wrong place. He had a strong personality, he was tall, he was good on the ball. He played over 450 times for Stoke and I feel comfortable in saying that if Rio or Nemanja hadn't been available Ryan could have stepped in and done a capable job. He could have also been among the centre-backs to have played for the club after they both left, too. We were spoiled with defenders, and Craig Cathcart was another who went on to play many times at the top level.

Gerard and Giuseppe Rossi are probably the two players from that reserve team who received the most attention and

I have to say I loved Giuseppe. I really did. Breaking into the first team and establishing yourself revolved around two things – opportunity and confidence. I don't think the timing ever worked out for Giuseppe that he could have a long enough run to overcome the doubts some had about him. I felt he was a fantastic player, a mix between Hagi and Stoichkov. He had great technique, that low centre of gravity, a great dribbling style. He scored four hat-tricks for me and ended up with more goals than games. He also had a great career, but it was a shame he never made it at United – yet if you think competition was tough for Gerard, look at the established players in front of Rossi. You had Ruud, Rooney, Ronaldo, Giggs, Solskjaer, Smith and Saha.

Phil Marsh was another young striker facing that dilemma. And he had Rossi, Campbell and Ebanks-Blake to contend with. Phil had a lot of qualities – you couldn't find a more honest person or player. He'd done so well to get back in the fold – and after Christmas, when Danny Simpson went on loan to Antwerp, we had a bit of a shortage of right-back options. I spoke to Phil and discussed his positive attributes and how I felt he might be a good progressive option in that department. Remarkably, he bought into it. On the other side, Kieran Lee, who was struggling to get a game in the middle of the park, agreed to play at left-back to replace Adam Eckersley who had gone with Danny to Belgium. They were both fantastic for me.

When I watch games in the English leagues now, I see plenty of players I worked with during my time at United. I'm proud of my own work in that regard but it is a testament to the legacy of the club and their philosophy that even if those players don't have long-term careers at Old Trafford, many of them go on to have lengthy careers at other clubs in the professional game. And often the attitude of those players is a credit to the clubs they moved on to. United have had generations of incredible success with their own youth and academy players in the first-team squad, but they have also had a much greater influence across the English game than any other club.

At the end of the season, we won a clean sweep in the reserves. That conclusion hadn't even been a part of my objective when we set out at the start; I wanted the players to feel that they belonged, that they could feel good about themselves, and to see a more positive outlook in their career progression. Yes, winning is in United's DNA, so we played well, and we played to win.

As we came closer to achieving our total success, we defeated Oldham in the Manchester Senior Cup and then lost our last Premier Reserve League game at Liverpool – we needed to get some momentum back ahead of the play-off against Tottenham.

I told the players to consider what I described as the Federer moment – and that, in effect, was to deal with what was in front of us. I found five clips of Roger Federer serving the ball, all from different stages of his matches in different tournaments. I asked the players to write down what tournament it was, and what set, game, and point. The only thing they were able to get with real accuracy was the tournament. I had watched an interview with Roger where he was asked about his volatile temperament when he was younger and how he had changed into what he had become; the cool-as-a-cucumber, almost emotionless, elite professional. This is what I was trying to get across to the players – only focus on what's in front. What happened before to get us where we are is gone. It doesn't matter. I would employ that same story a little later with the senior team.

Federer's explanation was attached to a game where he'd

won the first two sets of a match and then lost the next two. He was battling away in a close fifth set and at 5-4, he was up 40-30. And that was the moment. When he won that point, he wins the set, he wins the game – and whatever he did to get there is irrelevant. It's a psychological tool to address the value of momentum; when you have it, you try to keep it, and when you don't have it, you try to dismiss its relevance.

Everybody associates Federer with greatness, but they also acknowledge his mental strength under intense pressure. In football, you might well find yourself behind in the game. Are you going to lose your composure or are you going to be able to keep doing what we practised? Make sure we don't concede again. Make sure we create chances. Where the mind goes, I told them, the rest will follow. Tennis players in a singles match are in control of their own thoughts. In doubles, you don't know what your partner is thinking, but it is key that you think the same thing. In a team of 11 players, and the opposition is engaged within your pattern, you have so many variables at play; so if you can keep your composure, it's a crucial tool to implement if you get it right.

The first decade of the 21st century saw huge changes in European football, possibly still coming to terms with the after-effects of the Bosman ruling. Foreign coaches were now coming to England more frequently too, and they were beginning to have a strong influence in the way the game was played. In 2004, Jose Mourinho became manager of Chelsea, and Rafael Benitez took over at Liverpool. Both coaches believed in a pragmatic style where the emphasis seemed to shift towards not losing, and closing games out, rather than winning and entertaining.

As a coach, you always need to try and evolve and to be creative with playing systems and your approach. You must observe the trends across the game – for years everyone played 4-4-2. Then it was 4-3-3. Many teams then moved to play with three at the back. Within those team shapes, if you can develop players who can meet the technical requirements of the modern game – because the game is quicker, more physically and technically demanding and in less space – and make the intelligent decisions, that will always outmanoeuvre a team that has a fundamentally negative approach.

In any event, playing only to avoid defeat and not to win would have completely conflicted with Sir Alex Ferguson's vision of what Manchester United and football was supposed to be about. Our resolve to this new, defensive wave of football was to simply improve. Become more creative. Find new solutions. Break those defensive walls. If the players have the attributes, what else can we do? Find flexibility in our systems and be smart with the squad rotation.

A little further down the line, to just make a quick reference, we had Ronaldo, Rooney and Nani in our front line. Those three players could play anywhere across the front line and that gave us the potential to create unpredictable combinations to areas of defences they found vulnerable – we trusted them to do that and asked only if they understood the defensive requirements of the area they were in when the ball was turned over.

I would say that 75-80% of our preparation concentrated on us and our approach. We would never be dismissive of an opponent – we would analyse their style, their key players, and key strengths. But we would run through our own strengths and look where the passing of Scholes, the penetration of Giggs and Ronaldo, or the power of Rooney could cause the most damage.

Chapter Six

DENMARK CALLING

BEFORE the summer holidays in 2006 I had a post-season trip to Hong Kong with the youth team. On our return, I received a message from Sir Alex asking me to come into Carrington. I thought he was going to discuss the plans for next year.

"I've got a request from Brondby," he said. "They want to talk to you about being the new manager."

I asked him for his thoughts. He said he felt I was doing a good job, but he knew I'd managed before, and he could see it being a good opportunity for me in Denmark. If he had said there and then that he didn't really know, but he wanted me to stay if I wanted to, then I would have just ended the conversation there and then. But I left his office a little confused and with a promise to speak to Brondby.

Brondby are a fantastic club. They're magnificent. Their historical standards in terms of their stature were the same in Denmark as United's are in England. They should always be challenging for the top honours and always expected to do so.

They always had the ambition and resources to be the top club in the country.

At any club, there is the seduction of the history versus the reality of the present – I confess I did not spend enough time to undertake due diligence of the situation I was walking into. I was offered a three-year contract, and of course the contract of a manager differs from that of a coach. I accepted it even though there was this nagging, gnawing feeling instinct I had telling me it was the wrong decision.

But I signed that contract in good faith and to show my commitment I moved my entire family out there. That's just the way I am – when I make the decision to start something, I'm going to show it my full commitment and put everything into it. I wanted to transfer that ideal of how things were at United and give the best support in the country the best football to watch. I wanted us to play on the front foot. That would mean pressing high. When you press high, you leave spaces, so you need a goalkeeper who can sweep and a backline that is quick enough to anticipate danger.

I inherited a squad which didn't have the qualities to successfully play this way from the start. The cornerstone in defence was Per Nielsen – he was 33, the club captain and effectively Mr Brondby. He was immensely respected and rightfully so. But where I wanted him to push up, he was cautiously dropping off. This is just one example, and Per was far from the only player who had trouble adjusting, but it's the quickest way I can make the reference. I had four players in their 30s on good, long contracts that they did not want to give up.

If I'm being totally honest, I was only a few weeks into the job at this moment and I was already feeling as though I really should have brought someone familiar with me as an assistant. You need to have an aide to pass on your messages, that's part of the healthy balance of a squad – though, having said that, the strength and conditioning coach was René Skovdahl and he became my assistant. He was superb and a big support to me. But the benefit of having your own people rather than people who were already at the club is that you know when times are tough, you don't have to wonder about which direction they're pulling in.

Every day is a learning experience and in football it is very rarely the truth that all the changes you want to make have an instant impact. Yes, it goes without saying that I wanted to impress my own philosophy and style of football, and I laid that out from day one. When a squad is met with a fresh approach, you generally get a strong initial reaction, so long as you've put forward a strong enough impression. You lay down some basics such as timekeeping, you discuss your expectations and how they align with the club, you talk about values, and so on. You discuss your game plan in a very simple way to begin with. How are we going to set up defensively? Is it pressing high or a low block? Do we play long in possession or play out from the back? You have these initial conversations and the more you get to know the squad, the more you adapt your approach.

That process took me a few league games. We started the season quite well — unbeaten in my first nine league games — but at a club like Brondby (and you could make this argument for most clubs) it's really difficult to assess the strength of the squad until you're a fair few games into the season and you can see what is working and what isn't. Pressure and expectation from the fans and the press can turn a player who was looking superb in pre-season into one who is struggling.

I did make two signings – Adam Eckersley and Mark Howard, both for free from United. Adam was an aggressive left-back going forward and Mark had an assurance in defence.

I was hoping that they would help get the message of what I wanted to achieve across, but it was proving difficult. There were also comments leaked to the press and I found that to be a major disappointment, as it was disrespectful to the other players at the club. I knew this from my experience at United – the press loves it when the King has fallen over. They write about it every day. Feeding them seems as unnecessary as it is counterproductive.

In mid-September we came up against Frankfurt in the Europa League. The German side were favourites, so, as always, in times of such disparity, I turned to psychology. I utilised this before I went to Denmark and afterwards because I'm a strong believer in that principle I explained earlier, of the rest following where the mind goes.

Understanding psychology and how the mind works will help a coach or manager to get the best out of his players and team. It can be seen as a complex aspect for many players, but if a person can take control of his thinking and emotions and is able to choose his desired attitude towards anything, he or she will have a by far better chance at achieving what they want. Every person balances on a lifeline where on one end of the spectrum is what you don't want and on the other side of the spectrum is what you do want.

The power lies in the ability to steer your attitude and behaviour towards what you do want, your ambitions and dreams, rather than let it slide towards the other side where fear will be the biggest culprit in dragging you into what you don't want. We cannot always control what we hear, see, smell, or feel. What we can control is how we react and translate those feelings and emotions and how we turn them into positives rather than negatives.

Human mentality has a fight or flight instinct and as a coach you are always aiming to achieve the former quality. If a small animal is up against a predator, they will try and escape. A brave animal will stand up and fight.

The disparity between the sides might have had our players feeling inferior, and to make the Frankfurt players be a little more apprehensive, our own must be confident and aggressive. I tried to instil the concept that they were lions. They couldn't be pushed aside.

We got to half-time 0-0. We were doing well. Straight after half-time we were given two red cards. Two penalties were given against us. On balance, 11 against 11, we were doing well. We lost 4-0. So much for psychology, some would laugh, but to me it proved only that football is unpredictable and things happen outside your control. The result however had an unwanted effect on us mentally. We were eliminated from Europe and suffered a bad run of form in the league, losing big games against Copenhagen and FC Midtjylland and winning just two from the next eight after that.

I felt we needed a new heartbeat in the set-up to create a new sense of vibrancy and revitalise the entire club. I talked to the hierarchy of the club to explain what I felt were three groups within the squad.

The first, possibly the smallest, were the eldest group of experienced players who were clinging on – and I understand that, because nobody wants to accept that they're saying goodbye to the best years of their football career. There was the massive middle group who didn't have many stars. Then another small group of promising young players who I felt had what it took to represent the club – but they weren't there yet. There was a significant imbalance, because the middle group needed to be the one with the most quality.

I tried – I made an early attempt to sign Thomas Helveg,

one of the most established Danish professionals of all time. He wanted to come in a player-coach capacity and that was an ideal situation for me. I felt so confident after my conversations with Thomas, which were held over an international break, that when I returned to work, I had this urgency to impress upon everyone that my wish was to address all our concerns, establish a clear vision for all of us, and create a positive environment within the dressing room.

The executive director and chairman of the club was Per Bjerregaard, who was a doctor by trade; we had a decent relationship, but he was the sort of man who wanted to try and have a say on everything that was happening at the club. I mean everything – marketing, ticket sales, the team, you name it.

"Per," I told him. "If someone comes to you with a headache, an infection, or the flu, you can help them. But if a person has a serious heart condition and needs surgery, you send them to a specialist, don't you?" I was trying to impress upon him that to progress as a club we would need specialists in many different departments.

He appointed his son, Anders, as the technical director. When I returned from my break with my hopes of signing Helveg, Anders informed me he'd signed another defender whose name I can't recall and who I was unfamiliar with. I had to Google him and I discovered he had barely played and had a track record of injuries. I met Anders the next day and asked him what was going on.

"We didn't want to disturb you on your break."

"What's this?" I said, pointing to my mobile phone. I tried to bring up the subject of Thomas Helveg and Anders seemed to avoid the question by saying we couldn't afford it because we hadn't offloaded certain players. I'd already had conversations with agents of players we were looking to move on, and I knew for certain we had offers on the table for every single one. I knew something didn't smell right so I picked up the phone and made the call to Sir Alex for advice.

"René, what you're thinking is the right thing. What you want to do is the right thing. Starting out as you are, you need to make tough decisions. No negotiations. No concessions. No emotions. Stick to what you believe in and make sure you get what you want, because it's these decisions which will determine if you can be successful."

It was the best advice I'd ever had. It gave me an extra sense of confidence to go back to Per and explain to him that we were travelling towards a dead end and that the plans I was putting in place would have us challenging for the title within a year or so. The response was blunt – that it was impossible to offload the players. My own reply was equally stubborn. I said without this sort of movement and progression, the club was doomed to stagnate, and I would be the one who would suffer the criticism for it.

At the time, my mother was very ill with cancer, and her experience was the bluntest way I could articulate the message to the chairman. "The club reminds me of my mother. The medication doesn't work anymore. It needs direct surgery." The conversation provided nothing but a clarity that we both wanted very different things.

The club and I went our separate ways. It would be 2021 before Brondby won their next league title, by which time FC Copenhagen had overtaken them as the most dominant club in the country. It was sad to see the problems I envisaged play out, and just as sad to see how long it took them to be resolved.

I had other spells in management, but I already had a feeling – that was later reinforced – that coaching senior players with all the extra pressure that comes with being a manager was, effectively, indulging in everything that I loved about the game, but also forced me to deal with the things I didn't enjoy quite so much. I'm not saying that I couldn't have enjoyed the elements like picking the team or facing the press, in fact I did, but if you are taking on those pressures and you don't have the support you require to succeed then it's a very different proposition.

I made another phone call to Sir Alex. I explained what happened and that I would be leaving Brondby. I also went one step further and revealed my reservations at having left United in the first place. If he felt I had a role to play, I told him, I'd be more than happy to come back before even entertaining a serious offer from elsewhere. I was told that Sir Alex discussed it with the senior players at the club – and they all encouraged him to bring me back into the first-team set-up. I suppose, in a sense, I have the move to Brondby to thank for that, because prior to taking the job I was still seen as someone who was predominantly associated with the academy and youth structure at the club.

"Most coaches wouldn't have done what you did," Sir Alex told me after I returned. "They would have stayed and taken the money. I admire your values and principles."

My family had taken to the move quite well. We liked the area in which we lived. My daughter was enjoying figure skating. My sons were playing football. I had to tell them that it hadn't worked out. They weren't very happy to be making such a big move again, even though they liked Manchester, as it was a lot to take in twice in a matter of months. I understood, and I felt bad about it. In football you can never make a guarantee, but I made a personal vow at that time, that I would ensure I wouldn't put my family through another period of this instability.

Chapter Seven

COACHING THE ELITE

BACK in Manchester, Sir Alex was pushing for the league title for the first time in four years. A new great team was realising its potential and the development of the chemistry even in the few months I'd been away was clear to see. Patrice Evra and Nemanja Vidic were now settled in English football and Michael Carrick, signed in the summer, looked like he had been at the club for years. On such a strong platform, Wayne Rooney and Cristiano Ronaldo were able to show their power.

I noticed some subtle differences in the approach to leading the players as opposed to when I first came to the club and saw the likes of Keane and Beckham. I could clearly recall Steve McClaren's sessions having a lot of energy whilst under Carlos Quieroz there was a lot of calmness. The difference in techniques was always fascinating to me and in my time away I'd noticed the subtle challenges that were presented when coaching professionals versus coaching elite professionals. I would observe the sessions and try to identify the buttons that specific players needed pressing at certain times to motivate them or prepare them. With normal professionals, you need to maintain a consistency, you need to keep coaching them and reminding them through repetition.

At this elite level, where players had so much experience at the top level, you needed to create a pathway where you were informing them about the next opponent, facilitating the right sessions whereby the players get a clear idea of what's needed in the upcoming game and encouraging them in doing the right thing. It's about purpose, challenge, quality, and intensity. If you have those four objectives in a session, players generally enjoy it more.

I remember a succession of breathtaking performances in the months after I came back to the club. Ronaldo and Rooney were exceptional against Bolton in the league and against Roma in the Champions League. It was remarkable to watch – you're lucky to have one player with this star quality in a team, but we had two, and in combination they were too much for the league to handle. Their personalities were completely different though. Both were great professionals. Cristiano looked after himself to achieve the level he wanted to get to – his focus was unmatched. Wayne was a different animal who played a lot on instinct and just enjoyed playing football for Manchester United. The two were perfect for each other on the pitch.

I had worked alongside Carlos, but he was the one setting the tone in training, he and Sir Alex were the ones who were responsible for the strategy as I found my feet in my new role at the club. I was just delighted to be back at Old Trafford and share in the moment as the Premier League came back to the club for the first time since 2003.

Sir Alex decided to add some significant additions to our squad over the summer of 2007. One player he had coveted for a while was Owen Hargreaves, the midfielder who had tremendous experience playing for Bayern Munich and England. Everybody knew he had a fantastic technical level and that he had a certain tenacity, and even though there was a concern about a long-standing injury issue he had, when he arrived at the club he was training very well. Some players get haunted by little injuries and it is a challenging process to get involved with.

At this time, Carlos was still the assistant to Sir Alex, so my main responsibility was not too far away from what it had been earlier in my first spell at the club – I was helping with the sessions and spending time with the players who were returning from injury once the physiotherapists and doctors felt they were ready. I would take that opportunity to implement skillwork in game-related settings and Owen Hargreaves, a nice guy, was one I spent some time with in his first year.

Anderson was a typical, bubbly Brazilian character. He loved to play the game and he had some great qualities. I thought his ability to drive with the ball and burst between the lines was exceptional, and he also had an element of creativity and healthy risk in his game. Defensively he suffered from lapses of concentration when it came to doing the job that had to be done, but he had so much potential. Nani came from Sporting Lisbon and naturally invited lazy comparisons that he was just like Ronaldo because he was following the same path and he played in wide areas.

They did share similar qualities, but Nani was his own player. He was a unique athlete. He was powerful, quick, able to play from both sides and use both feet. He was direct and a scorer of simply unbelievable goals. He could take players on and was quick enough to play behind the defence. There was room for better decision-making, but he was still young, and a tremendous asset in our attacking line. The whole squad had a great balance of experience, quality, and youth to inject some energy and drive into the team.

Carlos, with his Portuguese background, helped those players settle in very well. He was the main man doing the team sessions. Over the course of the season, I was given more licence to do specific work with the forwards. Carlos then wanted me to get more involved with skills drills in warm-ups or passing-based exercises. It was enjoyable getting to work with the bigger groups and it was a very important period in my time at the club because now, for the first time, Sir Alex could see for himself the work I was doing with senior players.

As the season started, Carlos Tevez arrived. He had been at West Ham and performed very well. He was a great example of the difference between South American players and European players – all he cared about was winning. You do get single-minded European players, but the mentality is slightly different – the attitude towards the game revolves only around winning in whatever form it takes. Training, for him, was a necessity, something he had to endure.

If you were doing scenarios based around the upcoming game, he would be great, no problem. But if you were going over tactical drills, for example repetition of a sequence, you could tell that was not his cup of tea. Carlos was very close with Patrice and Park Ji-Sung – three men from completely different parts of the world who had an instant connection. Perhaps they bonded over their way of playing – high-energy, intense, getting on the front foot, qualities associated with the club. Carlos would never stop running and working and he was great at it. It gave Sir Alex fantastic options. This is as good a moment as any to pay tribute to Ji: in every successful squad, sometimes you ask certain players to carry out instructions in specific games.

Ji was massively important for us. He was so versatile. Whenever you wanted to change the system, he could always be the missing piece, whereas other players might only be able to do one job. Ji could play wide, in the pockets, as a midfielder. What I respected most about him, and I'm certain this is a cultural thing that had much to do with his background, was that he was very much a player who said, "I'm here to do what you tell me to do." He never moaned, he never questioned. He appreciated every moment he had and he gave his best. He was exceptional. If you were to ask the average person how long Ji played for United and for how many years, I'm almost certain they'd underestimate it. He was technically very good and he never overdid it. If he made a mistake, it would always be an honest one.

A funny story regarding Ji is that my wife Marieke still claims till this day that she signed Park Ji-Sung! Well, that needs some explanation. As Ji was transferred from PSV, Holland to Manchester, his medical reports were in Dutch. As I was away with the first team at the time the club secretary Ken Merrett asked if he could drop by my house to have Marieke translate the Dutch medical documents. She did and Ji got signed after everything got approved on the same day.

Another player in a similar mould was Wayne Rooney. As Cristiano started to flourish at the start of the season, and he started to roam from his natural position, a few critics observed Rooney's contribution in comparison, and they came to some form of conclusion that he had taken a sacrifice to help the team. I can tell you that Wayne would not have seen it that way. He would have seen it in quite the opposite way – he would have seen Cristiano's movement as something that helped his own. It helped him play to his own strengths and it was clear to see he enjoyed playing.

He was always involved in the play and always involved when we countered in those rapid attacks. He really loved being involved in the start of the play all the way through to the end. He truly enjoyed great passages of football and an assist as much as he did scoring goals. As we sought to turn Ronaldo into more of a goal threat, Wayne achieved greater freedom to drop back and feature more in the build-up.

Over the autumn, as the team found their feet with the new players, Rooney, Tevez and Ronaldo were in remarkable form. Our play was based on energy, dynamism, running, getting in behind the defences, and there was a gelling and an appreciation for each other. We scored four goals against Wigan, Aston Villa, Middlesbrough, and Dynamo Kyiv, twice, in the space of four or five weeks – it was an extraordinary run of form. It was mesmerising at times. The interchanging of positions, the complete fluidity of the attack, it was so fun to watch.

In the span of six or seven years the faces had changed on the training pitches at Carrington, but the intensity remained. It was Carlos and not Steve McClaren leading the sessions and these were often tactically oriented, so you might say that the intensity was led by the direction and not necessarily the individuals in the same way as Roy Keane was doing it, for example. My observation was – and it was a massive learning curve for me – that at this level, the pace of your sessions was so important when it came to all of the elements; purpose, challenge, quality, intensity. You want players to enjoy training and players who are that good need to know why you are doing what you're doing, they need that process to be facilitated. They need to be immersed.

I compare training to cooking – and as coach of Manchester United, you have the best ingredients, so you can make a five-star meal. But you can cook the same meal every day of the week and by the fourth day you're sick of it. It's the same with training sessions. You need to get the same message across – so train the same way and work on the same patterns – but dress it up in different ways. The most important part was that the natural flow was maintained. Carlos and I would ensure that we discussed the sessions with the players as a group and individuals so that they always knew it was their game. We wanted them to enjoy the training. It didn't matter how much money they made or what club they played for, so long as you were making training captivating, purposeful and fun, they'd put the effort in, no problem.

While the first team was making positive strides towards retaining the league title, the reserve team, once my domain, was now under the leadership of Ole Gunnar Solskjaer, the legendary striker who had recently retired. I had countless conversations with Ole, going back to when I was in charge, and he was regularly playing for the second string. He was always observant, always reading the game, and always asking questions. Twice a week, over several months, we would sit and have long conversations where I would discuss my ideas and philosophy with him. I even served as assistant to him on a handful of occasions, and I used those conversations and opportunities to get a greater understanding of the players Ole was now working with who would be hoping to make the step up to the first team.

Amid our run of scoring four goals every time we played, we had a trip to Arsenal – Arsene Wenger had rebuilt his side and this season they looked like genuine contenders. They were playing good football too, and in the build-up to our match they were tipped as the more aesthetically pleasing. These things are determined and influenced by the media. It made no difference to us – we concentrated on ourselves and our own way of playing. The game ended 2-2 and we learned a few things.

Arsenal's game plan was centred around a few key players. The major link was Fabregas to the centre-forward, in this case, Adebayor. We knew if we stopped Fabregas getting on the ball they'd have to find different solutions. Arsenal were was so open on the ball so we knew we needed to adapt our defensive strategy so that our defenders were not necessarily behind the man they were marking but side on, as we knew they always played it to feet.

By pushing Park, for example, on Fabregas, we could limit his time on the ball. He gets frustrated and other players take their chances. We could set traps that way and the moment they play the ball in, they would be open defensively. From that moment it's about picking the right pass – and there were multiple occasions where we exploited this, with some famous goals and sometimes quite heavy score lines.

One thing I'd noticed about Sir Alex over the years was that his drive had always remained the same. I am certain that his attitude towards the praise other teams got in comparison with United was that he was never bothered. But his attitude towards the drive he had for his own team had probably changed over the years. At the start, he had to rebuild so much of the club that he would have had to have been much more hands-on.

By the time I was working as a first-team coach in 2007, he had established United as one of – if not the – top clubs in the world. Certainly the club with the highest expectation and therefore, the club with the most pressure. And yet, on a day-to-day basis, I never felt any of that pressure. Not once. That was purely down to Sir Alex's management of the players and of the staff. His own expectations and standards were probably higher than those demanded of us from the outside. But he was so relaxed and his attitude to delegation was so trusting. You might think that delegation would be a transfer of pressure, but that is not even remotely close to being true. It was a routine. He instilled a cultural winning mentality and we all worked together to keep that mentality. Through it all he would always ensure he got the message across – the players had an obligation to entertain the supporters.

The boss was light-hearted and had a great sense of humour when it came to engaging with staff, especially during lunch time in the canteen. Whilst brewing his own cup of tea you could bet on it that he would put the red-hot teaspoon on your hand if you just happened to stand next to him. Ouch! Mike O'Donnelly was our chef. An outstanding chef I might say, as the buffet he, Carol and Tina prepared was outstanding. He had a great demeanour about himself. He loved to crack a joke and it was great to chat to him from time to time. I recall one incident that made me giggle. Carlos Queiroz was filling up his plate and asked Carol, "What is this?"

"Nowt to do with you, just get it down your neck!" Carol replied. I stood behind Carlos and was pissing myself laughing. So much for Manchester hospitality.

The next time we played Arsenal was in the FA Cup in February. We won 4-0, even with a few changes. It was our 13th win in 17 games, a level of consistency that was becoming as much a product of psychology as it was quality. One of Sir Alex's mantras was to say that if we were no more than five or six points behind the league leaders at the end of January (if we weren't on top), then we were in a good position. From that point he'd pick a more consistent 11 in the league to develop continuity. He spoke of the importance of our individual talent and how that would win games – but it was a team effort that would win us trophies.

That individual talent was clear in the form of Ronaldo. By the end of February, he'd already scored 30 goals in all competitions. He was already on such a strong trajectory with his form.

"I know exactly what you want," I remember saying to him in one of our sessions.

"Oh yeah?"

"I'll say it. You want to be the best player in the world. And not once. Not twice. You want to establish yourself as one of the greatest of all-time… and that's great. You have a focus. You have an aim. And people who have an objective are much more successful than people who do not. So, the question is, where you are going and where you want to be, will you be considered that way tomorrow?"

"No," he admitted.

"Next week?"

"No."

"Next month?"

"No."

That's where the different conversations came in. He needed to be more effective in the deployment of his incredible gifts. He needed to score more goals to help United win more games. If he did that then United would surely win more trophies. And winning more trophies is part of the sequence of achieving greatness.

His form was incredible. Multiple times he scored twice in games to put us in control early on. He had embraced what he needed to do. Chances were turned into goals. The perfect goals he wanted arrived, as I had assured him. The free-kicks he scored against Sunderland and Portsmouth were breathtaking. It was not a surprise to me or any of us who saw him every day. He was relentless. Get better. Score more goals. Win more games. Get better. Score more goals. Win more games. He reached his target of 30 against Newcastle in February. "Great," I said to him after. "You've done that, but now you've got March, April, and May. What's next?"

"I'm going to try and reach your target," he said, referring to my opinion that he should get 40 goals. I'd made a DVD for him titled *From Good to Great*. I wanted to get him into a mental state to maintain his incredible form and still look to improve each time he went out. I asked him to watch the DVD three times – the first to just watch. The second to focus on the words and quotes that were said. The third and final time was to analyse the clips and to consider why I'd chosen them. The purpose of the video was to sharpen the perspective that he was so important as an individual to make the team achieve what they wanted – but without the team, he was nothing. The two were complementary and without each other they wouldn't work.

We were challenging for the Treble. To achieve it you need greatness, and you need some luck. Luck deserted us against Portsmouth in the FA Cup; but we responded by winning seven of our next eight, putting us in a strong position in the league and in the semi-finals of the Champions League, where we came up against Barcelona.

Before travelling to Spain for the first leg we drew at Blackburn, late on, thanks to a Tevez goal. We drew against Barcelona. Ronaldo missed an early penalty, but we drew 0-0. We went from there to London, to play against Chelsea, who had once again emerged as the rivals for the league after Arsenal dropped away. We were four minutes away from a draw when Chelsea got a lucky penalty and won the game.

The momentum of three draws would have been very different to the two draws and a defeat. I didn't travel to Spain or London, and when the squad arrived back in Manchester, there was a downbeat mood. At that moment I had a conversation with Sir Alex. I discussed the Federer moment with him. We were in that position.

Beat Barcelona and we were in the final.

Beat West Ham and we were in control of the league title race.

Rather than looking back at the last two results and letting that influence where we were going, we needed to stop and look forward. Press the reset button. The anxiety of the previous results needed to be replaced by the excitement at the prospect of what winning would bring. Winning against Barcelona would get us in a European Cup final. That would generate positive momentum for West Ham.

I wasn't present at the team meeting before Barcelona, but Ole later told me that Sir Alex used the analogy with the squad.

Frank Rijkaard's team had won the Champions League in 2006. They were already well on the way to moving into their peak side which Pep Guardiola would inherit in the following months. Lionel Messi was already at the top of his game, much like Cristiano.

There were a few narrow escapes to say the least. Paul Scholes scored a sensational early goal. It was one moment in a game, a game of thousands of interactive moments where you need to be on top and aware, or you'll be punished. The intensity was incredible. I was watching it from the stands where you are caught up in the moment. It was in the aftermath as I reflected, obviously in a positive mood, that we were Manchester United and, especially at Old Trafford, we should have been the team putting the other under pressure and asking all the questions as well as being well-organised in defence. It worked, but I felt it depended on such a narrow margin because Barcelona had excellent individuals who could have changed things in a split-second.

Nonetheless, we had reached the mindset of the Federer moment. We defeated West Ham comfortably. We played Wigan on the last day in the rain. Cristiano scored early on and Giggsy sealed it late on. It was as professional as we needed it to be. This was the third time I'd experienced United winning the title when I was at the club, but the first time where I'd felt this level of involvement, and it was a very special feeling, I must confess.

Chelsea were the other Champions League finalists. They were not unfamiliar to us. Jose Mourinho had been dismissed early in the season and Avram Grant, his successor, was a little more adventurous. The preparation was handled by Sir Alex and Carlos and it focused on us taking the game to them. We went 1-0 up through Ronaldo and should have been 2-0 up but they equalised through a scruffy Frank Lampard goal. Giggsy and Carrick both had chances to win it before it went to penalties.

We had practised penalties in the build-up. They say penalty shootouts are a lottery – you can certainly make it that way if you don't prepare the players adequately. I was sitting in the stands next to my wife as the shoot-out began, and I told her I just had a feeling that it was destined to be a special moment for Edwin van der Sar. We had very good takers, I knew that for sure. Tevez, Hargreaves, Carrick, Anderson, Nani. Ice through their veins. Ronaldo missed. So too did John Terry, right when it looked like Chelsea would win it. Perhaps they both had a moment where they thought about themselves and not the team. At this level, every moment of concentration is crucial.

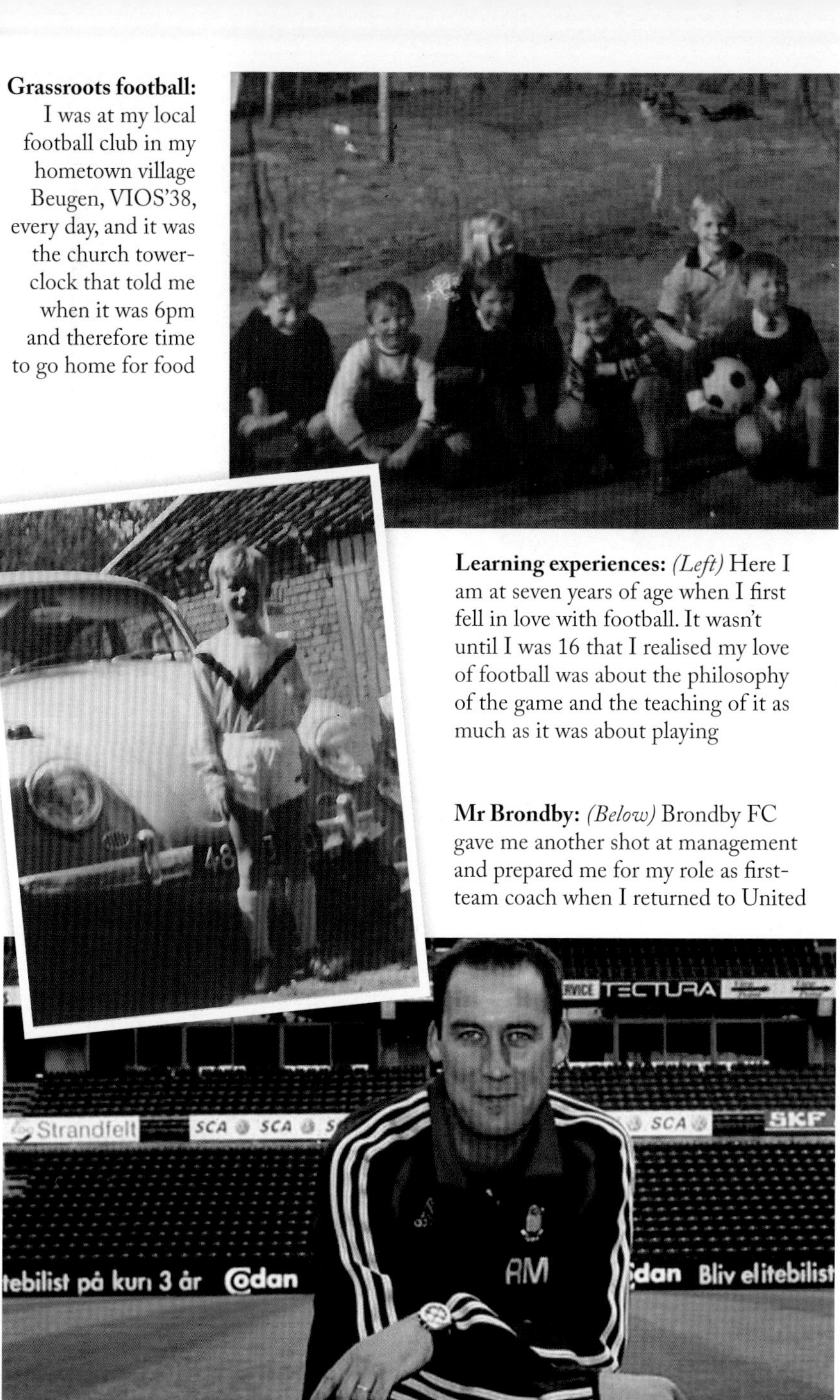

Grassroots football: I was at my local football club in my hometown village Beugen, VIOS'38, every day, and it was the church tower-clock that told me when it was 6pm and therefore time to go home for food

Learning experiences: *(Left)* Here I am at seven years of age when I first fell in love with football. It wasn't until I was 16 that I realised my love of football was about the philosophy of the game and the teaching of it as much as it was about playing

Mr Brondby: *(Below)* Brondby FC gave me another shot at management and prepared me for my role as first-team coach when I returned to United

Rising stars: The reserve team is the most difficult team at any club to coach because your squad is always changing. You want players to do so well they get called to the senior side

World champions: The Club World Cup was Wayne's time to have his individual moment in the spotlight. He scored twice in the semi-final against Gamba Osaka and then the only goal against LDU Quito of Ecuador. As far as I'm concerned, I always considered this one of the pinnacles of club football

United philosophy: Sir Alex always spoke of the importance of the players' individual talent and how that would win games – but it was a team effort that would win us trophies

United weigh: I can remember the first time I tried to lift the Champions League trophy; I was surprised by how heavy it was. The Premier League trophy was even heavier!

Go big or go home: The element that sets successful teams apart from the rest is a winning mentality. All those teams that have won numerous domestic and international trophies have this in their DNA

United overseas: *(Above)* The boss loved pre-season trips, I felt he was always very relaxed there. Here we are watching a friendly match between Orlando Pirates and Manchester United in 2008

Winning mentality: *(Right)* Cristiano knew exactly what he wanted. He was very focussed and determined and took everything on board to help him become the best player in the world

Goal getter: Robin fitted into our group easily. He was a top professional. There was no arrogance about him

Quality players: Danny was technically outstanding. He was deceivingly quick. He was also fantastic at 'back defending' – lurking around defenders and pinching balls from them

Keen to learn: Wayne Rooney, would always walk up to me before training and ask, "What are we doing today René?"

More silverware: Myself and the rest of the coaching staff celebrating United's Carling Cup win against Aston Villa in 2010. Michael Owen and Wayne got the goals in a 2-1 comeback

The final whistle: Sir Alex Ferguson lifts the Premier League trophy after his final home game as United manager, against Swansea City in 2013

Exciting times: I don't think there was a game where I took my seat on the bench at the start of the game and thought we weren't going to do something special

An unexpected promotion: I tuned into Talksport – the breaking news was that Martin Jol had left Fulham and René Meulensteen had been appointed manager

Proud dad: My son Melle *(above)* plays with Vitesse Arnhem in the Dutch Eredivisie. My daughter Pien *(right)* is a sports presenter, and my son Joppe won promotion to League Two last year with Stockport County

Socceroos: We wanted an identity. Football is the fifth sport in Australia – Football, though, unites the nation like nothing else

John messed with his armband. He wanted the spotlight. He got it, but not in the way he'd planned.

Giggs scored. Anelka stepped up. My gut feeling was right – Edwin made a fantastic save, and we were European champions.

I was disappointed to not have actually travelled with the team and to be on the bench but there were only so many places available, the boss explained, so I was just happy to be there in the stadium and, of course, to be a part of the celebrations afterwards. It was a late kick-off anyway and I'm pretty sure it was 2am before we even got to the dinner. I remember getting back to the team hotel after only having breakfast before getting the flight home.

You live for those moments – life at Manchester United is the pursuit of them. Life at Manchester United involves the pursuit of those moments from the moment you taste them. That means preparing for the next one while you're still celebrating the current one. I have no doubt that Sir Alex was in the midst of that when he received the news that Carlos would be leaving to take over as manager of Portugal. We had already reported back to pre-season training, getting ready to travel to South Africa. Mick Phelan and I were called into the manager's office and we were told that we'd have to look after the pre-season training. So we did. Our organisation came naturally – I took charge of the field sessions, together with Tony Strudwick, and Mick was happy for that to be the case. I knew I wanted to incorporate a lot of football activities, working in big areas and then more intensive in smaller areas. We had to work closely with Tony to ensure we got things right from a strength and conditioning point of view. Everything went smoothly. The results went well, but more importantly the preparation seemed strong and solid.

We won the Community Shield on penalties and opened our league campaign with a draw against Newcastle and a win against Portsmouth. Then there was an international break, and it was at this point the manager made his decision. He called Mick and I into his office at Carrington in separate meetings. I learned Mick had been appointed assistant and I was to be promoted to first-team coach. I was also given the responsibility of running and planning training sessions.

"I don't have to tell you how to run them," he said. "It's clear the players love it. But I just wanted to have this quick chat, so we are on the same page. If I close my eyes and picture the best Manchester United team in my head, this is what I see."

He had a flip chart next to him and he started talking through everything that was on there. On the first page was the defensive strategy: "I want us to be able to press high, to press from the front aggressively with a high line," he explained. "At times we'll need to be compact and then press from a block. We'll need to be clever, sit in a bit, let a player come at us with the ball, set traps and hit the spaces they leave for us. There will be moments we have to defend deep and, in those moments, we'll have to make sure we don't give time and space to those opponents. We always need to make sure that when we do get the ball back, we're able to counter. Everything is based on the principle of a quick transition of play."

He went through the importance of defensive set-pieces and then flipped over the paper to the second page. Possession: "This is key," he said. "We must always have possession with purpose. Our purpose can be to come straight out of the blocks and blow them away with an early goal, or to settle down into a game and keep the ball moving. The most important aspect of possession is rhythm." As he spoke those words, it really hit home to me.

"The best midfielders create rhythm; they maintain rhythm and they change rhythm when they have to. If we build up from the back, it's a one or two-touch rhythm. You get over the halfway line and into more condensed areas, and then you need to switch to one-touch. The purpose is to open the opponent up through switches of play, breaking lines, get behind the back four and create chances. If you have possession, you can take the initiative in the game. If you can turn possession into creating chances and goals, you're taking control of the game. The advantage, when having control of the game a team can then dominate the game. You can be so strong in your pressure that even when they reclaim the ball you can counter-press a mistake and regain the ball easily. Those are the three key phases of momentum in a game, which is the pattern of every game of football. Initiative, control, dominance."

He flipped over to the last page.

"This is the most important one," he says. "Attack. When I see United attack, I want to see us attack with speed, power, penetration, and unpredictability. I want you to instil these four things in every training session you take control of."

He then ran through attacking set-plays and stressed that these were the three elements around which his philosophy of play was centred.

"And if that doesn't work," he said, mischievously, taking a red pen and writing these two words in big bold letters and then underlining it, "we gamble!"

I loved that. And everyone reading this will know exactly what that meant. But how do you teach it? I interpreted it as maximising the time left in a game to create as many goal-scoring opportunities as possible. If there were 10 minutes left on the clock, we'd average perhaps an extra four minutes, and I would calculate that from that time we would want to get seven or eight good crosses or entries into the box to create an opportunity. When the clock goes down to eight minutes, four balls. When we get into injury time, we need two good crosses into the box. We would do scenario training for this. We'd have a defence against attack and have them play out the last eight or nine minutes. I'd make changes with our attack to create different combinations. Your intention is to suffocate a defence.

I took that conversation and those instructions as my parameters for how I would coach Manchester United. You have two ways of training in football. You can work on general strategies or specifically planning for an opponent. The four words: speed, power, penetration, and unpredictability, they took on a cadence and rhythm of their own in my head, a masterplan that underpinned everything we were trying to accomplish at Carrington. We did wave sessions, box to box, game-related distances, many different patterns, everything to achieve attacks in the vision of Sir Alex.

It should be clear by now that this was music to my own ears, particularly the unpredictability element. Unpredictability, as I saw it, was all about switching up rhythm and movement when you were in possession. Can you move to one-touch, can you overload, can you overlap, underlap, beat opponents in 1v1s. Could you have a team that can do all of these things so opponents just don't know what to do?

Mick naturally gravitated towards the defensive players and worked more closely with them. We were both invested in making sure the players understood what we wanted, and while I found myself more invested in the attacking dynamic and overall structure, Mick would look at those defensive performances and would have the space to give pointers and have conversations with players on an individual basis.

Emboldened by this, I felt cheeky enough to go one step further. One day I went with the boss in his car to watch our reserve team play. We were listening to the Champions League draw on the radio.

"Listen boss," I said. "I think we need to go back to what we're good at. What we've always done. We're Manchester United. Home and away we need to play with no concessions. Play on the front foot. We go out there, we play to our strengths, we play with our hearts on our sleeves. We've got so much quality and if we don't beat them with that, we'll outrun them, we'll outwork them, we'll outsmart them."

He smiled and agreed.

There were some notable squad adjustments over the summer. Dimitar Berbatov arrived for a club-record fee. He was not a player who was going to add pace or energy to the front line; he did things in a very laid-back and stylish way. I wouldn't say he was a loner, but he was an individual, and I think it took a little while for him and the existing squad to get to know each other. He was an introvert. I had conversations with him at United and in the spells where we were together afterwards. He was perhaps a little insecure.

Berba was a fantastic player. He was a joy to watch. The boss loved him and was delighted to get him. But he was a very different player to Carlos Tevez; and when Carlos wasn't playing, he was not the easiest guy to have around the squad. Berbatov offered us different solutions and a unique option. He wasn't a footballer – he was an artist. We also brought in Rafael and Fabio Da Silva, the Brazilian twins, who usually played at full-back, and they had a lot of character.

Perhaps the biggest move we made was keeping hold of Cristiano. He quite openly wanted to join Real Madrid, but the boss had convinced him to stay an extra year. Credit to him because as soon as that decision was reached, it was business as usual. No sulking.

The players took it in good humour. The first day back in training, Scholesy said to him, "Seeing as you wanted to go to Real Madrid so bad, you can wear a white bib all season." Cristiano was great for us, and I think in hindsight he would have been happy he did stay with us for that extra year.

Now I was with the first team, although Paul and Ryan had even more experience, I wasn't keen on replicating what I'd done with the reserves and having the senior players explain things. It worked with the reserve team because it was helping development but with the senior squad there had to be a clear definition between the coaching staff and the playing squad. To achieve the same goal, when there was an issue, Mick and I might pull the defenders to one side and run through solutions to problems together, asking them for their thoughts and opinions as a collective used to playing with each other and understanding their strengths and weaknesses.

Even though the squad I was coaching were the reigning European champions, we still had an objective to improve. I must stress here that this was a mutual understanding. This wasn't a written edict; it was not a message from Sir Alex. It was the way of life at Manchester United and it was the only way you could exist at the club. It wasn't a discussion. It wasn't a topic. This was the expectation of the club. We wanted to win the league. We wanted to reach every cup final and when we got there, we would want to win them.

We were also chasing the league title in an historic manner. Winning it would take the club to 18 overall, matching Liverpool's record. I must be completely honest and say it was not a factor for me personally. It wasn't even a consideration. I was too focused on the immediate demands on me after the change in role and I was keen to explore the ways I could inject something of my own personality and philosophy into the team. That's what life is like at the club.

I wanted training to be vibrant, I wanted it to contain a lot of speed. I wanted every moment to be utilised, I wanted everything to have a challenge and a purpose for the players to be stimulated. So the challenge for me was to get on that treadmill of perpetual motion which was the everyday demand of being at Manchester United – a result and a performance in every single game.

I've no doubt that Sir Alex would have been aware of the significance of the season that laid in front of us. He would use different analogies before seasons and before important games. I remember one where he spoke about the great mountain climbers. The view once you're at the summit is magnificent, but you only get a limited time before you must go back down. Then someone else is up there experiencing the view. They're your competition. How hungry are you to climb the mountain again? That's the question he'd ask of the serial winners like Giggsy and Scholesy. Did they want to do it, or did he have to find someone else? Can those players make the other ones excited to have the same journey?

Sir Alex was a master storyteller. The greatest. Without equal. His ability to inspire and motivate was extraordinary. It was a strong and healthy dressing room, able to take those lessons and use them positively. There was a good mix of characters, those who were laid-back, those who were loud and opinionated – the young lads coming through.

It was an established set-up, so when I came in it wasn't a case of suggesting drastic new formations. We played in a shape that you would say was a fluid 4-4-2 in defence moving into a 4-3-3 in build-up and attack. This depended on whether we played with one holding six or two holding and one more advanced. We might play with Carrick and Scholes holding and we could be assured our build-up play would be okay.

We had such a good variation of skills in our wingers and full-backs that we could decide for any individual game whether we might want to play wide or with them coming inside; that would inform the decision we made on the full-backs, though Patrice Evra was usually the one constant. On a game-by-game basis we evaluated the opposition – not in any great way to put the emphasis on them, but to look at the way they played, their style, their tendencies, their key players, and then look at our own set-up and try to predict where we might be vulnerable.

At least 80% of our preparation concentrated on our own strengths and how best to utilise them in the specific game. I based my strategies on the general idea we were playing an extremely fluid 4-3-3. I think we tried a three-man defence once in the entire time I was there, and we never really played with a diamond as we generally defended in a 4-4-2. If we were playing at Old Trafford, we'd press higher and if we were away from home we'd usually press from a deeper position. We had the tremendous benefit of being able to field a stable and consistent defence and goalkeeper, so we had so much opportunity to indulge in the quality of our options.

We had a slow start to the season. Cristiano was out injured and we signed Dimitar who made his debut at Anfield. He set up an early goal for Tevez and we played with those two and Wayne up front, using a compact midfield of Carrick, Scholes and Anderson, because of how well Anderson had played there in the previous season, where we won. Against Rafa Benitez, we knew games there would be tight and tough. We knew we'd have to be at our best and to be clinical. Liverpool turned it around and Nemanja was sent off late on. Mick Phelan talked to the press afterwards and said we didn't take control of the game, suggesting Liverpool took advantage of our unfamiliar shape. He probably had a point.

Our reaction to that defeat was strong and coincided with Cristiano coming back into the team. Eight wins from 10 – Cristiano scoring seven, Wayne scoring five, Berba getting five. The confidence was back but we came off a hard-fought game at Celtic to play down at Arsenal three days later. On this occasion we gave Arsene Wenger's team too much respect. We allowed them to play their natural game. They took a two-goal lead and we got some of that much-needed energy back into the side which was crucial against a team like Arsenal when we brought on Rafael and Tevez. It was a defeat that provoked another reaction. This time we didn't lose a game of significance until mid-March, a stretch of 30 games (the sole loss we suffered was against Derby in the first leg of a League Cup semi-final, which we overturned in the second leg).

Just before Christmas we travelled to Japan for the Club World Cup. I thought it was a fantastic experience and I loved the competition. I've always been a good traveller, and I'm usually okay at adapting to new time zones, probably because of my past. I remember on this trip Sir Alex struggled massively with that. His entire body clock was screwed up. I was sitting next to him on the team bus, and he was sending a text message. Someone ended up getting "aaaaaaaaaaaaa"!

Earlier in the year we played at Chelsea. There was an incident which had gone viral – Mick and I were sitting either side of Sir Alex on the bench. A balloon floated by and Mick grabbed it and popped it – taking Sir Alex completely by surprise and causing him to air a few choice words. Anyway, that little clip had gone viral, and before a team meeting, during the Club World Cup in Japan, Simon, our video analyst, showed him the video on the big screen. He was in hysterics. A complete fit of laughter. He couldn't stop. We must have replayed that clip for him a dozen times. The more we played it the harder he laughed. Then Mick walks up.

"Show it again, show it again!" the boss orders. Then the players. It lightened the mood tremendously. Sometimes when you're a long way from home, in a different time zone, with a need to be completely professional, you call on that togetherness. I'm not saying that it was a deliberate act of team-bonding, it was completely opportunistic, but really that's the sort of mood-reading the boss had developed a knack for controlling. It wouldn't be the last time this season that this quality would prove to be influential.

The Club World Cup was Wayne's time to have his individual moment in the spotlight. He scored twice in the semi-final against Gamba Osaka and then the only goal against LDU Quito of Ecuador. As far as I'm concerned, I always considered this one of the pinnacles of club football.

As a kid I watched Ajax take on Independiente and when they won, it was huge. As a coach it was great to test myself against peers from other continents, an opportunity that doesn't always present itself. We had such a good squad that ultimately, we justified our position as favourites and came away from that trip with nothing but positives. We had to work hard – the final was tough – but it was a hugely rewarding trip.

There's the potential for things to go wrong – imagine if you go away, you underperform for whatever reason and return with a low feeling. But we had a nice break from the pressure of the Premier League and Champions League, and returned feeling the high of victory which helped us keep momentum in our domestic form.

The trip was just before Christmas. While we were away, the boss gave me a tip about a horse. He was certain that it would win. He also said he was so sure, I should tell my neighbour, Stuart, who sometimes gave me and the boss lifts; I wasn't big on horse racing, but it came up in conversation on those journeys. So I sent Stuart a text and told him the gaffer had a tip. He put a bet on for both of us.

You can guess what happened. The horse did nothing.

Stuart sent me a picture. "You can show Sir Alex this." It was his Christmas tree with just one present underneath it. "Tell him this is the only thing I could afford to get my kids this year!" The boss was laughing when I showed him.

A few weeks later I was giving the boss a lift and we were stuck in traffic. A car pulled up beside us with a familiar face. Stuart. The boss wound the window down.

"How's the horse betting going?" he joked. "Hope you had a good Christmas!"

When we were travelling for away games in the Premier League, we would always set off the day before in the afternoon, having trained in the morning. We would normally jump on the train in Wilmslow where we had two first-class carriages to ourselves. I would always share a table with the boss, who sat opposite me, and Simon Wells, who sat next to me. However on this day, we were to depart from Macclesfield station.

Normally the boss and I would share a ride but not this time. Whilst waiting at the station I didn't see him anywhere, so I thought he must have jumped on somewhere else. When I got on the train, only Simon was in his seat.

"Where is the boss?" I asked.

"No idea."

We asked Kevin, the conductor, if he had seen him. "No, not seen him."

I stood up and walked to the next carriage to see if Mick or anyone else had seen him. They also said no. Then Albert the kit man's phone rang. It was the boss!

"Albert, where the hell are you?!" he fumed through the phone.

"We are on our way to London, boss, where are you?"

"In the car park at Macclesfield station, I missed the bloody train!"

"How?"

"I was watching the horseracing on my phone and forgot what time it was!"

We all cracked up, but the boss was less amused as we found out later at dinner. "You're all fined a week's wages."

So we all assumed the horse hadn't won either. We all did have a good laugh about it though. When we arrived at the hotel, the players would have their evening meal at 7pm in a nicely set up room. We, as staff, would congregate in the hotel bar around 7.30pm, after which we would have a meal in a different room.

The reason why I mention this is because to me it was such an important time where we would be together as staff in an informal setting. It wasn't just Sir Alex, Mick, myself and Eric. No, everybody else on the staff was there. The doctor, all the physios, masseurs, Karen the media officer and, of course, Albert the kit man. It was a great moment for the manager to discuss things in an informal way where all staff were present. I fondly remember those dinners; the nice red wine, the many jokes and stories the boss would share with us. We would often leave the dining room crying of laughter. It was another testament to the boss's great management skills.

Our first game back in England was against Stoke City on Boxing Day. Tony Pulis was a good friend of Sir Alex but their way of playing football was very different. Stoke were very direct, long throws with Rory Delap, constantly looking to win set-pieces. If they get a free-kick anywhere in your half, they're flooding the box. Bolton under Owen Coyle did the same. We made a big effort on this in training and our approach. We had to avoid fouling. Yes, put pressure on the ball, but also, allow them to have the ball. They're waiting for the contact to go down. If we showed enough patience, we'd get the ball back anyway, because we were better than them.

It's a great psychological contest. With Stoke we thought that corners were better to give away than throw-ins, but our preparation for this was always very strong. Set-pieces are the great equaliser in football because it comes down to height, physicality, and quality of delivery. Eric Steele was always fantastic in how he would help organise the defensive structure to give the goalkeeper the best chance. We would front and back mark the player nearest to Edwin and we'd always have one player defending the near post and one player dropping back on the line, if the ball had been headed on.

They liked the ball dead or in the air. We wanted it moving and on the floor. You must turn the game around to control it. Games at the Britannia were always indifferent because of the pitch and the conditions, particularly in winter. Earlier in the season we'd beaten them comfortably at Old Trafford – Danny Welbeck scored a magnificent first goal for the club in a 5-0 win – but the game at their place was tough. We won through Carlos Tevez in the 83rd minute as we started to click into gear with our late-match scenario routine. A few weeks later we won in injury time against Bolton.

The quality and experience in our team seemed to take us to

another level through the season. We seemed to have answers for every opponent we came up against. Even in the games we lost, I always had this sense of feeling that we could do something. We sometimes just ran out of time. In fact, I don't think there was a game where I took my seat on the bench at the start of the game and thought we weren't going to do something special.

The solidity of the defence came into its own – we kept a record number of consecutive clean sheets, which was immensely valuable as we came up against sides who had no ambition besides trying to stifle our attack. After the Arsenal defeat, we went 14 games without conceding a goal. Eight of those games were won 1-0. Three, including the Stoke and Bolton games, were won in the last few minutes, when we had to roll up our sleeves and find a victory in a different way. Sir Alex would always reiterate that the 1-0 wins were the most important ones.

Some managers and coaches – and there are some very famous examples of this – have such a single-minded approach to the game that their plan B is only ever perseverance with plan A, even if confronted with an opponent where being more inventive with your approach is likelier to succeed. They complain about the tactical set-up of an opponent. I loved those challenges. I loved trying to find solutions and working with the players to help them see that we could find an answer within our own talent.

At Old Trafford especially we would often find ourselves against teams playing with two banks of five. We'd set up with a training pitch that was effectively condensed to 45 yards because even Rio and Nemanja would be over the halfway line. Within this heavily populated area you're trying to achieve two things – the first is to manipulate the areas to find whatever space you can.

The second is to try and force errors in their back line by encouraging players to step up and leave their position. We used an imaginary midline, which runs from box to box from penalty spot to penalty spot. We effectively split the pitch in half vertically and used this to drag teams over to one side; if we could drag a compact team to one side of the pitch, we knew we had players like Scholes who could switch the play and exploit the space that would inevitably be left. From that moment you might be able to get a 1v1 or 2v1 – and then you can get in behind them. Once we did that, we had the best players in the world to put teams away. But the spaces were always very limited and that's where you need patience and a lot of clever footwork. You need the clever interplay, the one-twos, the over and underlaps to open them up. If the defence is really deep, then you need players comfortable on the ball outside the box. Someone who can pick a pass. Someone who can get a shot away from distance. Someone who can break through by dribbling, like Ryan Giggs did to score the match-winning goal against West Ham.

One of the greatest challenges as a coach, and one of my biggest objectives, was to ensure that our players embraced and enjoyed those difficult scenarios. You can imagine what it must be like – the repetition of playing football against a team who are playing compactly and with fear. They're not playing an open brand of football and it reduces your capability to. That's when it becomes about the business of winning games.

You engage and empower the players by subtly relaying the message – opponents are doing that because they know our players are better. It's a mark of respect. If you can make the players enjoy the task of trying to break down an opponent, that will transmit to the support. You paint the picture. The more we won games, and the more the players bought into the success of our preparation, the more they realised that together we'd been painting a picture. They could step back and appreciate that. They knew the information was good and they could trust us in our direction.

At certain points throughout the season, I approached players individually for their feedback on our sessions. Were the points we were making valid? Did they find the sessions constructive? Did they get enough information? Did we provide too much information? I was always trying to keep a healthy awareness of the balance.

After one session we presented the squad with some analysis of an opponent in the Champions League. It showed a team with a lot of quality.

"Are they really that good?" Patrice asked. "From the video clips... bloody hell..."

The next clip we showed them revealed some weaknesses. "Look, lads," I said, "they're good on the ball, but here's where we can hurt them." I could never waste a moment or opportunity to emphasise that affirmation. We're Manchester United. We're that good. If we do what we can, nobody can live with us. Sometimes it was necessary to present a reminder of the danger of an opponent so that the basic principle of earning the right to play was never lost on the players.

So much of the game is psychological. You could not question our squad when it came to that side of things. Sir Alex was always looking for an edge, a bite, something to keep that focus strong. I think it's certain that he enjoyed the rivalries and the mind games because for elite professionals who have already achieved and won everything, the challenge is the next opponent. It always must be that way.

He enjoyed looking at the bigger picture and observing how his rivals worked under pressure. I recall one conversation, probably just before we left for the Club World Cup, where he asked our press officers for some stats on penalties. He mentioned those stats in his press conference. He was planting the seed.

In January 2009, Liverpool emerged as the main contenders for the title. Considering our objective for the season, it couldn't have been more poetic or fitting that it was our greatest rivals. They were due to play at Stoke. Rafa Benitez faced the press and gave one of the most memorable statements in Premier League history, where he complained about Sir Alex, complained about referees, and mentioned the word 'facts' multiple times.

I saw Sir Alex later that day and he had the widest smile. He had Benitez exactly where he wanted him. He thought it was brilliant. My personal observation was that Benitez did neither himself nor Liverpool any favours. When he was asked about it at his next press conference, the boss just laughed it off. Liverpool was a great side, and they were keeping pace, but this was all the evidence Sir Alex needed that if there was to be a crucial moment, they would be the ones to suffer from a lack of composure.

Benitez would have seen things very differently after they came to Old Trafford and won 4-1. We'd taken the lead, before they turned it around, and at 2-1 our hopes of getting anything out of the game were gone when Vidic – dismissed at Anfield – was sent off against them again. A week later, Scholes and Rooney were sent off at Fulham and we lost again, giving Liverpool hope and throwing our season into a very difficult moment. We'd only recently won the League Cup, taking us to two trophies for the season when we defeated Spurs on penalties. We respected every trophy that we won and when we got to the semi-final stage, we were in it to win it.

Our game management was such that we were planning three games ahead. We'd look at who we were playing next, if it was at home or away, and then consider what we might need one or two weeks down the line. We managed the group in two sections – the high-energy lads below the age of 30, and the experienced players above that age. We knew we weren't going to play Ryan Giggs and Paul Scholes every week. We were fortunate to be able to pick and choose their games. We looked at the attacking qualities we might need in these certain games and our decisions were informed in this way. It was never something revealed to the players – just conversations between the boss, Mick, and me.

When you get to the second half of the season you must be smarter with your preparation. You don't get too many weeks where you are able to have more than one or two sessions dedicated to a particular game. So even in recovery sessions I would try and implement some drills that were disguised, including elements that would be important in the forthcoming game. If it would be important to break the lines or switch the play, I'd make sure that was featured in the passing drills.

You get used to the routine. At United, we very rarely had days off. Even if we travelled to Europe and we got back at 1-2am, we'd be in the next day at 9.30am for training at 10.30am. I could speak for a long time about the value Tony Strudwick brought to our preparation, but it was incalculable when it came to changing up the intensity. He suggested training with low intensity two days before a game, whereas many other teams would use that day to go the hardest.

Tony also changed the way we did things for European away games. Normally we'd travel in the morning and the players would get some bed rest before training in the afternoon. Those sessions, in the stadium of the opposition, were the best training sessions I'd ever see from the players. They were buzzing. But the next day was a long day. A lie-in. A walk before lunch. A team talk after lunch. Then it's a long wait and often we found the players couldn't get going when the game came around.

We changed it, so that we would train at Carrington, then travel to arrive in the early evening. Dinner, bed. You have the same long day on the match day, but you can't do anything about that, so changing what we could about the day before had the players buzzing to get on the pitch.

You do all these things in the pursuit of controlling what you can. There are some things you can't do anything about, and no amount of squad management or fitness preparation can help. Suspensions to Vidic, Scholes and Rooney ruled them out of our home game with Aston Villa. Wes Brown, Owen Hargreaves, Rio Ferdinand and Berbatov were all injured. We were 2-1 down against Villa after 58 minutes.

We had two teenage forwards on the bench – Federico Macheda and Danny Welbeck. Macheda was making his debut when he came on in the 61st minute. Welbeck had played a few games and he came on late on, just after Ronaldo had equalised to make it 2-2.

There are a few things to say about Federico – Kiko. It was clear as soon as he came to the club that he was a born finisher. Give him a half chance with either foot; bang – goal. I can still vividly recall though how he would react to the frustration of senior players. One session I think Pat and Ryan were on his case.

"Fucking hell René," he complained, "why are they always shouting at me?"

"You should be very happy that they are," I told him. "Look at those boys there and what they've already won. They shout because they believe in you. They shout because you're not doing what they think you should. Don't listen to the volume. Listen to what they're actually saying instead of putting your barriers up. Tell them to tell you what to do. That's the information you want to know."

You saw the benefit of his single-mindedness on that day though. He'd been called up into the squad late because of the injuries – he'd scored a hat-trick for the reserves which meant he was good for a place on the bench. In our last session we were doing finishing drills and using different scenarios – getting on to a cross in front of a defender, what to do when a defender's tight and you've got your back to goal. In that case, do a little Cruyff turn, create a yard of space and get your shot away.

We practised this and other turns with Kiko in training during a finishing session. When the ball came to him, after 90-odd minutes in a high-profile, high-intensity game, his execution was with the composure of the kid on the training ground.

Two days later I saw him in the boot room at Carrington.

"So, what's it going to be for you?" I asked him. "We had that conversation the other day about those older lads who've won everything. You came on and won the game for us. And I know how it made you feel. You're on the back pages of the papers. What is that going to mean for you? Is it going to be the kickstart of a great career? Or is it going to be the moment you look back on?"

He came off the bench a week later at Sunderland and scored the winner again. But then Rooney was back from suspension. Dimitar was back from injury. Kiko didn't get much game time before the end of the season. We have the benefit of hindsight to inform us that it was indeed the moment Kiko will look back on – a very important moment – but it also tells us how the expectations and demands on your personality and attitude, as well as your talent, are so crucial to your chances of succeeding at that level.

In the Champions League we'd continued to progress. We hadn't been beaten for a year and a half in the competition and came up against Inter Milan in the first knockout round. José Mourinho was their manager and was in the process of implementing his defensive strategy. Going to Italy for the first leg was therefore a strange experience. There was little ambition from them to win the game and again, you must adopt a strong psychological stand when confronted with this approach. The principle was that away goals counted double so the value of a score-draw at Old Trafford would mean they would qualify. We drew 0-0 and tried to remind our players that 0-0 was still a neutral score but kept in mind that we would need to score twice at home.

With that in mind we made a very clear tactical decision in the days before the game. We told the players to come flying out of the blocks. Terrorise them. Be aggressive. Pin them back straight away. Make them feel what Old Trafford, on a European night, can do. Within four minutes, Vidic had scored. Even at 1-0, Mourinho wasn't likely to make any big early gambles, so we controlled the game to the break and told the players to go again. Ronaldo, four minutes after the restart, gave us a two-goal lead that saw us qualify. They had nothing to say. We executed the plan perfectly. Mourinho was then forced to change things – and you know from the moment that's happening, he doesn't have the control he wants.

Ronaldo was unbelievable for us in the knockout rounds. At Porto he scored that fantastic goal from far out that brought us to the semi-final. He'd been named the best player in the world and was living up to the billing. He was incredible – quick, powerful, brave, relentless. He was unbelievable in training, a top professional. He was in a great team that were playing in a way that maximised his potential and he was at the top of his game. He was as happy as Larry. And, I want to reiterate, he was a fantastic trainer. Always doing extras. No problem whatsoever.

After winning in Porto we had the FA Cup semi-final. The boss was convinced that it was impossible, this time, to win everything. He was insistent that he would have to rotate the squad after the heavy schedule we'd had and were facing. I said I could see where he was coming from and agreed we needed to keep the right focus on the right games.

His response was that the youngsters we had in the squad had to get experience at some point – and the experience of playing in a semi-final at Wembley, win, draw or lose, would set them in good stead for the future. The boss made a huge statement against an experienced Everton team managed by David Moyes. Rafael, Fabio, Gibson, Welbeck and Macheda all started. Foster, Park, Anderson and Tevez, none of whom had been first-team staples for the past few months, also came in. Some of the senior players were upset – but the manager didn't want to risk picking up more injuries if the game at Wembley went into extra-time.

We drew 0-0. Lost on penalties – and we should have had one in the actual game when Welbeck was fouled. If VAR had been in place there, we'd have been in the final. The rested players came back in against Portsmouth and did a professional job, winning 2-0. But when we were 2-0 down at home to Spurs at half-time three days later, there was that horrible, mixed feeling that the momentum we'd fought so hard to maintain was slipping away from us.

At half-time the gaffer wasn't ranting or raving. I'd seen him like it before – he was always at his most fascinating in these moments of adversity. Earlier in the season I'd observed his long game in terms of mind games on the opposition. You can strategise and plan all you like before a game. You can even marvel at the decision making in the heat of the moment – for example, bringing on Welbeck and Macheda against Villa. That was a decision where you felt he was truly pressurising Villa, making them believe something spectacular was about to happen. And it did, perpetuating that feeling. It was all about rhythm and pulse. A decision to influence what he was watching. But at half-time the manager is with his players, involving himself in their collective mindset.

"Another mountain to climb here," he says, moments after he announces Carlos is coming on for Nani. "But remember this. If we score one, believe me, we'll score three."

If we score one, we'll score three.

Brilliant.

None of this, try and get one back and see how it goes. Start fast and keep the foot on the gas. I thought it was remarkable management. Three? The power of that remark lay in the subconscious of the players who, after scoring one immediately think, we need two more. It ended up being five.

Tevez led the barrage. His pressing and aggression was so intense that Spurs had no idea what had hit them. He didn't score, but he inspired the comeback. The other three forwards on the pitch did score. Ronaldo with a penalty. Then five crazy minutes as their defence folded. Rooney equalised. Ronaldo scored again with a minute. Rooney scored three minutes later. Berbatov made it five. It was some second half.

Fulfilment as a coach generally comes from a perfectly executed plan. When things don't go your way in a match, the key is to not become emotionally attached to the action. Supporters can't help it. But that's our job as players and coaches. We lost two goals quickly in the first half. We had to analyse, in a very short space of time, where the goals came from. How did it happen? Was it opposition brilliance? Sometimes you must hold your hands up)? Was it an individual error? Was it an occasion where we weren't doing what we were supposed to be doing?

In the five or 10 minutes before half-time Sir Alex would ask me for my observations. It became something he always did – so I made sure I was properly prepared for when the question came. He was a fantastic listener. It wasn't always the case that he'd adopt everything you'd said, but he would always take on board everything and pick out what he felt were the key elements.

Against Tottenham, I didn't think we were playing poorly. That informed and reinforced the instinct of the boss that he should throw everything – every forward we had – at them. In the short passage of time before he spoke to the players, I worked with Simon Wells, our video analyst, to get the clips of the goals. We didn't want the manager to be in a position where we were shouting at the players if the pictures didn't back it up. His speech to the group was only ever short. Two or three minutes maximum. He'd instruct Mick and I to talk to individuals. Mick would talk to the defenders. I would speak to the midfielders and forwards. It was just our natural instinct; we weren't ordered to speak to particular groups. Mick had a good instinct for defensive issues that needed to be addressed.

We knew what Spurs would be thinking at half-time: 2-0 at Old Trafford. Let's try to hold on.

Nobody ever held on.

When that pressure and atmosphere builds, it's impossible to deny.

We'd changed the momentum of the season. The 5-2 win was followed by a 1-0 victory at home to Arsenal in the Champions League semi-final first leg. The clean sheet was valuable to our game plan. We rotated for the weekend's game at Middlesbrough and won 2-0. It was nicely poised for the return with Arsenal.

We knew from our experience playing against them, that Arsene Wenger wasn't going to change. They were going to leave a lot of space. We had an exceptional plan for their approach. We decided to play Ronaldo through the middle. We knew he had qualities that Arsenal's defenders didn't have answers for. With Rooney and Park wide, and Fletcher and Anderson in the middle, we had the energy to prevent that passing route from Fabregas to Van Persie or Adebayor.

They attempted to play high up the pitch very early on – and in the eighth minute, Ronaldo had already wreaked havoc, pulling the defence wide and crossing for Park. He kept his composure when the Arsenal defender Gibbs slipped. 1-0 – away goal.

Three minutes later Ronaldo stood over a free-kick. If you were to look at a highlight reel of the goals he scored from free-kicks, You must have noticed that his run-up and approach to the ball had changed over time. I always felt his run-up to the ball was too straight. It was a completely different way to how David Beckham or Owen Hargreaves would strike the ball. So, we talked over the technique at Carrington.

"I know what you want to do," I said, "but it's almost technically impossible even for you. When you're so straight on with the ball, you simply don't have the physiological positioning to get the strength and direction on the strike." So, he started to change his stance – that's where the two steps back and one step left came in.

From 40 yards – he pings it. Flies in. Typical, he scores a goal like that in the Champions League semi-final when the eyes of the world are watching. The blistering pace on it. He leathered that thing. Manuel Almunia had no chance.

From then on, we were in complete command. Ronaldo had another chance. Rooney went close. Ronaldo had another free-kick saved. We played with the confidence and swagger of a team certain they were heading to the final.

Early in the second half, Rooney was millimetres away from making it three after an aggressive and imposing passing move. And if you thought that was good, the third goal, when it finally came, was even better. Pure satisfaction. It was something from the playbook – a play straight off the Carrington training pitch. It was indefensible. It was Manchester United at their very best. The pace of the attack – Vidic cleared. Ronaldo with the back-heel to Park. Park wide to Rooney. Rooney released the ball at the perfect time, and Ronaldo was there to finish the move.

I'd seen that play many mornings in Manchester. We did those counters in twos, threes, and fours, box to box. There's nothing like being a player scoring a goal, but the euphoria of seeing a plan play out perfectly, in one of the biggest games, in one of the biggest competitions, the feeling is phenomenal. If we're being clinical, at that point, the game was ours. It was unlikely Arsenal were going to score the four goals they needed before we struck that final time. Yet Sir Alex celebrated with all the enthusiasm as if it was the first and decisive goal. Why? Because that was Manchester United playing in the way he envisioned.

A perfect evening. Almost. At the end, Darren Fletcher is sent off. It's a complete injustice, but he won't be able to play in the final, and we have no recourse to appeal. If I'm being completely honest, once the game is over, and you know you're in the final, Fletcher's dismissal wasn't something that impacted our preparation, because we knew we wouldn't have him. Our disappointment was more on his behalf – of course he was a miss for us – as he provided the perfect balance in midfield. But especially for himself because how many times do you get that opportunity in your career? Speaking in football terms, though, you must be prepared for these eventualities. Someone gets injured or suspended and another player steps in.

Ronaldo hit another one of those free-kicks a few days later against Manchester City. Carlos scored to make it 2-0. We turned a 1-0 deficit into a 2-1 win at Wigan a few days later, Carrick scoring late on to put us in the position where we needed just one point to win the league. Federico's goal against Aston Villa marked the start of 10 wins in 12 games. The recovery was magnificent and some of the performances were outstanding. There was never a day where I didn't enjoy watching Manchester United play, but I must admit that this period was very special; Villa, Spurs, Arsenal, I know those games will be as memorable for supporters as they are for me and for all of us.

I loved watching us play. I loved Edwin's control of the backline. I loved Neville's passion. Pat's enthusiasm. Rio and Vida's no-nonsense defensive power. Scholes with his passing range. Carrick with his simplicity. Giggs with his disguise. Ronaldo with his speed and power. Rooney with his strength and energy. Nani with his unpredictability. Ji with his versatility.

It was a strange game against Arsenal. The previous encounters had been about confronting their game plan and not allowing them to settle. This time it was about not doing anything silly, not taking any unnecessary risks. A point would mean we could win the league in front of our own supporters.

And then it does start to sink in, about the enormity of the occasion. Drawing level with Liverpool on 18 league titles. The Champions League final, against Barcelona in Rome, was still 10 days away – we had the opportunity to celebrate.

Those were, obviously, the best days to spend in the dressing room. The players were bouncing up and down. All the staff would come together. Legends would come in. Bobby Charlton would be there. Denis Law. You'd be able to get pictures with them and the Premier League trophy.

You indulge in that moment and then you decide to break off from the squad and celebrate by yourself. It's great to have that moment of togetherness. But you also need to maintain a distance and discipline. You don't want to have one or two drinks too many and make a fool of yourself to the extent that the players don't respect you. You need to keep the distance. I went back home, invited a few friends around, and already found my attention drifting to Rome.

Chapter Eight

A SEASON OF CHANGE

HINDSIGHT is a wonderful thing. I felt that our preparation for the Champions League final in Rome was fine. We had plenty of confidence and some good strong form going into the game against Barcelona. If you look at the numbers from the end of the game, they don't paint the picture of one team being massively better than the other. Ball possession was equal. We had an extra shot, and we had more corner kicks. The most important number is goals scored, of course; and Barcelona scored two, while we scored none. They scored goals at the right time in the game which completely killed our momentum.

In the discussions before the game, we looked at all kinds of line-ups and strategies. My concern was that if we showed too much respect to Barcelona, they'd keep hold of the ball and drag you everywhere trying to get it back. We needed aggression in the team, we needed legs, but we also needed players who ensured that when we did get the ball back, we kept it.

We certainly had enough of the ball, but this is where the eyes on the game are more important than the numbers, because it's about the quality of the possession and the chances you're creating.

A game never finishes how it starts and you have three moments where a coach or manager can have a strong influence on the momentum of the game – the start, half-time, and the changes midway through the second half. We started very well. Everybody talks about that. Ronaldo had a chance. We should have scored. We didn't. Ten minutes in, Eto'o scores. The pragmatism of Xavi and Iniesta and their effortless ability to keep hold of the ball once they had a feel for it necessitated a change from us.

It was so disappointing. We brought on Carlos Tevez at the break to inject some energy. I felt we were getting back into the game – then we brought on Berbatov, who was strong, holding people off. For a moment we were getting into good areas, pinning them back. Then Messi scores a header if you can believe it, and that's that. They were poor goals to concede at bad times. Those goals came against the run of play and disrupted and deflated our entire rhythm. We brought on Scholes and he was booked immediately – maybe the first tackle in anger we'd made in the entire game. But it also illustrated, probably, the lack of aggression during the game. Was this because we showed Barca too much respect or was it because they moved the ball so quick that we couldn't get near them? A bit of both, I think.

It really is only at Manchester United where you can come out of a season like the one we'd experienced – three trophies, history made in the process with some seminal memories – and feel as deflated as we did that night in Rome. It sucked the life right out of us. Finishing the season on a low with no game to put things right… Well, the disappointment of it all sets a low tone for the summer and creates mental fatigue.

This was another example of why we were lucky to be managed by Sir Alex. For other clubs, the lows might be particularly hard to handle because you don't know when you'll be challenging again. When you're at United, under Sir Alex, the expectation is to win every game and be in every cup final, so, in effect, it creates a perfect balance where you don't get too carried away with emotions in victory or defeat.

The best thing we could do is to go about business as usual. That meant getting the major transfer activity over and done with as swiftly as possible. Real Madrid made an offer of £80m for Cristiano and the transfer went through quickly. It's a fee that looks like a bargain in retrospect.

Ronaldo was such a big presence that we had to have conversations about what we would do moving forward. His single-mindedness had obviously been a great quality for him and for us but a comment from Scholes in training had stuck with me – that Ronaldo had become so obsessed with scoring that if he got the ball on the attack, Scholes would either hold his position or drop back rather than join in the play because he knew he wasn't going to get the ball back. I felt that the transfer gave us an opportunity to spread the goals around the team.

The way I see Tevez's decision to move to Manchester City comes down to a simple fact. Most people, when they come to Old Trafford, they become consumed by the club. They become attached to its DNA and they become a part of it. Those players couldn't go to Liverpool or Manchester City. I wasn't a player and even I would have found it very, very difficult to have said yes. When you represent the club and what they stand for, I couldn't envisage moving to a rival. Yes, it's more of a supporter issue than it is a coach issue, but I still felt he didn't truly care about the consequences of what moving across the city meant. He always gave everything on the pitch and we would miss that quality. As far as I understand it, there was a difficult period where Carlos wasn't playing as often as he wanted and talks around keeping him at the club had cooled off. By the time we went back to negotiate, Carlos had made his mind up to leave.

The decision was taken to move Wayne into the centre-forward position. It was not an easy change; he always wanted to be a part of the action, and we had to instruct him to stay away from the build-up, let others do their job, so that the balance of the team isn't affected and that there is always someone there to get on the end of crosses. He bought into it fully; he became a great success, and he enjoyed it.

During the summer I received a call from the boss.

"Listen," he said, "I just want to run something by you. We've been presented this opportunity to sign Michael Owen. What do you think?"

I admitted that I didn't think it fit in with the profile of the players we usually signed. He was 29 and had a record of injury issues. My assessment was, on the face of it, that if we signed him, he wasn't going to be a regular starter – but he did have a strong history of scoring goals, and he had played for some top clubs and for his country at tournaments, so his experience couldn't be questioned.

In his first training session with us I could see what a clever player he was. His movement and positional intelligence – the economy of his use of the ball and the timing of his runs. All these qualities were top class. He was a delight to work with. He understood his role in the squad and accepted it – and made sure he was always ready for whenever he was called upon. His contribution to United was not insignificant.

Antonio Valencia signed from Wigan for around £16m. He was a very humble, very quiet boy, and his English wasn't the greatest. Sometimes that doesn't matter – that's where football becomes a universal language, as they say. If the quality is there, the other players will embrace you, and they certainly did that with Antonio.

Everybody loved him. His appreciation for the opportunity to play for United was reflected in every training session by his commitment, dedication, and work-rate. That willingness to work so hard was greatly appreciated by his teammates. He had earned some good reviews for his performances at Wigan, but we were all taken aback by how quick and how powerful he was.

The challenge for me was working on the area of his game that still needed a bit of work – the quality of his final ball when his pace got him beyond defenders into that final third. We wanted to add tools to make sure that he had a good variety. Yes, he was known for his effective bursts and fired crosses. I wanted him to understand that he had to come on the inside as well, to make defenders confused about how to stop him. If he could be effective cutting in, then they wouldn't know what to do.

I encouraged him to play 'give-and-go' with the outside of his right foot as he wasn't too comfortable with his left. He was a big asset for United – you don't get to play for United as almost first-choice for nearly a decade without having some serious quality. He was a versatile player and he later proved to be an outstanding right full-back as well.

We had our pre-season in Malaysia. We were supposed to go to Indonesia but there was a bomb scare, so we stayed a little longer in Kuala Lumpur, Malaysia in the Mandarin Oriental Hotel, right next to the impressive Petronas Towers. One morning I was having a coffee and David Gill joined me. We were talking about the future.

"I think your biggest challenge," I suggested, "is managing this club after the departure of Sir Alex. You must start thinking about a succession plan. There are two tracks you can go down. You can make him part of that transition plan and you go for a continuation from within, using somebody who knows the culture of the club. Let's say Ryan Giggs, just as an example. You keep everything else the same, but at some time you start that process, get Giggs more involved as a coach over the season, and then the boss can step back when the time is right, and there'll be no big changes in vision or philosophy whereby the continuity and stability will remain.

The other way is to go from the outside with the understanding that a new manager will bring in all his own people. He'll have his own ideas, vision, and experiences. Unless that person has the knowledge and experience to run a club the size of Manchester United (and at that time the three obvious names would have been Carlo Ancelotti, Pep Guardiola and Jurgen Klopp), you might find he struggles." After such a successful season, though, the manager was showing no signs of losing his appetite, even at the age of 67.

In the early part of the season Dimitar played alongside Wayne but eventually we moved to a 4-3-3, especially for the big games, because it just started to make sense with the quality we had available and the form that the players were in.

We started the season quite well, aside from a blip at Burnley in the second game. In late September, Manchester City came to Old Trafford. They had spent over £100m in the transfer window under their new chairman Khaldoon Al Mubarak. It was an eventful afternoon to say the least. Three times we took the lead. I distinctly recall Ben Foster being in goal and being powerless to stop an injury-time equaliser from Craig Bellamy. The strike was a cracker after he gained possession after a silly turn-over and off he went.

Michael Owen had his most memorable moment in a United shirt during that game, certainly at Old Trafford. It was a moment that showed everything that he was capable of. A moment where the value of all that experience was shown. We were running through our scenario football – we had four minutes or so of stoppage time, so it was about maintaining our composure, pinning them back and getting quality balls into the box. A ball gets cleared from a cross and falls to Ryan Giggs. Giggsy had already put in a man-of-the-match shift, setting up a couple of goals for Darren Fletcher.

Only two players in the squad could have done what he did next, and Paul Scholes wasn't on the pitch that day. Giggs observed the situation with ice in his veins and waited for the movement of the forwards. Owen peeled off the pack to the left-hand side of the box and Giggsy's pass was inch-perfect. The value of Michael's experience in this moment was the split-second of time he had to take a touch – from that position, he can finish with all the clinical composure he is renowned for. It was one of the moments at Old Trafford which truly evoked goosebumps – Mark Hughes, the striker who had been responsible for some of those himself, was now Manchester City manager, and was livid about the lateness of the goal.

After the game, Fergie described City as the 'noisy neighbours'. He knew, much like Chelsea, that if their new owners were sticking around, City would quickly establish themselves as a major rival for years to come. They were not in the same situation as Chelsea were when Roman Abramovich took over, so their journey would take longer, but we were waiting to see when they would win their first trophy.

Over this season, we enjoyed two more last-minute winners against them – first at Old Trafford again, when Wayne Rooney sealed the League Cup semi-final, and then at the Etihad, when Paul Scholes' late header sent us all into ecstasy. It was a result that kept us fighting for the title and had an influence on stopping them getting into the Champions League. Those results only delayed the inevitable. Another £140m spent in the summer made them even stronger – and they finally won their first trophy in over 30 years, the FA Cup, defeating us along the way. We knew from that first trophy that they would now be serious contenders.

We lost at Anfield and Stamford Bridge but won tough games at Stoke, and then scored four goals in visits to Portsmouth and West Ham. It didn't come without cost. At Upton Park we ended with Darren Fletcher at right-back, Michael Carrick at centre-back and Ryan Giggs at left-back, as an injury crisis engulfed the squad.

At Fulham our defence was Fletcher, Carrick, De Laet and Evra – we lost 3-0. At Manchester United the headlines speak for themselves and what normal people might understand as reasons, others see as excuses; the injuries in defence were compounded by the loss of Fletcher and Carrick from their usual positions in midfield. The players did the best they could in challenging circumstances. It was without question that this run of results had a major impact on where we ended up at the end of the season.

Overall, I felt the squad had adjusted brilliantly to the loss of Ronaldo. There was a vibrancy about our attitude. We tried to emphasise that any success would depend on a truly unified team and squad effort. Other players would have to chip in.

Once the defenders were back fit, form quickly recovered – big wins against Hull, Wigan, Burnley, and Hull again were followed by a trip to Arsenal and a real test of that team spirit. For maybe a year or so, Nani had struggled with confidence. I didn't feel the weight of expectation was necessarily fair on him and, especially since Ronaldo had left, the idea that he was supposed to follow him was suggested in the media. They were two different people with different personalities.

There is a culture, particularly in modern football coverage, where because one player isn't quite as good as another, this can be portrayed as a criticism. Ronaldo was the best player in the world. Nobody was as good as him. It didn't make other players poor. We were waiting for that moment where Nani's confidence would return and he would show everyone what a great player he could be in his own skin. That moment arrived at the Emirates Stadium – it was a five-minute spell.

First, he did this incredible skill to flick the ball between two players and then chip the ball in from a tight angle, over the goalkeeper, in the back of the net. Then, minutes later, he did for Wayne what Wayne did for Ronaldo a few months earlier on the same ground – carrying the ball in a rapid counter-attack, timing the pass to perfection and allowing Rooney to finish off a fantastic move. Nani's selfless movement gave Park the space to score a third on the break early in the second half.

It was another hugely satisfying victory which, without Ronaldo, showed that we played in that exact fashion. It was the start of a period of between 18-24 months where he was brilliant for us.

On the last day of February, we won the League Cup – a great turnaround victory against Aston Villa, where we conceded an early penalty. Michael Owen equalised, but then came off injured. Rooney – not a bad replacement – scored the winner, a looping header from a Valencia cross, which was possibly our most productive combination all season. We played some good stuff on the day.

In the Champions League knockout stages, we were paired with AC Milan. They had a great, if ageing, team. Ronaldinho. Seedorf. Beckham on loan. And Pirlo. Our analysis informed us that Pirlo had such a strong influence on the rhythm and pattern of their play. I estimated that three-quarters of their play went through him and therefore the obvious answer was to diminish that threat. He was a bit of a floating six. The two ways we had of dealing with it were to either pass on that responsibility between our zones or to do something unconventional and put a player on him. If we were going to do that, we needed a player who would run off him when we attacked, because he didn't defend. The player we needed to use had to have energy, tactical discipline, and the mental desire to embrace the challenge. Ji-Sung Park was perfect for it.

The plan was executed masterfully. Pirlo was forced to retreat into left-back looking to get on the ball and Ji followed him even there. I must admit – Milan started the game strongly, Ronaldinho scored early on – but our overall plan was extremely successful, and we limited Pirlo to probably a third of his usual output.

Our comeback in that game was strong, our control was outstanding. We won 3-2 in the first leg in the San Siro, a fantastic experience in those awful dugouts where you can barely see anything, and from the off at Old Trafford we implemented an aggressive approach which caught them off-guard. Rooney was outstanding in both legs, scoring twice at the San Siro and twice at Old Trafford where we beat them convincingly 4-0. Our other goals came from Park and Fletcher.

After coming through that tie, we had Bayern in the quarter-final. It's one of those ties that makes you think 'shit' as soon as it comes to mind. We were in control – Rooney scored early on. Late on, Ribery equalised, but 1-1 would have been okay – we should've seen out the game in better fashion, but we made an injury-time mistake, Olic scores to make it 2-1, and Rooney hurts his ankle in the process. There was a lot of frustration and angry shouting in the dressing room afterwards.

The return game was even more frustrating. We took the risk to play Rooney and maybe that helped the atmosphere. We absolutely blasted them away in the first half. Darron Gibson scores a great goal early on. Nani scores a sensational flick. Nani again for 3-0. We were on fire. The performance was fantastic. Then Rafa is booked for a foul on Ribery and Carrick slips up and makes an uncharacteristic error which allows Olic to score just before the break.

At half-time we discussed what to do with Rafa. We were going to bring him off – he insisted he wanted to stay on. Four minutes into the second half, Ribery does him again; their players surround the referee. Rafa gets sent off – yes, he played into their hands, but he should have seen it coming. Everyone else did. From then on, we were hoping to protect the lead, especially when Wayne had to come off – it's about the critical moments. Nani switches off on a corner and Robben has the space to strike a volley. We won 3-2 but we were out on away goals.

It was a bitter feeling, and I wasn't impressed by Louis van Gaal, the Bayern manager, in the gaffer's office afterwards. I was pouring the wine as they both took a seat.

"Do you know why we won the game?" van Gaal asked Sir Alex. "It's because I gave a better team talk."

I might have deliberately been a little energetic with my pouring of his wine – missing the glass and getting it over his trousers and shoes.

"Sorry about that," I said, with much less polite words running through my head. I normally enjoyed spending time with rival managers after a game – that was one occasion I was quite happy to leave quickly.

Bayern went to the final to be defeated by Inter Milan. Their opponents in the semi-final were Lyon. It seemed like a great opportunity missed for us to have won the trophy, especially with Wayne in the form he had been in. It was a hard one for Rafa to take as he felt and bore the responsibility of us getting eliminated. He played with his heart on his sleeve – that's why everyone loved him. That's why I loved him. But there was no escaping the fact that he was sometimes rash, sometimes naive. I had a conversation with him about it. There is nothing wrong with making mistakes, it's part of a learning process – but when it's the same mistakes being repeated, and there's a trend, we must try and identify the reasons. It's a difficult thing to do when part of that impulsion is part of his quality. I knew it was a long-term process, but at a club like Manchester United you must learn quickly.

The game had been a good example of the positive influence of Darron Gibson. To have the composure to score a goal of that quality against such a good team at such a high level spoke volumes about him. He had a big frame, he wasn't afraid, and he had some great moments. I was surprised that his career didn't really kick on. Life at the top can be cut-throat. You need a very strong mental toughness and resilience to be able to sustain some consistency at that level. It's the same principle as the Nani and Ronaldo comparison. We had Scholes, Fletcher, Carrick, Anderson; it doesn't make a player less good if they're not quite Paul Scholes, and Darron made a very good contribution.

In between the games against Bayern was the critical league

game against Chelsea at Old Trafford. They took an early lead and scored a goal that was clearly offside through Didier Drogba. Macheda pulled one back – but they held on to get the three points.

We won our last four games. City away, Spurs home, Sunderland away, Stoke at home. Stuck four past Stoke. Chelsea had Wigan at home and Wigan didn't even turn up. Chelsea stuck eight past them and won the league by a single point.

Where was that point? You might argue it was the head-to-head at Old Trafford. You might hold your hands up and say Carlo Ancelotti had turned Chelsea into an entertaining side as well as a great team. For me the biggest issue was the pre-Christmas form. We lost five league games before the turn of the year and two right in the middle of our injury crisis – at Fulham and against Aston Villa at home. The difference between winning the league and not was becoming so marginal.

When you discuss an injury crisis as being an influence in a title race, you're walking on a tightrope between reasons and excuses, especially as far as the media are concerned. You can tell a lot about a squad's mental strength by their reaction to adversity and if they feel sorry for themselves, that can be natural, but it can also be a representation of using an excuse. At Manchester United, we were built differently; we worked to our own standards. It was difficult to lose by a single point, but it was an experience that reminded us of the need for consistency.

After our experience against Barcelona, we now witnessed Inter Milan as European champions under Jose Mourinho. They knocked out Barcelona along the way, playing the most pragmatic game you could imagine; Mourinho used Wesley Sneijder as a breakaway player who launched the attacks and Diego Milito to finish them. Sneijder was in such a rich vein of form that I raised the suggestion of him being a long-term successor to Scholes. I know there were some conversations, but nothing really materialised.

Milito scored twice in the final and Inter won the European Cup. Barcelona, the holders, had been the key team to stop, and now we'd seen a defensive display stifle them, in a much more obvious way than our performance in 2008. I watched those games and still felt convinced that although winning was important, your own identity, winning in the style that represents everything you're supposed to be about, meant more. I was convinced that Sir Alex felt the same. I don't know if he would have felt comfortable winning something and then somebody afterwards said, "That wasn't you. That wasn't United."

This was the philosophy that underlined all our decision making. If it didn't work, it didn't work. Mourinho didn't care. If someone said you won that trophy but played terribly, he wouldn't care. He would point to the medal, to the trophy, as the ultimate answer. It was a victory for Inter Milan but not necessarily for football. When we tasted victory with Manchester United, we wanted it to also be a victory for the sport.

Chapter Nine

TIKI-TAKA: THE ART OF RHYTHM

THERE was an established narrative in the spectrum of football that fed the idea that tiki-taka (a style of play characterised by short passing and maintaining ball possession) was unbeatable, unplayable even, and Spain's success in the 2010 World Cup helped enforce that idea. Spain, with Xavi, Busquets, and Iniesta, won all their knockout games, and the final, by a scoreline of 1-0.

Spain was coached by Vicente del Bosque and because of the heavy Barcelona influence they shared many traits. The five-second rule, for example, reflects the short time in which the ball had to be won back after losing possession. After 2004, clubs seemed to become more pragmatic, now there seemed to be a widespread intention to imitate this style. The issue with it comes with patience and concentration. There were some in the game who even felt that tiki-taka was boring; but that's where you must watch closely.

I understand, and agree, that possession without purpose

is, well, pointless. It can be boring to watch. That's where you must study the rhythm. Tiki-taka is about rhythm, especially when it comes to movement in tight spaces, this is where you can notice the significant and profound difference between a team who is keeping the ball for the sake of it and a team who is keeping the ball ticking over, patiently waiting for a move to pounce like an apex predator. The pass is played with the objective of drawing an opponent away from their position; to take advantage of their momentary lapse of discipline. It's a mentally frustrating tactic for opponents because they can't get the ball back; to execute it well you need to have players who are technically proficient and understand that need for rhythm and taking advantage at the right moment. Precisely why it's a very tough strategy to coach.

Most great teams look to keep possession. It's part of the game. We did it at United – but always with the primary goal of finding a space to penetrate and hurt the opposition, rather than frustration. You could see the difference in the number of vertical passes and risks taken. There was dynamism in our play, there was so much energy. I think what made our Manchester United squad so great – we had a great versatility to our play. We could perform a standard of tiki-taka that was greater than most teams because we had the technical capability to pull it off; however, the invention and individuality of certain players would always add a different dimension. We could counter with power and pace with the likes of Valencia and Rooney.

Rhythm is important for the success of most tactics and in the most successful teams you can see a certain comfort in the way they carry out a plan; it feels smooth, it feels natural. That's rhythm. At United I worked hard on establishing this in different ways. In training I might put two teams of eight players on one and two touch and three link players on one touch, and then switch it around. The higher the level you play at, the greater the economy of play. The lower you go, you will see players take touches they don't need. Therefore, stopping the rhythm.

I would give the players this straightforward example. If five players touch the ball twice the passage of play can last 10 seconds. But if those players play one touch, you can cut that in half and increase the speed of your play in a very meaningful way, especially if you manage to create a play up, back and through situations.

Some players would get frustrated with the repetition of those drills. Cristiano, before he left, was one.

"Why all this one-touch, two-touch?" he'd moan. "Why can't we just run at them and play?"

I'd explain that there would be moments where that would naturally occur in a game, but first he had to see the drills in the context of how we wanted to play. In this certain part of the pitch, we needed to build possession in a certain way to be able to create space to break the lines. There is a universal truth – all top-class players are excellent at playing one-touch football. They see the game and solutions quickly.

We never wanted our team to be predictable, and I think that is what made us unique. Maybe Carrick and Scholes would not perform tiki-taka in the same way as Busquets and Xavi, but it's just as true to say there are things that Carrick and Scholes would do that the other two wouldn't, and those qualities helped our penetration and helped us achieve our own style of play.

Those ingredients have always been there in every great Manchester United side. I can only refer to anecdotal evidence of the Busby Babes but certainly when we look at the most successful and most loved sides since then. You have the European Cup side, with the midfield quality of Pat Crerand and Bobby Charlton, the lethal and inventive nature of Denis Law's goalscoring, and the individual magic of George Best. You can make similar comparisons in the sides that followed.

I have spoken at length of my main influences being Coerver and Cruyff, but I feel that method perfectly fit into what was already happening at Old Trafford when I joined in 2001 and it perfectly fit into the overall remit of what the boss told me he wanted when he appointed me first-team coach.

Here's a thing to note – whenever you ask anyone what attacking football looks like, chances are they'll describe most of the same qualities. Creativity, speed, unpredictability, skill. My job as a coach was to work on the drills and the patterns that helped the natural skill levels of the players create solutions on the pitch in a way that they seemed natural.

It's fair to say that the gamble Ferguson spoke about was part of what resonated so much with the United support. The gamble in the obvious sense – a late substitution for example – but also the gamble in the less obvious, and that is being somewhat accepting of the fact you can't control everything in a game as unpredictable as football, and then enjoying it and loving it for that. That's the distinction of the magic that sets United apart. And let me stress here – even then, as a coach, I'm trying to ensure nothing whatsoever is left to chance.

Imagine you have a blank piece of paper, and you illustrate some boundaries on an illustrated pitch – what you want to see from a defensive structure and what you want to expect from the attack. You can split that pitch into three and see clear messages – structure in defence and midfield. In attack, though, it's much less structured.

You can plan as much as you want – you run through the drills concentrating on quick movement and finding spaces. You can pick certain players that you think have specific attacking qualities that most frighten the opposition. You can look at the opposition and highlight their vulnerabilities – is one of the defenders slow, or are they susceptible to long-range shots or crosses? You set the parameters and consciously equip them in the best way possible, but then encourage them to paint their own masterpiece.

Do you know what freedom does to a great player? When they embrace it, they play on the base of their own intuition, and somewhere in their subconscious they still include all the elements of the good training that can inform their decision making. Giving freedom to players is also a way of saying you trust them. And when players feel the manager trusts them, they are even better equipped to bring the best out of themselves and perform at their best.

The most direct way that the 2010 World Cup impacted Manchester United could be found in Wayne Rooney's start to the season. Now, everyone knows what was happening and there are multiple different versions and ways of seeing it. At the time, you sort of knew something was going on in the background, but as a coach looking after a big group, you must take the decision to not get involved in case the manager asks you to. Wayne had been taken to the World Cup despite still carrying his injury. It hadn't gone great for him. He'd criticised supporters directly into a television camera. He had publicised personal issues when he came back and there was some speculation about another injury he was carrying.

I don't know what Wayne's motivation for putting in that transfer request in October 2010 was. I can only say that it didn't sit right with me – I could never see him playing for another club. Yes, when he eventually went home to Everton, but that was different – at the peak of his powers, he epitomised United, and that was his right and natural place.

What I do want to say is that this was an example of first-class management of a player and his football club by Sir Alex Ferguson. How he navigated that week was remarkable. First, let it be said that everybody wanted Wayne to stay. He was an integral part of our squad – of us. What did Manchester United stand for? What did Wayne stand for? Energy, dynamism, fearlessness. The boss was very firm. He dealt with a major incident in the space of four days, and he completely controlled it all. He nipped it in the bud and achieved a strong output for the club, with Wayne signing a new contract. After getting Tevez, Man City would naturally have been looking and hoping to entice Wayne over to the wrong half of Manchester.

Wayne was injured, and out for several weeks. Antonio suffered a broken leg in a Champions League game with Rangers. Thankfully the recovery rate for serious injuries like this has hugely improved, but it's never a good or nice thing. It's painful and psychologically traumatic to break a leg; we all felt so bad for him, especially considering how important he'd made himself to the team. That was our main route of goals over the previous year. Now we needed other players to step up.

They did. First, let's talk about Dimitar Berbatov. He'd been at the club for two years now and although he'd played plenty of times – 43 times in both seasons – there still seemed to be that element where he appeared to feel like he was outside rather than inside. One morning in training we had an 8v8 and the quality was on show as it always was. Fantastic football. Berba's team lost and as he came off the training pitch, he started complaining to me.

"Can't you help those players understand how football should be fucking played?" he moaned in a tongue-in-cheek way.

He sat down with a water bottle as Tony Strudwick took some of the players for some more running. I sat alongside Berba for a good couple of minutes and wondered how I could get the message across.

"Do you like music?" I eventually asked him.

"Of course."

"Any instrument in particular? If you could be the best in the world, what would you play?"

"The piano."

"Okay," I replied. "Let's assume you're the best pianist in the world. Everywhere you go, there's a full house. People come from miles to watch you play. They want to listen to your distinct style because it makes them fall in love with music in a whole new way. Now, do you see that group of players there? That's the best band in the world. They've got the best conductor in the world. Everywhere they go people fill stadiums to watch and listen. Your music is a little bit different but now the best band in the world and the best pianist in the world have come together. The pianist wants the entire band to play in his tempo and his style. I can tell you, that won't happen. The conductor has his own way. But if you, as the pianist, can tune in to the way they play – Berba, you'll elevate the whole orchestra. Do you understand where I'm coming from?"

I talked him through what we envisaged as United's main qualities. Again, those four attributes – speed, power, penetration, and unpredictability – were mentioned. We talked about how he could fit into that. I said if it worked well, the supporters would be treated to some unbelievable technical football.

We had a pre-season training session in Mexico – before a

friendly against Guadalajara – and at the end, when everyone was cooling down, I grabbed hold of Berba and said I was going to cross balls for him, so he could volley them in the goal. I said I was going to put every ball on a plate for him.

"You?" he joked in disbelief.

"You watch," I insisted.

Eight balls – every single one volleyed or overhead kicked into the net.

"It's all in the service, mate," I laughed; the truth is, I sometimes just loved to do it to enjoy watching his marvellous technique.

Early in the season, he scored a hat-trick against Liverpool, with one of the most outrageous and acrobatic overhead kicks the Stretford End had ever seen. He was on song; beautiful to watch, confident and bullish. That Liverpool goal was fantastic but against Blackburn, Berba scored one of the greatest goals I've ever seen. He started and finished the move, exchanging a couple of passes with Evra with some extravagant flicks, switching the play with a beautiful pass to Nani, and then advancing into the box to finish with style. That was the goal which sealed another hat-trick – but only the third of five for Berba on that day, who helped us win 7-1. That was the world-class pianist playing in sync with the band.

He was an exceptional player. Strong, much stronger than people gave him credit for. Sometimes you must look at what the person has been through before you cast an opinion on the player. The way that he presents himself after retirement, on social media – he's a great artist, he loves acting. He expresses himself and lives to do it. I loved him. I told him he was one of the few players who could turn our football into an art.

Chapter Ten

THE BARCELONA STUDY

IN 2012, Dick Bate, the elite coaching manager for the FA, asked me to present on the Pro Licence and my presentation included my analysis of the Champions League final against Barcelona in 2011. The document included my scouting report, the preparation in terms of our video analysis and training, coverage of how the game went, and then the conclusions.

I studied the second leg of their quarter-final with Arsenal. Arsenal won 2-1 – their goals coming from a Van Persie effort Valdes should have done better with, and Arshavin from a counter. Offensively, Arsenal only ever played one way, so I wasn't surprised by their short, quick, combination play, nor was I surprised that they found it difficult to get into that rhythm because Barcelona was pressing so well all over the pitch. Defensively, Arsenal had started by pressing high – but Barcelona had figured that out, so Arsenal dropped into a more compact, deeper midfield shape, then the visitors took advantage and scored through Villa.

I concluded that the key was to put Barcelona under attacking pressure and force them to defend. It's not as straightforward as saying doing so guaranteed victory. In the two years since we had faced them, they had matured and evolved. Eto'o and Henry were gone and Pedro and Villa – the smaller, diminutive players Pep Guardiola seemed to favour so heavily – were in. Every player knew his job, and did his job, when it came to applying pressure to win the ball back. They had a team of chasers and hunters. Not many teams could handle that sort of pressure. I felt we could get at them in defence, but they still played out from the back no matter what. They would always find a solution eventually because opponents didn't have the persistence, discipline, or endurance to maintain that high press.

Once they had the ball, they were masters in rotating it quickly, simply, and with intent. I calculated that 95% of their possession was one to two touches. Only Iniesta and Xavi, when changing the angle of the attack, would use turns to do so, or Messi in his trademark dribbles, ran with the ball. Villa, for example, always played on the shoulder of one of the centre-backs looking to find space behind them – and he'd often pull wide to the left to do so. They were experts at using the total width of the pitch to create and recognise the spaces to attack.

I watched Barcelona's second leg with Real Madrid in the semi-final at the Nou Camp and drew many of the same conclusions. The most joy Real seemed to get was from pressing high early on. They couldn't sustain it; Messi dropped back into midfield, leaving the visiting centre-backs wondering what to do. They had nobody to mark. Barcelona had more than two-thirds of the ball and it was clear that this was their style home and away – they'd never change. Their biggest strengths to me were their tactical discipline in defence – they pressed early and high – and their attacks, based on quick transitions, were relentless. They also benefitted from the respect many opponents seemed to show them. Teams dropped off and let them have the ball. I felt it was so important that any opponent must be unified in their approach if they wanted to have some success against this team – one thought, one mind, one action.

So, that was Barcelona. I then focused on our own preparation, and I felt we had three key defensive elements to consider, starting with our set-up when Valdes had a goal-kick. Would we press high or drop back? The first is the most difficult one. Dropping deep to try and contain them was not our style. Pressing high and stopping them playing out was more difficult. Barcelona was good enough in any event to find solutions to either approach – and so it was important for us to have energy and tactical discipline to sustain what we were doing.

What would we do when the ball was in their half in open play? Would we press or stay compact? I felt we had to deal with the inter-passing and balls around the corner – for example the pathway from Xavi to Messi. I felt it was important to press on certain players in certain areas for two reasons – to make it difficult for them to play out from the back easily. I felt the first 15 minutes of our final in Rome showcased that we could do that, and Barcelona's recent game with Real suggested that it was still an avenue we could pursue. The second reason was that the press from certain players would allow the rest of the team to get back into formation.

My suggestion was to play a compact midfield that would defend the area of the pitch that was inside the width of the 18-yard box and leave space in the wide areas. Barcelona did use the width of the pitch, but they'd generally do it with the full-backs coming high and the wide forwards coming inside. They dragged players out wide, picked them off and played around and beyond you. They created their chances through this type of clever interplay and movement. We needed to deny them this space in the central areas of the pitch and make them play around us instead – we could invite them to cross. There were not many players who were likely to score with a header.

What solution did we have in terms of personnel and team shape? I suggested a 4-4-1-1 shape with a possible diamond in the middle, or even a more flexible midfield. Michael Carrick in front of the back four, sliding across, squeezing up and dropping back into the back four when the ball is in wide areas. Valencia on the right, Ryan Giggs on the left, two sensible players who would understand their need to work. Park on Xavi, man for man, in the exact same role we had him in against Milan and Pirlo. And then Wayne Rooney off the front, dropping in on Busquets and supporting the wide man.

Defending in front of our own box, we needed to have compact defensive lines. We needed to watch and track the runs, intercept one-twos, and stop the dribbles. I felt it was important that we enjoyed the challenge of defending against them and set a clean sheet as one of the targets. We needed to understand what our objective was in different scenarios on the pitch – recognising the pattern and making the right decision. The best way to do that, I felt, was to stay compact and leave no space between defence and midfield.

That was the defensive strategy. How were we going to maximise the possession we were going to have, and create scoring opportunities? The key points for me were:

One, looking for early forward passes as soon as we got the ball. That meant recognising the spaces, appreciating the runs. Two, playing away and around pressure, and switching the play. Three, penetration in wide areas – we needed quality crosses and cutbacks. And fourth, of course, set plays. We needed to view each one as a serious opportunity to score. Pique, Busquets and Puyol aside, they were a short team. Everyone used to joke about whether they could have handled a wet and windy night in Stoke; I would have liked to have seen it!

Barcelona liked to have the ball. They liked a fluent and flowing game. Therefore, I thought it would be better to make it more erratic and hectic – something more like the Premier League. So that was going to mean more long kicks from Van der Sar to put pressure on their defence; the key to this was winning the second ball higher up the pitch. If we hit switches of play early, we were likely to find space behind their full backs. We had to try and break their lines of pressing as early as we could – playing in front of them would give them opportunities to press. If we had to pass back, then we must open out quickly to play around or through them.

Our mental focus and strength would have to be at its greatest concentration. Barcelona was not only great on the ball, but they were also great at surrounding the referees and questioning his decisions. Even their better players had a tendency to go down very easily, and Busquets was one of the best at faking injuries and disrupting. We had to make sure we kept our concentration and limited those distractions. We needed to keep our cool.

In our training sessions through the week before the final, we first concentrated on regaining the ball in the midfield and our tactical attacking phase down the right-hand side on Monday. On Tuesday we had a team meeting about Barcelona's strengths and weaknesses and then worked on penetration in wide areas as a specific phase of play, followed by a finishing session with Wayne and Javier and I did some angled-finishing work specifically with Antonio and Nani.

There's a lot of debate at times with regards to finishing. I see it as such an important element of the game, but in many clubs it's not practised enough for whatever reasons. At United we did finishing drills every training. On Wednesday we worked on our defensive block in midfield, and Thursday we had more finishing sessions after first holding a meeting with the defence that had been selected to play – Edwin, Fabio, Rio, Nemanja and Pat. We had a 10-minute 11v11 session where we worked through defensive and attacking scenarios and practised penalties also. On Friday we did our three-ball shooting and crossing routines and finished with a big 11v11.

My initial thoughts on team selection were: we had to pick players with the right balance of experience, energy and pace; tactical and mental discipline; and the courage and confidence to play. They were beatable. Everyone had to show the belief that we can win, and play with the attitude that we were going to win.

Chapter Eleven

THE HIGHS AND LOWS OF 2011

AS you probably know, Manchester United would always go on a pre-season tour. The boss used to love those trips as I felt he was always very relaxed. This time we were in Kansas City, USA. We played some friendlies there before heading to Houston. One early afternoon I was wandering around a shopping complex just outside our hotel when the phone rang.

"Hi René, it's the boss here. Do you fancy coming to a Paul McCartney concert tonight? He's performing in the city."

Absolutely! But first we had a training session in the afternoon. Rain, thunder and lightning stopped us from training so the boss organised an extra signing session for all the people who had come out to watch. We did get on the field eventually, but it was cut short as we had to go to the concert. You go and change, the boss told me and Mick. "I will finish the session." Before we entered the changing room, we heard the whistle blow.

"That's it boys!" he said, leaving all players in disbelief not knowing what was going on. About a half-hour later the boss, David Gill, Mick, Eric and I arrived at the concert hall. "You get the beers, David, whilst I get the hotdogs." I'll never forget when the boss wanted to put some ketchup and mustard on his hotdog. He pressed the handle that hard that all of it went straight on his shirt. You can imagine ours and his reaction.

After the concert we got invited to Paul McCartney's after-party in one of the private suites in our hotel. The boss quickly changed into a new shirt and we all took the lift up. When the doors opened, we stared at a security guard who looked like the guy from the Green Mile. He was huge.

"Who are you?" he asked in the deepest of voices.

"I am Sir Alex Ferguson, manager of Manchester United," the boss replied.

"Never heard of you," he said with a straight face. We stood there all wondering not knowing whether to laugh or not, but then the gentle giant burst out in laughter and with the biggest smile on his face he said, "Come in Sir Alex, Paul is expecting you, enjoy your night." And what a night it was.

That friendly in Mexico, by the way, was arranged because we signed Javier Hernandez. Hernandez – 'Chicharito' as his nickname went – was a great find. Credit to Jim Lawlor, chief scout at the time, and his team for picking a player like that out. You have two stages when looking at a player – being and becoming. Being is identifying a player who can fit in straight away with the starting 11 and play. Whereas becoming means that you are looking at a young player who has a lot of potential. Scouts are tasked with finding the right player who is becoming; and while it can sometimes be straightforward (not always) to identify talent, it's less obvious to identify personality and temperament, especially when it comes to judging how those traits can adapt to the relentless demands and the spotlight at a club like United.

From the first moment in the first training session, when I

als in there. I can't say
was. I would presume
hter after taking the lead.
ry rarely, if ever, did that
aid we should put an extra
when we'd implement our
all, keep the rhythm.
als, Wayne swore into the
a magnifying glass now. So
h and stadium that no word
tional game. Wayne released
'm not here to justify it at all.
ng children and I could under-
erhaps Wayne was unfortunate;
to swear and there were likely
broadcast from the pitch and
hear swearing. Those instances,
the camera and we, and Wayne,
found himself with a suspension
Cup semi-final.
e cup up until that stage. We faced
during a bit of an injury crisis in
an inventive solution. We had two
ments in natural positions, or look at
play and consider how we might use
ble to disrupt them like we normally
forward players who would press like
isrupting the game to force them to
nd Fabio had experience of playing at
nd they were both comfortable on the
to play as wingers with Rooney and
and Gibson and O'Shea in midfield. We

saw him in Houston during our pre-season, I liked him. If I had two words to sum him up, I'd use energy and bravery. He had the heart of a lion. He'd have no problem dealing with physical defenders. He wasn't as classy or fine-tuned as Berbatov, for example. But you need players who will get in and score the scruffy goals just as much.

On his debut against Chelsea in the Community Shield, Hernandez scored from a couple of yards out when the ball hit his face and went in. Early in the season we went to Stoke; he scored both of our goals in the win, his first coming from the back of his head and delivered with perfect direction. It really was remarkable. He had the instinct of knowing where to be at the right time. You knew that you could bring him on, and he could change a game through his tenacity and ability to put himself in positions that would cause headaches for opponents. And by the way – what a great kid, from a great family. I was fortunate enough to meet them a few times after games and they were the loveliest people. Chicharito was full of appreciation for the position he had found himself in but he absolutely embraced it with his bubbly personality. He was full of life.

The form of those two forwards, and Nani, truly compensated for the other issues we had – so much so that we approached the turn of the year still unbeaten in the league and through to the knockout stages in the Champions League. We went to newly-promoted Blackpool in January – the original game had been postponed – and we were 2-0 down when Rafa suffered a concussion and had to come off. Ian Holloway was their manager and had the sort of personality where you knew his teams would always have a go at home. And to be fair, they were giving a good account of themselves; they were mid-table, and had won at Wigan, Newcastle, Liverpool and Stoke, with Charlie Adam in particular in fine form. On this occasion we were able to take advantage of their naivety at this lev two-goal lead and a break in the play, they never reall up. You apply the pressure and score one – as we did – knew that we had to, as Sir Alex said often enough, gras nettle. Berba and Chicharito got the goals and we won.

Those comeback games are always great because they pro a tremendous boost for momentum over a more prolong period, and they also play a psychological part in the title rac

We suffered our first defeat of the season in February, a Wolves, but had the perfect game to bounce back, when we faced Manchester City at Old Trafford. Nani scored a magnificent goal in the first half, when Giggsy put him through with a sublime pass; his composure and quality finish was outstanding. Few people talk about that goal because of what followed late on. Wayne had been able to find his way back into the side in a more comfortable way because of the form of his strike partners; but I don't think he'd mind me saying he was having a bit of a stinker on the day. Nothing seemed to be going right. And then, in the 78th minute, Nani hits this cross, and a slight deflection takes it behind Rooney, who decides to throw himself into this perfectly arched bicycle kick. True to his form of the day, the ball comes off his shin – but fortune favours the brave, and the ball flies into the top corner of the net.

There was a moment earlier in his career people remember – where he was arguing with the referee, he was about to be brought off, and he scored this fabulous volley against Newcastle. Here you saw another moment that was typical Wayne. Things weren't going right but he still had the bravery and self-confidence to try something different. No manager or coach in world football manufactors drills where they instruct players to perform bicycle kicks. There were just certain players who liked to try it; people of a similar age or a little younger

noted the reaction to the team being announced. People were asking, 'What the hell is this?' On paper, it looked like we were playing eight defenders. The plan worked perfectly. We had it in place for around an hour and by that time, we'd harassed them into so many mistakes that we had a two-goal lead – Fabio and Wayne scoring – that we weren't going to give up.

Fabio was having his best spell for us, and though he played as a left-winger in this game, he was mostly playing at right-back in this period. The twins could play in different positions. I once imagined them both in the number six position, Rafa as more of a Keane and Fabio as Scholes. I tried to suggest to the boss playing them both down the right-hand side in the game, as I knew it would cause some confusion to opponents. Can you imagine an opponent going past Rafa and then sees Fabio! "Bloody hell, I've just gone past him and here he is again!" It was difficult to see them apart. I knew they'd both be up for it. They both had incredible potential; neither, for whatever reason, ever truly established themselves as permanent fixtures in the first team, which was a shame because they had talent. They were so desperate to do well; so desperate to not let anybody down. They are genuine guys and I loved their attitude – they were never fazed. I loved Rafael's energy, and I loved Fabio's coolness. He was technically a very good footballer. Fabio's move to right-back was partly as a reaction to the retirement of Gary Neville, which had come abruptly in the middle of the season after he had endured a difficult performance at West Brom. I remember him coming into Carrington the day after and complaining.

"That was fucking hard work," he admitted. "What did you make of it?"

"Gary, I have to admit, it reminded me of an old Toyota pulling a caravan up a hill."

He burst out laughing. "That's about right!"

Having beaten Arsenal, without Wayne, we were knocked out by City in the semi-final. Yaya Toure, previously at Barcelona, scored the only goal. This time, City went on to win the trophy. They defeated Stoke in the final and I can remember hearing the result when we were on the team bus having our own celebrations – more on that in a second. We knew the future was going to be different.

We were still favourably placed to win the league, as well as having a Champions League semi-final with Schalke to look forward to, so we weren't too disheartened by the exit to City. We were magnificent against Schalke and played two great games.

The first leg was in Germany, and we did a lot of preparation looking at Manuel Neuer, their world-class goalkeeper. When Simon Wells and I felt there were clear trends we had to expose regarding an opposition goalkeeper, we would do these specific video sessions to highlight those trends so players were well aware of it and understood their best options to convert chances into goals. We'd run through their weaknesses. It was all about empowering our forwards to give them the confidence, especially in one-on-ones, so we would study the goalkeeper's technique in those situations; for example, if he would throw himself at a player's feet, and so on. Neuer did the star jump, making the best use of his huge frame, but it left space in the area between the legs and the arm and leg if our players could keep composure. Giggsy did just that, scoring a superb goal through the legs. Rooney got a second a couple of minutes later and our professional performance was rewarded with a perfect result.

I felt tremendous satisfaction as we left the pitch – we had to get escalators to get back to the team bus, and as we did, we had the applause of the sporting German supporters congratulating us for our display. The win gave us the chance to rotate for the second leg; Valencia, having just returned, scored, and then Gibson got a second, with a great shot, to put us in complete command. Anderson got two late goals to make it 4-1 on the night and 6-1 on aggregate.

In between those games we went to Arsenal and lost 1-0 to a Ramsey goal. It was one of our poorest performances against Wenger's side, and we never really did anything. Thankfully we knew that if we got a win against Chelsea that defeat wouldn't have hurt us too much. We knew Chelsea would have been anticipating a bit of a hangover from us celebrating getting to the Champions League final, so we made a deliberate plan to come out aggressive and strong from the first whistle. We were a goal up in 60 seconds thanks to Hernandez. Vidic made it two. From that moment it was a case of clever game management – see the match out and know that we only need one more point, from two games, to win the title.

And so, to Ewood Park. Blackburn scored an early goal. There seemed to be a bit of anxiety, more than usual; it wasn't a particularly strong opponent, but sometimes, the gravity of the occasion is inescapable. When we were awarded a penalty with 17 minutes left, the weight of history was on the shoulders of Wayne Rooney, an Evertonian – after all the events of the season, to push Manchester United ahead of Liverpool on league titles. Of course, you know he handled that pressure no problem, and our big moment had finally arrived.

With the symbolic nature of the 18th title success still recent enough, I knew – as did everyone – what winning this title meant. Nineteen was different. The celebrations on the pitch and in the dressing room at Ewood Park were special. Every title is; if you're lucky enough to experience it more than once, then the first one always holds a special place, and while you don't ever take it for granted, you start to appreciate certain milestones as a representation of your contribution to the magnificent history of our football club. It was one that set us apart from everyone else.

It was typical of life at Manchester United; you reach a landmark in British football, and you already must switch on to the next task. We had two weeks to prepare for our Champions League final against Barcelona at Wembley. Having explained our preparation, I was just hopeful that we wouldn't give them the time and space to cause damage. I still felt we started the game quite well. We were committed to pressing and turning them in defence. There was one ball over the top, where Chicharito was inches away, but Valdes swept the backline well and got there first.

We had hoped Wayne would sit on Busquets more; it didn't happen in the way we wanted it. You don't really need Barcelona having a free man in midfield, for obvious reasons. I'm not going to say we didn't have good players at holding the ball – we had Carrick and Giggs, two of the best, and in Valencia and Park we had another two with all the necessary energy to ensure we could press or stay compact. On top of that we needed them to break when those situations occurred and support the front players. But at the top level, football can be defined by tight margins. We had a good opening 15 minutes; they scored after 27, but we hit back immediately, and managed to settle down until half-time.

There was an argument going on between a few players; they were still complaining about the Barcelona goal. I noticed this as we came off for half-time and was desperate for them to refocus because the first 15 minutes of the second half were critical; this was the period where Pep Guardiola's team usually inflicted their greatest damage. We had to get through the next 20 minutes of the second half as we still had lots of options on the bench to use in the latter stages of the game, and by contrast, Barcelona had their best team on the pitch.

Every substitution they made would weaken them. But 15 minutes flew by, and this rattle of an argument continued. It's a usual occurrence in football; it's quite normal. But you must, at some point, say that we've heard it all and move on. They needed to focus as one. We never had a moment to redouble and concentrate on the task in hand.

Nine minutes in, Messi scores. It was Edwin's last game – he would not have been happy to have that footnote on his excellent career. Villa made it three with 20 minutes left. Game over. On the carousel, as the boss called it. They had enough quality to control the rest of the game once they had that two-goal advantage.

It was so frustrating. So disappointing. You can make a point that perhaps this was the strongest Barcelona side in history, at their peak, and that perhaps we were not. I still felt that we could have given more. That we could have done better.

Was that a great Barcelona team because of the individuals or because of the coaching? A bit of both. The players were obviously outstanding. Xavi and Iniesta had the perfect qualities to maximise the potential of that philosophy. But you need a great coach to create the best environment and to explain the concept with clarity so that the players can understand, engage, and believe that they can do it. They need that structure, and of course, it helped that Guardiola had spent time with some of these players in the B team before he took the senior job. The messages were the same. The players he inherited who didn't have the discipline or energy to execute that philosophy at that highest standard – Ibrahimovic, Eto'o, Henry – were all out. Villa in. Pedro in. It was the complete execution of his vision, and then they could grow and go from strength to strength.

Communication was optimal because most players spoke in Guardiola's native language. The messages were clear. The Spanish culture, the style of the league, was very similar – the Premier League, by comparison, is very diverse because of the different styles teams play.

I have a lot of respect for Guardiola and it goes back to a time before he was even in charge at Barcelona. I was looking after a young player, Hussain Yasser, over from Qatar who I initially brought over to Manchester United and had now come for a trial at Manchester City. I would go and see him at his hotel two or three times a week, to see how he was doing.

One time, Pep was there, as he was training with Manchester City at the time – and he was sitting with the player, having a coffee. I introduced myself and soon we got talking about my background with Coerver and Cruyff. Having played for Cruyff, he told me about him and started talking about his own philosophy of football. What he accomplished with his Barcelona side was exactly true to what he had envisaged and planned, and I made sure to congratulate him in Rome and at Wembley, although things were so hectic that we barely got a chance to speak.

In July, just weeks after the Wembley final, we played Barcelona again in Washington, DC on our pre-season tour. Before the match, we bumped into each other in the corridor. I asked him how he was doing. "You probably don't remember me," I said, but as I reminded him that we had once spoken about football for three hours in the lobby of a Manchester hotel, it was clear that the penny had dropped.

"Well Pep," I told him, "I have to say chapeau, because what we discussed, you made it happen."

"Yeah," he said, "but let's be honest, I have Xavi, Iniesta and of course Messi. Listen. At Wembley, if you had Messi in your team, you probably would have won. That's how good he was."

I told him that when the time came for Sir Alex to call it a day, he would be perfect to follow him. "With your philosophy, you'd fit like a glove, and build on what we've done here," I said. He asked about the owners and their relationship with the boss; I told him that as I understood it, they let him get on with things. It was a good conversation, but I must confess, it did nothing to make me feel better about the frustration of that summer, which had lingered much like Rome. Neither did beating them in the friendly – although we re-emphasised the same approach to our players, and this time it worked. Small consolation but our job was to get back to business playing good football and winning as soon as we could.

I should mention the significant achievement of the youth team. Under Paul McGuinness, the club won the FA Youth Cup that same year; the same generation of players who had carried that prediction I once gave to Henry Winter. I had been at the club a decade and to see the long-term success of the technical development sessions I'd introduced at grassroots and junior level, and then match that with four years of success – a period of success that was as strong as any in the club's history, at such a momentous time – is a spell I now look back at with the requisite fulfilment.

At the time you're not looking at it in that focus; you're dealing with the pain of the defeat. It's insidious. It creeps under your skin and relaxation becomes impossible. You can't even say that you've won the league and use that as your concentration. So, you redouble. You look at ways you can be innovative. You look to freshen it up because you can't do the same things all the time. You would spend the entire summer pining for that first day back at Carrington; you knew that as soon as you were back, everyone had been feeling the same way as you, and so you knew that it would be business as usual.

Chapter Twelve

ENERGY AND INTENSITY

THERE was a fresh air about the 2011 summer side. I think if people were asked to find two words to describe the Manchester United side of that period they would use 'energy' and 'intensity'. The internal drive in the squad was so strong that when we made several changes, as we did, it seemed to inspire and elevate the individuals to put in a string of magnificent performances.

As anticipated, Manchester City spent a lot over the summer before we faced them in the Community Shield. It was a famous encounter where City went 2-0 up before we came back in the second half, Nani winning it with the last kick when he went around Joe Hart. Our confidence at the start of the campaign was wonderful to see. West Brom were beaten, Spurs also.

Then Arsenal came to Old Trafford and that was quite an occasion. We were 3-1 up at half-time. This was a different Arsenal team. Over the summer they'd lost Fabregas, Nasri, Eboue and Clichy. In the midfield in particular, the passing lanes they used to exercise were hugely impacted, and it made our job easier on the day. We sensed vulnerability and the players smelled blood. It took a while for us to get going in the second half – we didn't score again until after the hour mark – but once we did, it was like we were scoring from every single attack. Four, five, six, seven, eight. You get these games sometimes.

After the game I went to my local to meet some friends from Holland who came to the game. There, I was approached by an Arsenal fan who recognised me. He said in a joking way – at least I presume it was a joke – how much he hated us, especially as we always seemed to beat them, and the wins were getting heavier. I admitted to him that it wasn't that difficult to prepare tactically to play against Wenger, as he always set up to do the same thing.

"Fair enough," the supporter said. "I have to admit, even though I'm Arsenal through and through, I do love to watch United play." From a rival supporter – of that team in particular – it was one of the greatest compliments I could remember receiving.

The vibrancy was down to a few factors. We had Danny Welbeck, Tom Cleverley and Jonny Evans around the first-team squad after very successful loan spells. I'd known them all for a long time. Danny was technically outstanding. He was deceivingly quick. He was also fantastic at 'back defending' – lurking around defenders and pinching balls from them. He was a player who could occupy any of the forward positions. He could score a goal – he could score tremendous goals – but for him it wasn't a must. What I mean by that is, for a player like Ruud van Nistelrooy, he had to score. It was hunger. I felt Danny could have added that, but the way he played was very beneficial to us at the time and he went on to have a great career.

Tom was a late developer in terms of his physical stature, but we took our time with him and once he was ready, he had bags of energy. He was an extremely honest player. Maybe sometimes he overran himself a little, in his eagerness. We hoped that with maturity he would let the ball do the running. The enthusiasm Tom and Danny showed was great. But then Tom picked up an injury in our 5-0 win at Bolton and he spent more than a month out of the team. Timing is so important in football – by the time of his return, we had other players coming back like Michael Carrick, and it was so hard for him to regain the momentum he had.

We also made several signings over that summer. Ashley Young moved from Aston Villa, he was a top professional. We had watched him for years; he had caused us problems for years. He was mobile, agile, tenacious. He was strong at running behind markers. He was a big asset for us.

We signed Phil Jones and David De Gea to add to Chris Smalling, who we'd brought in earlier in the year. Phil had a great start for us. He had all the requirements to become a top centre-back. Both Phil and Chris showed great potential. They were both strong, quick, and powerful. They had the attributes to make a fantastic player at United, but you don't know how a player can adapt to the unique pressures of being expected to perform at the top of their game, twice a week, over an entire season.

In De Gea, we replaced a goalkeeper of 40 years old with one around half his age. That was an interesting process. I can remember sitting in our video analysis room with Simon Wells when we had a knock on the door. It was Edwin. I can remember the conversations from around the time. Edwin was willing to stay on for an extra year – he was feeling in good shape and he was happy to stay around and serve as a back-up for David, who he knew we were bringing in. He felt it would take David time to get used to English football and so he was offering to stay on for another season in case his experience would prove useful. But when he suggested it to the boss, for whatever reason, it was decided that this wasn't necessary – and Edwin, feeling it was pointless moving to another club at that point, decided to retire.

"That's it for me boys," I can remember him saying. There was, as it happens, one or two moments through the course of the season where David did need a week or two out of the team, where we had to take him out of the firing line because of how teams were bombarding our goal trying to make him feel vulnerable. I knew he was of strong enough mind to deal with it. We just needed to give him some time to settle in. I'd been to see him play against Liverpool at Anfield for Atletico Madrid in 2010 and I was hugely impressed with his temperament. His composure helped his team win the Europa League that season.

Composure was not the word you would associate with our October 2011 trip to Anfield, where the game became almost inconsequential. I'd known about Luis Suarez since well before he moved to Liverpool. His antics playing for Ajax had attracted much notoriety. One sports show in Holland ran a feature on what he was doing – let's just describe it as gamesmanship. In Uruguay, some felt it was great. It was shown as a part of their culture. Win at all costs. Create aggravation to unsettle your opponent. Use every tool, as cynical as it is, to win the game.

When you spend so much of your time deliberately straddling the borderline of acceptability, it's not a surprise if you frequently step over it. Suarez did. Manchester United weren't the first opponent to experience it, and we wouldn't be the last, but this particular experience of below-the-belt behaviour was, to be honest, appalling. He racially abused Patrice Evra – Pat's reaction, in that he was able to professionally complete the game, was commendable. It happened right in front of the Kop, as hostile and as volatile as it could be.

The incident created a huge media storm and prompted an inquiry. Suarez was suspended and his first game back, as fate would have it, was at Old Trafford for the return. All the focus was then put on to Evra – would he shake his hand as the teams crossed over? It tells you everything about the personality of Pat that he offered his hand – and Suarez rejected it. It was incredibly poor behaviour.

Surely, he must have felt so embarrassed about what he did. You wouldn't want your kids to see you behaving like that. You have players with moments of madness – look at Zidane in the World Cup.

The problem with these moments of severe inflammation, other than the severity of the act, is the hostility which is created as a result. Coaches and managers like to control the game. When a moment like that happens, you are placing your faith in the self-control or discipline of a player, monitoring it, and feeling that you might have to make a change and take them off for their own good.

Pat handled it well. We won the second game 2-1. And then he started celebrating – I had to grab him at one point because I think all that energy was about to come out in a bad way.

A week after we drew the first game at Anfield, we lost an infamous match at home to Manchester City. It was like the Arsenal game in reverse. It was 1-0 at half-time and then Jonny Evans was sent off. They scored twice more to really command the game. Then we scored in the 81st minute – a fine goal from Fletcher. The fans and players got excited, thinking they could get something from the game, even with a man short. They committed themselves to a comeback, but City kept getting us on the counter. They scored three times in injury time.

The manager was, naturally, furious after the match. "Why were you still fucking running forward?" he blasted. He had a feeling goal difference would be crucial towards the end of the league. He never wanted games to run away from us like that.

To be fair, the response after the match was strong. Back to basics. Three 1-0 wins in the league. Then league form picked up. A 4-1 victory against Wolves, and back-to-back 5-0 wins over Fulham and Wigan before a midfield injury crisis contributed to defeats to Blackburn and Newcastle. Against Blackburn, we'd been forced to play Rafael in midfield.

Ahead of our trip to Manchester City in the FA Cup, we had an unexpected boost. Paul Scholes had retired the previous summer. He was still around Carrington every day and the idea was that he would observe the coaching, usually with Warren Joyce looking after the reserve team. But Paul was still training with them and so fit.

We would often talk; I'd ask about the younger players, if there were any players he would recommend taking part in the first-team group, things like that.

Before one game around Christmas, we were in the player's lounge.

"How's it going, Scholesy?" I asked. "Do you miss it?"

"Yeah," he admitted.

"Do you miss it badly enough that if the boss asked you to come back, you'd consider it."

"Probably," he confessed.

I brought it up in casual conversation with the boss. I suggested that if he opened the door, the impression I got was that Paul would come back. It wasn't the first time we'd discussed it. Particularly in the European games – we'd been eliminated in the Champions League at the group stage – we'd often expressed to one another how we missed Paul, and what a difference he would have made in certain games.

A quick note on the Champions League – it was a very disappointing campaign which saw us go into the Europa League. It was like going from dining at Michelin star restaurants to eating at McDonald's. Nobody says it. Everybody says it's a big trophy. We're in it to win it. But it doesn't feel the same. It doesn't hit the right notes.

We lost both of our home games – first to Ajax, but we'd done the job away from home, and then to Marcelo Bielsa's Athletic Bilbao, who eliminated us. Even the test of facing Bielsa didn't give me a great appetite. He was known as being a unique individual. We did our preparation and knew what to expect – it was a very admirable philosophy, and we were not at the races.

My opinion on his approach was that it could be very successful but would have a sell-by date – it was so demanding and had a steep tipping point. If you push your body to exhaustion, the moment you hit your target, there's a natural release. It's a normal human reaction. That release is the pivotal moment. The mental and physical fatigue kicks in. They had the desire and quality over the tie, and went to the final, where they were beaten by Atlético Madrid.

It was a surprise to everyone else but us when Paul pulled on his shirt again for the FA Cup game at City. We won that one – and a week later, he made his league return, scoring against Bolton and playing as though he'd never been away.

Once again, we could enjoy Scholesy's brilliance in games and training. Nobody was safe in training when Paul had a ball at his feet. If a player would go for a quick wee on the side of the pitch you could bet on it that Scholesy was going to hit his backside no matter what distance. One day he fired a rocket from 40 yards straight at myself and the boss whilst we were having a chat. The boss held a cup of tea in his hand and surely, that cup would've disappeared in the sky had I not stopped the ball in its tracks.

"Why did you do that René?" Scholesy said with a laughing face whilst jogging past.

"Bloody Scholesy," the boss murmured.

Another day he nearly hit Geoff, the window cleaner, from his ladder whilst cleaning the windows of the boss's office. Luckily it was only the bucket that came falling down.

The team's form again was great – we won at Arsenal, drew at Chelsea, and won at Spurs. Five goals at Wolves. Scholesy scores again against QPR. But we lost at Wigan, a game in which we were denied an obvious penalty – Phil Dowd refused to give it. It was blatant.

A couple of weeks later we're at home to Everton and 4-2 up when Pat has a great chance to make it five but he hits the post. This time we've only got ourselves to blame – they come back and score twice in the last few minutes. It was a true sickener. The sort of result that you know is going to prove influential for the wrong reasons.

You want a game straight away after that – we had to wait eight days to play in the crucial match at Manchester City. Social media had been around for a few years but was getting bigger. More players were using Facebook and Twitter. I remember a conversation with the boss about how much he disliked it; it was something out of his control.

I said to the boss, "Those opinions have been out there for thousands of years, the difference is that everyone has the tools now through social media to air his or her opinion. No responsibility and no consequences, no matter what they say. It's not going to go away! It's something we must manage."

The manager got especially upset about the fact that the line-up against City had been leaked shortly after we had our pre-match team talk in the Lowry hotel.

Yaya Toure played in an advanced position that was almost on top of Paul Scholes. We tried to adapt, but it was a tight game, decided by a set-piece on the stroke of half-time. They won 1-0 – the Everton result had come back to bite us, because now they had the edge on goal difference. That 6-1 defeat was now haunting us in a direct way.

We played Swansea at home. Won 2-0 – two goals before half-time. They were a good side. An attractive team. They liked to play, with Leon Britton conducting most of it beautifully. It's difficult because you're trying to drill home two different game plans. You must never take any result for granted. You must win the game. Then you must try and score as many as you can; the difficulty in those scenarios, especially when you're Manchester United, is that the opponent is all too aware of that, and their resistance doesn't buckle on 1-0 or 2-0.

It meant that we were realistically looking at results going our way on the final day. We were at Sunderland and City were at home to QPR. Sometimes in life you get gut feelings; like a period where something isn't going your way and there's nothing you can do about it. It could have something to do with the fact that my father had passed away earlier in the month, and I was naturally devastated about that, but I just had this strong sense that things were not going to work out for us.

We won 1-0. Try as we might, we couldn't add to the scoreline. The whistle blew, our game was finished. City was still playing.

I went straight from the bench to the tunnel to find Simon Wells. I was just about to get to the analysis room when Simon walked out. The look on his face told me everything, but he said it anyway.

"Bollocks," he said. "René, they've just scored. They've just scored."

I walked past him and into the dressing room. I was alone. The floor felt like quicksand; it was that, or I felt like collapsing into a heap on it. It was like a strange gravitational pull dragging me. Wigan, Everton. Both games flashed across my mind. Hitchcock couldn't create a film as horrific.

When I finally plucked up the courage to watch the City game I was even more frustrated. Rangers boss Mark Hughes was such an experienced manager, and I just couldn't believe what I was watching from his team.

Last minute of the game. QPR had a throw-in and gave it straight back to City. All that needed to happen from that point was to have the ball to go back to Joe Hart, and a QPR player to press him, so he had to kick it long. Huffle, shuffle, whistle. But there was no press – they had all the opportunity to cut through the middle, and Aguero benefitted from that space to score. The Sunderland supporters were ecstatic, I could hear them as our players and staff trudged back into the room.

Silence.

"Listen boys," the boss says. "Some of the older lads have been here before. But you younger players, I want you to remember this feeling. Remember those Sunderland fans cheering for City."

All the players have talked about it since and it has, quite rightly, gone down as probably one of the greatest team talks he ever gave. I don't know how he did it but from that moment all of us – myself included – seemed to carry this renewed sense of urgency throughout the opening weeks of the following season. We had a strong determination to make a statement from the start.

Chapter Thirteen

NUMBER TWENTY

I'VE talked about end-of-season disappointments and how they linger. They can really fester into your system and the 2012 defeat was one that was felt by the whole staff. In the moments before the players came back into the dressing room at the Stadium of Light, I can remember thinking that it was our shared responsibility to hide our own disappointment to ensure the players did not feel quite so fatalistic.

In his post-match address, the boss had transformed our entire mentality as a group, and we were immediately focused on regaining the title. No defeat is enjoyable, but the elite managers always learn and take something from it. That's quite difficult to do when the margin of defeat is so fine. But let's consider the nature of it – it was something that even our most experienced and successful players hadn't been through. That was their motivation to go again. And we did.

It's in moments like this, looking back and putting things into context, when I marvel even more at what the boss was able to achieve over such a prolonged period. I previously spoke about Bielsa's methods, and many might find a strong comparison in Jurgen Klopp's approach.

At United, we never suffered such dips, and I must put that down to the manager. We discussed what he did and how he did it, but the truth is that it's not easily replicated. The most stunning thing in all of this is that we were in such a pressurised situation, coming out of what could be described as a mentally draining way to lose the league, and at a club where you had to win and win with style in every game, I never felt any pressure for a single moment in the time I was first-team coach at Manchester United.

The defeats were turned into challenges. It's an extraordinary thing, and it is all thanks to the work of one man – Sir Alex! I know that fed down into the greatest compliments I got in my own career – that nobody ever came to me after a training session and told me it had been rubbish. The numbers backed up what we were doing; Tony was always fantastic with that, monitoring the heart rates of the players and observing the levels of intensity we would need to reach in any given session at any given time.

In the six years I was first-team coach, we hardly ever had a session where we practised 11v11 with exactly the side we were going to start at the weekend. The manager would never want to give his team selection away too soon, even to his own players, and that became a daily challenge – how can we put messages across to the players about what we expected in the game, without always giving too much away in terms of specific instructions? To create such a positive competitive environment at Carrington was one of the manager's most notable achievements.

Few people would have identified goalscoring as the problem

that summer. We had scored 89 goals, with Rooney on fire, and Welbeck and Chicharito chipping in. It was the highest tally since 2000, and the second-highest goal scoring tally we'd reached in Premier League history. So, I know there was a little surprise when our main summer transfer turned out to be Robin van Persie.

It seemed, to the public, to be a heist, capitalising on a contract impasse with the player at Arsenal. There's some truth to that; but the story of Robin's arrival at Old Trafford is much more complex than a simple opportunistic swoop. It went back to January of that year. I was contacted by Robin's agent – I knew him on a personal level – who told me that his client was not going to renew his contract at Arsenal.

"Listen, René," he said. "He'd love to play for Manchester United, but more than that, he really wants to play for Sir Alex Ferguson. What do you think?"

I promised I'd speak to the boss. So, I did. He raised an eyebrow and then listed some doubts. He was 28. That didn't really fit with the club's transfer policy. He had a track record of picking up injuries. That was even before dealing with Arsene Wenger. In the past we had explored the possibility of signing Samir Nasri, but we were never fully convinced by his agent, and he ended up moving to Manchester City. The boss didn't want to go through that again.

"What I would ask, boss," I said, "does Robin van Persie make us a better team? If the answer is yes, then I'd say let's explore. I don't know how long you still want to be manager of Manchester United – one year, two years, three years – but I would presume you want to remain successful. City aren't sitting still and if they get a sniff of him, they'll probably go in. Do we want that?"

On the back of this discussion, I wanted to check that injury record. The most prominent issue seemed to be an ankle problem – but he'd seen a specialist in Sweden and had played most of the last two seasons. A week later I spoke with the boss again. He said he'd talked to David Gill, and they still weren't sure.

I suggested raising the subject indirectly with the players – approaching a handful of our senior players and suggesting a couple of names to them. Robin was one, Luka Modric was another. We asked Scholesy, Giggsy, Rio and a couple of others. Whenever the subject of Robin was mentioned, their eyes lit up. Sir Alex was becoming more convinced but remained sceptical about how genuine it was from Robin's side.

I bumped into Robin's agent around this time and we got talking about the club. He asked about how training usually went – he was interested in Sir Alex's involvement, as Arsene Wenger usually took control at Arsenal. I explained how we did things and he seemed impressed.

"Regarding Robin," I said after a while, "How genuine is his interest in joining Manchester United? If he is only doing this to create a better position with Arsenal or another club, Sir Alex will drop this instantly. He won't even entertain it. But if you say hand on heart Robin wants to play for him and the club, I can guarantee you he'll do whatever he can to make it happen."

It wasn't the easiest of transfers. The club paid £24m for him. The boss has since said that he felt that while Arsene was reluctant, he was pleased not to lose another player to City. I was in the room when the deal was agreed, and he signed.

"I love the idea of playing for United, but more than anything, I love the idea of playing for you," Robin admitted. "So, I hope you're not going to disappear after just one year!"

The manager laughed. "No," he said. "I still feel good, I've got a good group and good staff. At least two to probably three years."

Robin fit into our group easily. He was a top professional. There was no arrogance about him. He was a bit quiet at the beginning, but he seemed to love the intensity of our sessions from the start.

After the first few sessions I was picking up some bibs and I heard the boss say to Robin that they needed to submit the squad list to the Premier League and Champions League, so he needed to select a number. There were two available – 20 and 21.

"That's quite easy, isn't it?" I interrupted. "It can only be 20. You're here to win the league. If we do, it's our 20th title. Carry that on your back and you will know what we're playing for every week."

That was it – decision made.

We made another big signing in the window. Shinji Kagawa came from Dortmund. I'd followed him over the previous couple of years and he had established himself as an incredible talent. I felt we needed someone like that playing between the lines. It was another one I suggested to the manager and Jim Lawlor. The boss and Mick Phelan went to see him, and later, David Gill. Everyone was impressed. Everyone loved him. The issue was finding the right place for him in the team. He was best in the number 10 role, but it was difficult when we had Wayne, Robin, and Danny. He could play off the wing, but you would want him to come inside – that would mean specific instructions for the full-back overlapping. Shinji would have been at his best if we'd been able to play him week in, week out in the number 10 role, because he was truly a magnificent player. Unfortunately, it didn't work out at Old Trafford the way we all wanted.

It was serious business at the club in the first half of the season. No messing about. We wanted to get on top, we wanted to create a gap, and we wanted to boss that league. Robin scored on his debut and then scored a hat-trick, including a last-minute winner, at Southampton. He'd earlier missed a penalty – but equalised from 2-1 down in the 87th minute. He came into the dressing room afterwards.

"Sorry for missing the penalty lads," he said. "I shouldn't have put us in that position. I shouldn't have got us in this mess."

He scored his next penalty – late on at Anfield – after Rafael had scored a beautiful goal earlier. We won 2-1. It was shaping up already to be Robin's season.

A trip to Stamford Bridge awaited us in late October. We had noted the strength of their defence over the years and had success once we decided to change our approach. There was no point putting crosses in at head height because Cech could gather it and if not, Terry would head it away. Crossing was to be low and hard in the six-yard box, or cutbacks from the by-line. We set traps for David Luiz. He liked to carry the ball forward and we decided to encourage it because he always tried a risky pass. We had to intercept the pass and then counter with pace into the spaces that were left.

We won 3-2 – Luiz scoring an own goal, a rebound from a Van Persie shot from a low Rooney cross. Robin got the second – a fine finish from a low Valencia cross. Chicharito scored the winner from a low and drilled Rafael cross. Later Robin explained in *Voetbal International*, a Dutch football magazine, that he was surprised at the level of detail in our preparation, which was nice to read.

The following week he admitted as much to me, when we

took on his old Arsenal side for the first time since his transfer. I was going over some video analysis with the players. It was Robin's first game against them since joining us. I was reminding the squad of our usual approach and highlighting key points in defence and attack. I would highlight the threats and what the solution was.

With no Fabregas, the strategy was to stop Jack Wilshere getting on the ball. I discussed the forward runs of Arteta, Ramsey and Cazorla and the movement of the forwards.

"Robin," I said, "if there's anything I've missed, or is incorrect, please tell us."

"No," he smiled. "Now I know why you always beat us."

He scored in the third minute – we won 2-1.

There were already enough memorable moments to fill a season, but arguably the most iconic of them all arrived in early December. We were at City and had taken a 2-0 lead, playing good football. Both goals had been scored by Rooney. They came back to level it up and thought they had the momentum to snatch another infamous 3-2 injury-time win. We were awarded a free-kick.

I can remember looking at it; I was right in line with it from the bench. Robin stepped up to take it, and I can vividly recall my gut feeling. If he is meant to be here, he's going to score this. Manchester United is a club which creates those kinds of storylines. The shot went in – the supporters were in heaven, and so were we!

It was a victory of authority, an exorcism of sorts, and an incredible boost for us which almost inspired us into this run of 12 wins from the following 14 games. To win at Anfield, Stamford Bridge, and the Etihad in the first few months of the season was a show of strength. The 12th of those wins came at Sunderland. 1-0. Six clean sheets in a row in the league.

Another cleansing. Another exorcism. Their supporters weren't celebrating this time. It gave us a 15-point lead with eight games remaining.

The determination and resilience of the players was outstanding. Twenty-five wins from our first 30 games. Four winners scored in the 87th minute or later. It was a squad which refused to accept anything other than winning the league title in convincing fashion. You can never remove emotion completely but at the top level you can achieve a distillation of sorts; you can compartmentalise that emotion, use it for motivation, rather than allow it to control your instincts. Emotional release is part of the beauty of football, but you can say without question that it was the drive and passion, the control, of the manager which had infiltrated the mentality of the rest of us at the club.

We played Real Madrid in the Champions League Round of 16. Away in the first leg, we drew 1-1. Welbeck scored a great goal, and we could even have got a win. Cristiano equalised, and David was in great form too. There were three weeks to go before the return leg. Sometime in the second week, the boss came up to me in the morning while training was going on.

"I'm not sure about the return leg," he said with uncertainty. "Something's not right." He was concerned about the referee appointed to officiate the game at Old Trafford after some media talk in Madrid. He didn't elaborate on it in great detail, but there was a strong sense of unease.

Our preparation was good. The boss decided we were going to play Danny instead of Wayne; a reward for how Danny had done in Spain, and we felt that the Real defenders would be unsettled by his tenacity to recover the ball. He had the skill-set that suggested he could do to Xabi Alonso what Park had done to Pirlo, and then join in the attack himself. He had a great chance in the first half. The tactics were spot on. At half-time we impressed upon the players to keep going. Early in the second half we had our reward when Ramos scored an own goal.

A few minutes later Nani goes into a challenge with Arbeloa. Arbeloa goes down in the most theatrical way. Get up, Nani. That's the initial reaction. Get up and get on with it. To the incredulity of everyone inside the ground, Cakir pulls out a red card. I was gobsmacked. There was a moment of absolute silence on the stands; nobody could believe it. These are the moments that completely change the game plan. When everything you'd prepared for changes, and you must react to and in the moment. The future is unpredictable.

Unpredictable to everyone except one person. Sir Alex Ferguson. He knew his own destiny at this point. Nobody else on the staff did. He jumped up and remonstrated. He's arguing with the fourth official. Suddenly his remark at Carrington flashed through my head. He'd been worried – now I knew why. He was still arguing minutes later, as I noted Jose Mourinho bringing off Arbeloa and bringing on Modric.

Mick and I were looking at how to combat that with our response. Yes, we had 10 men, but we still had the lead and we had home advantage. We planned to go to a back five, bringing Giggsy back on the left and tucking Evra in. We knew a storm was coming – we just had to weather it. The supporters had been magnificent all night and they would probably have got us over the line. We couldn't get through to the manager, who, unbeknownst to us, was battling with the realisation this would be his last chance, and the frustration that it could be undone by a terrible refereeing decision. It was a highly intense moment and logically, with the benefit of hindsight, I can now see why he was so affected. I'd seen him angry. I'd seen him animated. I'd been in the dressing room when we appeared to lose our concentration on the bigger picture for just a split-second. A split-second was all it took. We couldn't make the change before Modric equalised. Within three minutes, Ronaldo had made it 2-1, and our reaction was to a completely different game scenario. Rooney, Young, Valencia all came on. We had chances – enough to win.

We all felt a sense of injustice. The bigger picture was playing in the manager's mind. The final was at Wembley that year and looking back at how it went in the quarters and semis, we should have got there. I knew the boss always felt like he should have won at least one more European Cup so I can understand his frustration. At the time, my frustration was that the tie was still there for us, despite the awful decision.

It all snowballed into a difficult moment in the season. We lost in the FA Cup to Chelsea, and we lost at home to City in the league; a reminder that we needed to regain that focus as a collective, quickly. Robin hadn't scored for 10 games. Our next game was at Stoke, not a place you would normally want to go if you're in a moment of difficulty, but on the other hand, the perfect place to go to get back on track.

I talked to Robin about the drought. I felt he was trying to chase it too much. He seemed anxious and he was trying to force it. I put a small video together, clips of him in this recent spell, missing chances. I followed it with other clips of him from earlier in the season where he was scoring and assisting. I wanted him to see the difference, and the difference was that he was taking too many touches and delaying his decisions. At his best, he was sharp, direct, decisive, and clinical.

"You're so eager that you're almost fighting against yourself," I told him. "You're playing a game within a game. You're so desperate to score. But in these other clips you're just enjoying playing with us in a great team creating many chances. The difference is that there is a fluency in these clips. Don't worry about scoring. Play your game, play for the team and the goals will find you."

We were 1-0 up at Stoke when we got a penalty in the second half. Robin tucked it away to give us the points. He ran towards me on the touchline to celebrate – but the boss was celebrating too, and Robin reached him first, so gave him a hug. "I was running to you," he admitted afterwards, then added, with a big smile on his face, "but I couldn't ignore the boss!"

As we were preparing to face Aston Villa, Robin talked about coming up against our fellow countryman, Ron Vlaar, who played in the heart of their defence. He said he felt Ron had a weakness when dealing with a runner around the back of him, chasing the ball over the top. We ran through a routine with Fabio and Rafa as the two full-backs, Scholes and Rooney in midfield and Chicharito and Van Persie up front. The exercise was that the attackers would do crossover runs around mannequins.

In the game, we played with Pat instead of Fabio, Carrick instead of Scholes and Kagawa instead of Chicharito, but what I saw in the 13th minute was straight from those sessions. Rooney dropped deep to collect the ball and Robin set off on one of those runs. The long pass was perfect, and I mean perfect. Inch perfect. And it was artistically finished off in the way that only Robin could, caught on the perfect, beautiful volley which flew into the net.

It was a fantastic moment – the moment we knew we'd sealed the title. He knew he had done it, carrying that number 20 on his back all season. Mission accomplished: 20 league titles. I'd have to confess to some personal satisfaction, yes from that goal, but also in the actualisation of the moment. I'd been involved in trying to create a picture for Robin, something he could envisage. Everything we'd hoped for came to pass, and I was delighted that Robin had one of the greatest seasons of his career.

Robin completed his hat-trick in the first half. The title was officially decided at the final whistle, with four games to spare. It was a decisive message, a flex. We didn't come back and nick it. We dominated that title race from the opening weeks, and we left nobody under any illusion that we were the best team in the country.

We started talking about pre-season. We were going to China and Australia. The boss seemed as involved as ever. He was talking about some nice wine regions we were going to visit and as far as I could see, it was business as usual.

Chapter Fourteen

THE END OF AN ERA

ON a Tuesday evening in May, my phone pinged. It was about 11pm and the call was from Simon Wells, our video analyst. He'd been on a golf day the club was holding.

"Some of the players have been getting messages that the boss is retiring. Have you heard anything?"

I didn't know what he was talking about, so that's what I told him.

Seconds later my phone went again. This time it was my neighbour Stephen, a West Ham supporter. "Is it true?"

I headed downstairs, switched on the computer to have a look and I saw the headlines coming out. On Wednesday morning we turned up to Carrington and there was a heavy camera presence outside the gates. Mick, Eric, and I were called into the office.

"I'm really sorry you've found out this way," he admitted. "I wanted to tell you. I'm disappointed because you should have been the first to know. But it is what it is, and it's true,

I'll be stepping down at the end of the season." He explained how the death of his wife's sister had affected the family and played a part in his decision. We were sympathetic. After a few moments the conversation naturally turned to what came next – for the club, for us.

"What does that mean for us?" Eric asked. "What's the plan?"

"Well, we have already decided to bring in David Moyes," the boss said. "But David Gill and I have had a good chat with him, and we have told him how important you've all been. We understand he's only bringing in Jimmy Lumsden as a sort of sounding board."

I thought about the moments which surprised me over the course of the season which now started to make more sense in hindsight. The agitation he'd felt against Real Madrid. The tiny changes that you notice in someone when you've worked with them for so long which I could now attribute to him knowing the size and scale of his announcement and how much it was going to impact all of us, including him.

There were a couple of games left in the season. The penultimate match was at home to Swansea. It was an iconic and emotional moment in United history as Sir Alex addressed the crowd, and, at the same time, all of us as the staff at the club. I couldn't help but reminisce about the great times we had enjoyed together and it's funny because that was the one thing we never did for too long at Old Trafford. It was always about moving on to the next challenge.

The size of the occasion was not lost on anyone. The way we won the game, with a late goal from Rio, was typical. The reaction to that goal was remarkable, considering there was nothing riding on it. The title had been put in the bag long ago. This was about something different – this was about what it meant to have the standards set by yourself on a game-by-game basis. That's what Sir Alex instilled upon the club more than anything else and so it was fitting that his last home game was won in such a fashion.

The curtain came down on the Sir Alex era with a 5-5 draw at West Brom. The second half was a complete circus. It was, at the very least, entertaining, and a memorable way to conclude the most successful reign in English football history.

I recalled Johan Cruyff's end at Barcelona, where he lost in the Copa del Rey final, suffered elimination to Bayern in the UEFA Cup and a home defeat to Atletico Madrid which ruled them out of winning the league. Even the greatest of managers don't always get to pick and choose the perfect way to go out and at least there was nothing riding on the West Brom game – if there was, there would have been a few hairdryers. As it was, Sir Alex's time as United manager ended as it began, away from home, with 1,498 games between his first, at Oxford, and last. He addressed and thanked United's travelling support, the best in all the land.

I know Sir Alex came back to Carrington to clear out his desk during the following week but there was no big song and dance about it. It was quiet, understated. At that time, routine weighed heavily on my mind. Things were going to change. Everything we'd built was going to go and new systems were going to be put in place.

Over the couple of weeks following the announcement, the boss called me into his office. He told me he had talked to David, who was keen to meet me and work with me. I was happy to see what he had to say.

The season was still going when I went to his house to have that conversation. I don't know what I expected. In a perfect world, the conversation might have gone something like, "I'm the boss now, I'm the one sitting in this chair, but I have heard what you, Mick, Tony and Eric do, and I'm going to watch that and feel my way in."

The conversation with David initially seemed to go fine. I told him how we did things from my perspective, explaining the delegation and routines we had and the importance of the individuals in the process. I told him that I ran the training sessions and the trust the boss placed in me was so great that he didn't even ask me about the content of them. He knew there was enough variation and purpose to maintain the enthusiasm of the players and create new challenges for them. He was there, he knew what we were doing, and he was close enough to know that if it was rubbish, if it wasn't working, or if there was something he didn't like, he could have interjected to make his own assessment. He never felt the need to.

I discussed how we utilised video analysis. We used it to make specific points but there was too much going on, too much external pressure and too much emphasis on what came next at United to procrastinate. We didn't watch full games back – we identified trends and tried to provide the players with positive feedback so we could always seek to improve.

David asked what system we played. I explained that we didn't have a set system due to the flexibility of the players we had in the squad. We had a game plan which was centred on creating spaces, exploiting spaces left by the opposition and then creating overloads. That could be in a 4-3-3 that turns into a 2-4-4 depending on the players we had on the pitch.

"Can I ask you a question?" I said, as I wanted to know what guidance he had received from the Glazer family regarding the staffing set-up.

"I can do as I see fit," David replied.

"David," I said. "Do you realise how big this opportunity is? I know you've had a great career and you have earned all the respect you have in the game. You've done great things at Preston and Everton and it's obvious that Sir Alex respects you enormously. But this is different, and I can tell you that now. I do not want to be disrespectful to Everton, but you are going from a yacht to a cruise ship." I just needed an analogy to explain the huge difference between the two clubs. "In the smaller boat you have everybody in who you want to be in, you've got a megaphone, and everyone is doing what you tell them to do. United are so much bigger than that. You cannot do that at United. You have all these different decks and you're going to need captains who run each one. My advice is to lean on us. Use us. Let us get on with it. See how we operate. Try to get a feel for how we operate. You'll then find your own way."

"I'm too young for that," he insisted.

Delegation isn't an art. But the way Sir Alex delegated was. It's a quality you need to have as a leader and in those latter years I'd describe what the boss had as almost an autocratic metronome at the club. I left that meeting with mixed feelings. I knew he would probably talk to Mick, Tony and Eric and he'd probably hear a lot of similar things. I couldn't envisage a reasonable scenario where he would speak to those people and not come away with the strong feeling that Sir Alex had trusted them and so that was a compelling indication that he should too. In football, though, especially when you are going into a new job, there is always that feeling of a new manager wanting to go in and just do his own thing regardless of what's been said before. I'd hoped that I'd gotten through to him.

Usually, managerial changes happen because things aren't working. That clearly wasn't the case. And United was an institution. It wasn't any football club. Yet those last comments about his age, and me knowing what I did about the work he did at Everton, still left me feeling that something wasn't right.

He had those chats with the others and a week later we met in Wilmslow. This time it started to feel clear. When you're at a club like Manchester United, the first thing is that you are doing a job you love, and the second thing is that you have immense pride to work for them. In this period of change I naturally started to think about those 12 years and everything we had achieved, and how I had contributed towards that. A lot of people might have the sort of personality which said no matter what role you're given in a reshuffle, you would stay. That's not me.

The second conversation started strangely.

"Have you thought about it?" David asked.

"Thought about what?"

"Well, I would like you to stay…"

I was agitated. "Have you talked to the others? Eric?"

"Yeah, Eric's a great guy," he said, "but I let him know that I'll be bringing in Chris Woods as a goalkeeping coach instead."

While I was still reeling from that news, he came out with this question. "How important is the assistant manager's title to you?"

"Not at all," I said. "Mick's the assistant. I'm the first-team coach and I've always been happy with that. Unless there are other plans."

He said he was speaking to Mick after me and that he wouldn't be kept on either. I told him that we'd been led to believe we'd all be staying at the club. I asked that if I was to stay, what my responsibility would be.

"Well, I know how important you've been to the training sessions," he said. "But I am young, I am hands-on, and I do want to do all of that myself."

"How is that going to work?" I asked him while the following thoughts were running through my head: With all due respect, how many Premier League titles have your staff won? How far have they gone in the Champions League in previous years? It's going to be all your staff, and me. And everything I did; you're going to do yourself. So how is it going to work?

I didn't really get an answer. I just wanted him to be direct with me. I even tried to say it for him. I said I knew he wanted to do things his own way and with his own staff. I asked him to look at the path that laid ahead. If I stayed, and did effectively nothing, the players were going to ask questions. If they don't like what you're doing, they'll come to me. Then I'd have to go to David and tell him. If I do that a few times, he will think I am disloyal. If the players didn't see a reaction, they would question me. I didn't have much of a choice in the matter, and I wasn't getting a straight answer, so I decided to ask different questions.

"Can you give me an idea of how you're going to run the squad?" I asked. I was thinking of the fact that we had two groups – the high-energy years and the high-experience years were managed in different ways so we could get the maximum out of them.

His answer went along the lines of a traditional, general training session, that didn't incorporate either the age profile of the individuals nor the quality and experience of them. I just kept thinking to myself. This is Manchester United. This is different. You must be different. My gut feeling was telling me it was wrong. It felt wrong for several reasons. If I stayed, I knew I'd be the unhappiest man in the world.

"Listen," I said, "the last thing I want is to leave the club. But I just don't see how it's going to work."

"Well, I want to keep the continuity of the club," he said, perhaps not realising what he'd said in the wake of what he'd just told me. I felt as though I left that second conversation in the air, still willing to discuss the future if he could provide me with a vision of what that future looked like.

A few weeks later I was presenting a coaching course in Holland and we had a telephone call. I still didn't want to leave, but we had no resolution, so I said to him, "Look, I've got a feeling you want to do it your way, with your people. I don't think I'm the right fit for that based on what you've told me and how you would like to run it."

Shortly after that conversation, I got another call, this time from Sir Alex.

"David tells me that you're thinking of leaving," he said with some surprise. I admitted that I felt I had no other choice, explaining what had happened, especially with Eric and Mick. The boss seemed surprised that they had been let go too.

"I keep asking what my role is going to be," I said, "because David keeps telling me he's going to do everything I did. So, I'm asking him what I'm going to do and we're going nowhere."

I've been quite thorough with the way I've described those conversations because I don't want things to be left to misinterpretation and, in the same spirit, I want to go on record as saying I have nothing against David Moyes. I've got a lot of respect for him and what he has done in the game. I was never resentful or bitter towards him, and credit where credit is due, winning the Conference League is an unbelievable achievement for both David and West Ham.

There was sadness but no acrimony. I was frustrated during those conversations, and that was natural, because the last thing I wanted to do was leave. That was, however, the end of my 12-year association working for Manchester United.

Chapter Fifteen

NEW CHALLENGES

I COULD consider myself fortunate that I wasn't short of offers upon leaving United. In my life I considered I had three homes – Holland, Qatar, and England. I'd maintained close links with my past and utilised the connections from time to time. One winter we had an early exit from the FA Cup, so I leaned on Tariq Al-Naama, my connection in Qatar, to help us set up a warm weather training break in Doha. I regularly received offers to return but I was committed to United.

When I left, I was immediately offered an opportunity to work with Aspire in Qatar, and I was interested – interested enough to prepare a presentation that centred around the country's approach to the 2022 World Cup, which had been awarded to them in 2010. There were different men involved in the Qatar FA, and I felt some blew in the direction of the wind; that when Spanish football was popular, when Xavi and Iniesta were at their peak, they wanted to imitate the philosophy. For a while Belgian football was popular so they wanted to copy that, and these approaches were favoured over creating their own identity. That's what I wanted to try and implement if I was to go into that sort of set-up.

I wanted to work with reasonable expectations – so I told them that I hoped they weren't expecting to win the tournament. Their objectives had to be, a) off the pitch, everyone complimenting them for a job well done hosting the tournament, and b) on the pitch, hopefully winning a group game. I envisaged that I would work with the Olympic team and build from there, but I discovered my vision was not one shared by officials at key levels, so those conversations ended almost as swiftly as they began.

During that period I was also approached by FC Nürnberg who played in the second Bundesliga. I met with Martin Bader, the Sporting Director, at Düsseldorf Airport. It was a great meeting and they offered me a three-year deal. But because I was still in negotiations with Qatar I felt it was not right to take it. One of my biggest regrets, I would say.

We were still in the summer when I was approached to become Guus Hiddink's assistant at Anzhi Makhachkala in the Russian Premier League. I'd always respected Guus and I felt that situation suited me more. When I discussed it further with Guus, he explained that he wanted me to do exactly what I did at United, arranging all the sessions and so on, so it seemed like a good opportunity. There were some good players there – Chris Samba, Lassana Diarra, Willian and Samuel Eto'o in their ranks.

Hiddink had enjoyed a really good season the year before, finishing third in the league and getting to the last 16 in Europe. He seemed to enjoy a good relationship with the owner, Suleyman Kerimov. It was a strange experience to begin with, I must admit. We were training close to the Luzhniki Stadium in Moscow, but our home stadium was based in Dagestan, two and a half hours away from Moscow by charter plane.

On our arrival for our first home game, the first thing I saw when we landed was another plane, on its side, completely wrecked. We got in the bus and saw tower blocks with their windows blown out and bullet holes everywhere. In the middle of the city, a remarkable brand new 26,500 seater stadium, resplendent in vibrant green and gold, a strong contrast to the ravaged city that surrounded it. Football gave the locals something to look forward to.

Our opponents on the day were Lokomotiv Moscow. We were 1-0 down. Eto'o equalised. We then went 2-1 up. In injury time we conceded an equaliser – but there was still time for us to be awarded a penalty, which seemed dubiously given. Eto'o took the longest run-up I've ever seen for a penalty kick – and missed. We drew 2-2.

Kerimov came into the dressing room after the game and Hiddink completely ignored him. I remember being confused by it all. A few days later we played at Dynamo Moscow. We went a goal down then had a man sent off – but our response was good, and when Samba scored in the 83rd minute, it looked like we'd get a point. More late drama – another penalty, this time to Dynamo, three minutes from time. Voronin, the former Liverpool player, won the game for them.

In the fallout after the game, Hiddink was alleged to have pushed an official, and there was immediately talk that he would be suspended for six weeks.

Guus had originally announced his intent to leave the post earlier in the year but had been convinced to stay on after attempts to lure Fabio Capello and Laurent Blanc failed. The dust hadn't even settled on the game when the news came out that Guus was now leaving for good. I received a call from Kerimov's agent.

"Are you ready?" he asked.

"What for?"

"To take over the team."

Confused, I tried to contact Guus, but he didn't reply to my text at the time. I was picked up by the agent to go to Kerimov's office the next morning, we travelled with a translator and the club secretary. We were racing through Moscow in a huge 4x4 with blacked out windows like we were in some action movie. His office was somewhere in the middle of Moscow. We parked up in an underground garage and took the lift, which was guarded by a 6'7 armed bodybuilder. We were told to go into the meeting room, and I remember being struck by this bowl that had miniature candy bars in it.

Kerimov entered the room. He was a distinctive man. A few years earlier he had been involved in a car accident that had left him with serious burns, to the extent that he had to wear protective sleeves. He began talking, through the translator, about his decision to part ways with Guus, and how pleased he was to have brought me in because he'd heard the players were responding well to the new way of doing things.

He proposed to change my deal from a one-year to a three-year deal, with a significant increase in salary. Then he informed me that if we qualified for Champions League football my bonus would be a Bugatti. It was only at that moment I realised I'd eaten one of the little Mars bars without even taking the wrapper off, I was so astounded by the liberal way he was promising riches. Hiddink did get back in touch. I told him that I was happy to leave with him and show solidarity, but he insisted I should take the job.

In my first game, we drew 1-1 at Krylia Sovetov, and in my

first home game, we lost 1-0; Rostov taking all three points through a goal that to me was clearly offside and the survival of a penalty decision that should have been given our way.

It seemed to be a constant theme that we'd have some controversy on the pitch, but it wasn't confined to there. Just before I'd arrived the club had signed Igor Denisov for 15 million euros. Zenit St. Petersburg were quite happy to get rid of him because he held some controversial political opinions.

Denisov reacted angrily to me substituting him, to the extent that Eto'o arranged a small team meeting to discuss it when we were training next. Kerimov was alerted so he arrived at the Luzhniki Stadium in a convoy of these large black cars with armed guards stepping out of them. That's how we had our meetings. Eto'o told Kerimov that Denisov was a difficult character, that he shouldn't have been signed, and furthermore, he wouldn't be stepping foot with him on the pitch again. It was agreed that Denisov would be sent out on loan, after just three games.

Then there was an international break. I flew back to Manchester to see my family for a quick break – when I was back at my apartment in Russia, I received a message from Stijn van den Broecke, the strength and conditioning coach at the club, who had been at the club for a few years.

"Have you seen the newspapers?" he asked.

"Well, even if I had, I can't read Russian," I laughed.

He informed me that Kerimov had not only sold Denisov. Yuriy Zhirkov and Aleksandr Kokorin went with him, and several of our star names were all on the transfer list too. The fire sale of the squad was done to raise some money quickly after the owner had run into some difficulties..

Upon learning that he was to be transferred, Willian begged me to get him to Manchester United. He was desperate. He's a mad United fan. So, despite how everything had ended with David, I made the call. I was able to provide a sound judgement on his ability and I advised David that Willian was a top professional and a quality player who could occupy any position in the front line. I assured him of his mentality to take the step and said he had that great talent of being able to beat a man and score a goal. Giggsy called me to continue the conversation.

"You know me," I said, "and you know I know what a United player looks like. You can't go wrong with him."

Nothing happened. He went to London – he was supposed to go to Tottenham, before Roman Abramovich exercised his friendly relations with our owner to take him to Chelsea instead. Willian was fantastic for Chelsea – an opportunity missed for United.

That wasn't the end of it. Gadzhi Gadzhiyev, who had managed Anzhi on four previous occasions, replaced me as manager. I discovered that after these unforeseen developments, I still hadn't signed my new contract as the head coach – I was waiting for my agent to come to Russia to continue that negotiation, but he had some passport and visa issue that was due to be resolved in the week of my return.

In my next conversation with the CEO, I was informed that my original contract as first-team coach was the valid one, and I wouldn't be receiving a new one. I couldn't get hold of Guus to get some advice, so I made a call to Sir Alex.

"The only advice I can give," he said, "is that if you decide to leave, make sure you get the payment of any agreement as quickly as you can before you leave the country." He advised me to play hardball but to take the pay off and deal with it swiftly.

It was great advice, but it was not a fantastic situation to be in, considering I was still labelled as René Meulensteen, sacked in 16 days, however, I expected that people in the industry would see past this ridiculous run of events.

It happened at such a head-spinning speed that there was barely any opportunity to really consider the prospect of a long-term implementation of my ideas and how that might translate in the Russian game. I was already considering what my next move could be and the English season had barely begun.

I was offered an opportunity in China so I flew to Hong Kong for some conversations, but it just didn't feel right. Alistair Mackintosh, a director at Fulham, got in touch while I was out there to propose the idea of working with Martin Jol. I was still weighing it all up when Shahid Khan, the Fulham owner, called me and said Martin was enthusiastic about the idea of me going to London. I agreed to fly to Jacksonville, Florida and meet Shahid. I was impressed.

Shahid was a self-made billionaire and had bought the Jacksonville Jaguars. I was curious about his intention and motivation. He was a very nice guy but didn't seem to have much knowledge about soccer. I was introduced to the team coach at the Jaguars and had a nice meeting at the stadium. Afterwards, in the parking lot, I asked Shahid's assistant in a blunt way: "Why did he want to buy Fulham?"

"Well," came the replay, "he originally wanted to buy Everton. But then we found out Everton was not in London."

I nearly fell out of the car. He explained that they were driven by the prospect of taking American football to London. There seemed to be no genuine insight about the direction of the club – no interest in its day-to-day philosophy. What they did seem to enjoy was operating their 'moneyball' strategy, crunching data and buying players based on numbers. They bought full-backs from the Swiss league based on their numbers, thinking that would naturally translate to the same numbers in the Premier League.

It took me a little while to be convinced but eventually I was, because at least I knew the Premier League, and I knew Martin knew the game. He'd had a great first season and a decent second season, so I felt I could put my concerns about the bigger picture to one side.

I do have to admit though that even when I looked at the football set-up at Fulham and I considered the profile of the squad – there was quite an old average age, and several contracts were coming close to the end, and that to me was a recipe for a team who could well face a struggle. I confessed to Martin that this factor also played a role in my delayed decision to accept the job.

We lost my first game there against Swansea at home. The next week we were at West Ham. We missed Berba as he was injured and I felt we gave a good account of ourselves in the first half. In the second, we conceded early, and then two more late on, the sort of late capitulation you often suffer if you're a team suffering in confidence.

The next day, I went to the training ground to work with the players who hadn't taken part in the game the day before. At about 1pm I told the lads I was just going to nip across the road because there was a DFS furniture shop, and I still needed some things for the house I had moved into.

I was sorting that out when I looked at my phone and saw three missed calls from Alistair. I went back to the car and tried to return the call. He didn't pick up, so I just turned the radio on as I went back to the training ground. I tuned into Talksport – the breaking news was that Martin Jol had left Fulham and René Meulensteen had been appointed manager.

Excuse me?

I immediately telephoned Martin.

"René, I needed to go," he admitted.

I eventually got through to Alistair. "What is this?" I demanded. "I'm suddenly the manager and you didn't even ask me. Why do you think I hesitated to come here?"

He suggested that he come to my hotel that night to discuss it further. He did – and I laid it out bare for him the very dire situation the club found themselves in due to the squad composition. I asked him to explain how I was going to get the club out of trouble with a team which had many players who were above 30, of which a lot of contracts were running out and therefore not particularly motivated for a relegation fight. I said we needed to add quality, energy, and commitment. He agreed and said that there would be some room to make some transfers in January.

We had 24 games remaining and the fixture list presented us with many tough challenges against top-half teams in the first 12 of them – I felt if we could navigate through those, we had a fighting chance of accumulating the necessary points for safety in the last 12.

I made some calls to bring some staff; Mick Priest and John Hill, who I had worked with at United. They were both very good coaches and Mick was a great scout too. I knew Ray Wilkins from the number of times I'd faced Chelsea; he was Carlo Ancelotti's assistant and often Ray and I would be the first two in the room after our matches. I always enjoyed listening to him when he worked as a pundit; I often found myself agreeing with his point of view. I asked him if he was interested in helping and I was delighted when he said yes. It was the same with Alan Curbishley; a great man and a good manager with so much experience.

We won three of my first six games, which was a decent start before the window opened. I was impressed by how quickly the players seemed to adapt to playing in the way I wanted and even though we lost to Manchester City, we gave it a good go. I remember Alan remarking on how tough it had been on us because the games were coming so quickly. That schedule made it impossible for us to field a regular first-choice XI and inconsistent line-ups often bring inconsistent results.

January was difficult – we lost four on the bounce and that convinced the board to let me bring in some players late in the window. I felt that William Kvist and Lewis Holtby would provide the quality and energy in the middle of the park we needed. John Heitinga had plenty of experience in defence and I took a chance of bringing in Ryan Tunnicliffe and Larnell Cole as two United boys who I knew would play with the spirit I wanted.

With a week of preparation, we went to Old Trafford determined to give a good account of ourselves. We should have been 2-0 up at half-time. Steve Sidwell had scored for us early on. We started brightly. Kieran Richardson should have squared in a good position but went for goal himself. I knew pressure would build in the second half, but I was comfortable forcing them wide because we had big Dan Burn in the middle of our defence. I brought Dan back from a loan spell at Birmingham City and gave him his Premier League debut. They put in a record of 81 crosses – 81! I reckon Dan must have headed about 70 of them away. Their quality told – Van Persie and Carrick scored and looked to have won it for them – but we got a point when Darren Bent scored in injury time.

It was very strange to return to United so soon; to go into the visitor's room. It didn't feel right. I didn't have a drink with David after and I didn't see him after shaking his hand at the full-time whistle.

I was proud of the lads. They were clearly willing. A lot of those players had given so much for the club, but they were coming towards the end of their career and it was no surprise that it was in the last 10 or 15 minutes of games when we were really suffering. That's where we fell short.

As for United, well, I remembered seeing their first league game under David at Swansea. They won 4-1 and they played like the old United. The same ingredients were all there. But the first thing that happened in the coming weeks was that the one and two-touch football disappeared. It slowed the game down and looked pedestrian. They looked like they were running out of ideas. A good United team leaves you not knowing where to look. It was clear that it was not going as well as everyone had hoped.

As someone who had been connected to the club for such a long time, I was often – at this time and in forthcoming times – asked for comment by the media, particularly if things were not going so well. It does put you in a difficult position. On one hand, you know that everyone in the media is hoping to create or add to some controversy. The club gave me the best years of my coaching life and I love it. I would never comment on the club to add fuel to the fire, to jump on any bandwagon of criticism that is heading their way. The club faces that enough and I've been on the other side of it. I think I am realistic in my opinions, and I have an objective opinion which I'm not afraid to say. You never really leave United; if you have been there, it remains a significant part of your identity. So, you do always have some form of responsibility in your conduct and behaviour, though you can also put that down to respect for a former employer at a very basic level, and who you are as a person. If there is a witch-hunt on the club or one of its players, it's important that sometimes some of us are present in the press to defend them and provide a different perspective. There were certain occasions over the past few years where I wished things would not have been played out over the press.

It was, still, a very special place to go, and a last-minute draw was celebrated by our boys like a win. It provided a mental lift, and we were very aggressive and on the front foot in our next game three days later, against a Liverpool team challenging for the title.

In the following week I was tipped off by a friend in Germany and it caught me completely off-guard. He said he'd seen a representative from Fulham talking to Felix Magath.

I prepared our team in the best way and I felt we deserved something from the next game. Twice we took the lead against Liverpool, only for them to level up. We were still on the way to another good 2-2 draw when they were awarded a penalty in extra time. Riether made an unnecessary foul in the box close to the byline. Penalty.

It was devastating to us to lose the game in that fashion. If we'd won, or drawn, I would probably have kept the job – but they made the decision to sack me and bring in Felix, who was renowned as an unpredictable character and had no experience whatsoever of English football. William Kvist released a book a few years later where he said he went from heaven when I signed him to hell when Felix was appointed, within a spell of two weeks.

On the decision to sack me, I told reporters that I felt the club had hit the panic button. I wasn't the last one to suffer at the hands of that sort of decision-making. It was then that the club started to face all the teams around them.

Fulham were relegated by four points and 12 points were dropped in crucial games. I'm not saying we could have accumulated all 12 of those points, but for example, the club dropped four in the last two home games alone by conceding late equalisers, and I was sure we could have given it a better fight. Instead, all the issues I'd predicted in my conversations with Alistair came back to afflict the club in the most unfortunate way.

Chapter Sixteen

THE MEULENSTEEN METHOD

THERE has been an increased interest in coaching over the last couple of decades. People have loved football in a special way since the very earliest versions of the game were played but in recent times a fascination has developed with the methodology of coaches and managers. Because of that, sometimes that analysis can feel unnecessarily complicated, and it was always my intention when I decided to write this book that I would try and express and articulate my ideas in a way that could easily be understood.

The point is that the amount of work we do is comprehensive, and it is meticulous, but the success of any methodology is usually found in the economy of the message and how easily it is understood. For that reason, I have always tried, where possible, to lace ideas with hidden messages about mental preparation that can be used outside of football and assist with independent problem-solving. For example, with players, I would be careful with the terminology I used whilst I am coaching. I wouldn't say we need to change something to a player or team – I'd say let's add something. Add is more. It's positive.

You can send simple messages that make huge differences. After one game where a winger had been ineffective, I asked him how often he'd crossed the ball. How often did he beat a guy one on one? We set objectives. In the next game I wanted him to think that his specific target was to get between five and 10 quality crosses in. It is proven that people who set targets are more likely to achieve success because in merely doing that, you create a pathway. I'm a huge believer in the law of attraction and the power of positive thinking because there is so much evidence to support it.

I'm also a believer in exploring new territory. Life is short, we must enjoy the experiences and opportunities we are presented with, and it is well-established that I have always enjoyed trying something different and trying to implement my soccer philosophy in areas where it can have a widespread impact.

During my time at United I created a course called *The Meulensteen Method*, which was, simply, skill development in small-sided games. I got to know Fons van den Brande, who had a company called Sportpartners (now it is Voetbalscholing). With him, I held many three-day technical coaching clinics, starting in 2003 and continuing all the way up to 2017.

It started out as a taster course, where I tried to explain how significant it was to ensure that the approach for coaching U8s and U18s, for example, was different and engaging. We were hoping that 60-80 people would sign up, but 240 did. We did a survey afterwards asking if those who had participated would be interested if we expanded the courses to three days.

The courses were quickly established. We offered certificates to those who completed, and Fons was able to get those certificates recognised by the KNVB, marking a significant point in my journey, considering the trouble I'd had at the very beginning of my coaching career.

I had a lot of help setting that up in America thanks to Joe Cummings, who played a significant role in the rebirth of soccer in the US with the 1994 World Cup and Major League Soccer (MLS), and a childhood friend of mine, Erwin van Elst, who had played as a professional for a while before moving to America to study. He settled there and got married. As demand for technical skills development grew, we were able to run courses in new territories and as the reputation of the courses became more established, demand for it grew. Erwin was crucial in the organisation in America, holding camps and clinics as well as organising the the United States Technical Championship (USTC).

Joe called me after what happened at Fulham and asked me if I had any plans. He said he'd been having a conversation with Nick Sakiewicz, a shareholder at Philadelphia Union. They had been talking about doing something different at their club and my name came up. I was happy to speak to Nick over the telephone. My feeling was that the MLS had become heavily influenced by the influx of South American players, and that the North American players generally adopted a survival of the fittest mentality, whereby the most strong and athletic players thrived. Obviously, my strength was in technical development that had a unique European flavour and that would create a very strong and distinct identity to Philadelphia Union. Nick invited me over to take a closer look.

He too had a strong history in the administration of the game. He'd played as a goalkeeper in the original NASL and was instrumental in the recovery of the MLS. Along with Jay Sugarman, who had made his wealth in real estate, Nick had set about the project of establishing Philadelphia Union as a contender. Jay wasn't a soccer man. Richie Graham, the third key shareholder, was.

Richie was a fantastic man. He had an apartment in Vail, Colorado and he invited all the staff involved in the academy there to talk about his vision and ideas. I had been invited a few days earlier and we spent some time skiing. It was interesting to me as it really did strike home the following message: where you see excellence, you see simplicity. I'm not a good skier. Richie is, as he was previously part of the USA Olympic skiing team. When I saw him ski, with such grace and elegance, I was able to follow him. It was like I was tied to him by a rope. I felt it was the best way I ever skied, just by following him.

The conversations were productive, and a four-year deal was suggested. Jim Curtin was the assistant coach and named interim manager after the Philadelphia Union parted ways with John Hackworth – as I write this, he still is the manager now. My proposed role was to be the head coach and oversee the development of the young players into the senior set-up. Jim had just been appointed, so he still had a lot to learn, but he was an ambitious coach, a very nice guy. Credit where credit is due, he has done very well with the Philadelphia Union since he became coach. It is also testament and proof to the fact that when you give managers time, it will result in success.

I was impressed that the Union had a school connected to their academy, so a percentage of their time was spent preparing them for the possibility of a life as a professional soccer player and then the rest was a straightforward education in case they did not make it.

We saw out the rest of the season. The team failed to reach

the play-offs but improved from their poor start to the year; we did reach the final of the US Open Cup, which we lost to a strong Seattle Sounders side after extra time.

I invited Nick to Manchester just before the final and I discussed my observations from my time with them so far. I said one of the things that needed to be addressed for any club to experience success is to have a strong environment and good resources. The stadium was fine. I felt the training facilities needed to be upgraded; they were also too close to the stadium, and my opinion was that they needed to train in a different venue to make the stadium a more special place. More than anything, the staff needed to be right.

I invited Nick to have conversations with Tony Strudwick and Eric Steele so he could get a feel for the value of specialist expertise and experience. If I had to do it by myself, I would have to spend time educating people, but these were men who knew my way of working and would fast-track our process.

I explained that there was a potential issue which could come from the final, and it could come whatever the result was. We had a young team who had experienced a difficult start and if we won, great, there would be euphoria and a little boost that would come from that. But it was probably a bit of an overachievement and so they might struggle once the good feeling wore off. And, naturally, the risk of a low mood after a defeat was self-explanatory.

My feeling was that if we'd won the final, and then perhaps enjoyed the confidence boost that might have come from that, I'd probably have been given the job no problem. But we didn't, and suddenly Sugarman stopped the deal. It was a real shame because I thought four years would be a fantastic period to see some significant response and reward. Yes, it might take 18 months to start to see some real progress, but the long-term benefits would have been fantastic and seen across the game.

Nick, however, remained insistent that I stayed around in some capacity, and he suggested a six-month consultancy position. He said he wanted me to create an 'X-Ray' of the club. That much was straightforward as I used the same 10 key elements I used to navigate the success of Manchester United. So, I looked at ownership, organisation and management, the manager and support staff, players, hard work, teamwork, and team spirit, a clear game plan in terms of strategy and tactics, a desire to win or a winning mentality, and finally, scoring goals, stop conceding goals and/or keeping clean sheets. Those were the key points.

I oversaw the first team on their pre-season. Jim and his staff were able to tap into me whenever they felt they might need me. That didn't happen very often, but it didn't bother me too much. I was able to analyse the strengths and weaknesses of the team and the potential problems I could identify with regards their style and strategy.

My last report included an analysis of the games and exactly where our strengths and weaknesses had impacted our on-pitch results. Nick wanted me to present that report to Jay and the other members of the board. He was becoming frustrated by the situation, as he was convinced of my idea of direction. Ultimately, the decision was taken not to extend my spell there beyond my consultancy period.

Chapter Seventeen

SIR ALEX'S SUCCESSORS

MANCHESTER United experienced a difficult transition period in the spell after Sir Alex's retirement. David Moyes was given a six-year deal and I do believe managers need, give or take, 18 months to really see the value of their work pay off and to create consistency in the team performances and results. Unfortunately for David he seemed to be moving in the wrong direction from the beginning by disrupting the continuity and stability which were such important pillars of success in the Sir Alex era. If you're travelling in the wrong direction, the further you travel, the longer it will take to get back to where you should be. Yes, I do believe David should have been given some more time, but I also believe he needed help and advice to manage a club and squad of such magnitude. Would he have listened? Well, David Gill had left, so there was no continuity from above him. I don't think David listened carefully when he initially spoke to existing staff.

But let there be no mistake, the only thing I and the others wanted was to help David for Manchester United to remain successful. People say we were an ageing team and there was not much left in the tank, but I can guarantee you that if Sir Alex had carried on, we would've made some good signings and we would've been there or thereabouts to winning the league again.

David was succeeded by Louis van Gaal and, in my honest opinion, I didn't feel it was the right choice from the start. I haven't worked with him so I can't speak about that, but I do know he was a very polarising leader. Lots of players loved him. Many did not.

I did feel that he would struggle if he hadn't sufficiently analysed the Premier League, because he's so regimented in his own way that he would inevitably make it van Gaal United and not Manchester United. He would play possession-based football like he has done everywhere else – but the Premier League is so dynamic that such a playing style doesn't work if you can't be versatile. Keeping hold of the ball became more important than creating chances and that became a running theme at the club. He's achieved great success at other clubs, and he started at Ajax – but you can't make the mistake of putting van Gaal in the same school of thought as Michels and Cruyff.

Jose Mourinho had coveted the job for a long time. That much was obvious even before he was Real Madrid manager and said the best team lost in the tie where Nani was sent off. He was trying to cosy up, but he was not seen as the right fit at the time. Then, as time progressed, there was obviously a change of mind.

This is just my opinion, but it seemed to me that Mourinho was surprised by just how big United was. I think he struggled with the expectation that was on United to win and play an attractive style of attacking football because he's a pragmatic calculator. You must embrace unpredictability and emotion at Old Trafford, and he struggled in that respect to find a good balance.

Before he came to the club he had this tremendous character, he was seen as being a bit crafty, a bit sneaky; but the Mourinho who ended up at United had a lot of baggage with experience and titles, therefore his attitude was a little different. The way he conducted himself in press conferences seemed strange. He was representing the biggest club in the world. What a privilege. You want to show your pride at being in that position. At times it looked as though it was a burden for him to be Manchester United's manager.

Some managers have a short shelf-life. Their first year is a building year where they hope to achieve success and if they don't, it might arrive in the second year. In the third year, you're lucky if it goes well, but usually this is where everything starts to break down. Mourinho lost Rui Faria, his trusted right-hand man, and it seemed to me that it had something of an impact. He won the Europa League in his first season and finished second in the season after that. Then came the disagreement over the transfers and all the controversy which just seemed as though he was already manufacturing his way out.

The spotlight at Manchester United can be very difficult for some people to embrace. If you win and you don't play well, you keep most of the supporters onside because you're competing. But if you're not playing well and you're not winning – and you have a manager who is quite happy to court controversy – it can all fall apart very quickly.

When Mourinho was sacked, Ole Gunnar Solskjaer was hired as interim manager. He brought back Mick Phelan with him. There was a lot of speculation about whether I would go back, and I must confess I was half-expecting the phone to ring. I had a very good relationship with Ole when we were both there previously. I thought it was a smart move – there was a desperate need to rebuild a connection with the fans and there was a little bit of breathing space while the club could decide who they wanted on a permanent basis. I'm sure that even Ole didn't expect, when he first got the phone call, that he would become manager.

The response from the squad was a logical one – it was natural. Imagine a classroom with a teacher they don't get on with. As soon as that teacher goes, the mood is elevated. The way I see it, that period is a prime moment to re-establish a new system, a new tactical approach. Ole tried a few different things, but over time it lacked consistency. It would have been great to have been there and help with establishing that, but it wasn't to be. I did message Ole to pass on my congratulations, and we made a comment that we should catch up soon for coffee.

"You tell me where and when and I'll be there," I told him, although neither of us were able to do anything in the short term – he was obviously busy, and I was too, in my new position with the Australia team. There was one point where the dialogue completely stopped. Then, he was given the job on a permanent basis, after he'd enjoyed a strong start in terms of results.

You have to say that Ole exceeded expectations, but his tenure was always undermined by a lack of consistency. The team could always produce good performances and good runs but then there were critical moments which just didn't happen for whatever reason. The disappointment of losing the Europa League final was a big one. Ole would have been gutted to have missed out, whereas Mourinho and van Gaal could say they'd won something with United. I can't say that if I'd been there we would have won the Europa League. I just like to think I could have brought something helpful back to the club, but unfortunately, it never materialised.

The rumours of a return came around again after Erik ten Hag was appointed manager. Erik had enjoyed a good spell at Ajax where he worked with Edwin van der Sar. Edwin had sounded me out about the prospect of going to Ajax as Erik's assistant, but because of my obligations with Australia I couldn't make a commitment.

Chapter Eighteen

A STEP INTO THE UNKNOWN

THOSE experiences after leaving United gave me the feeling that if I did step back into club football, I would be tempted to do something myself and not necessarily be a coach or assistant. I had learned from the past and I knew I would do things differently.

I was in America attending the USTC, one of my skills championships organised by the MM (*Meulensteen Method*), when I was contacted by an agent who said Maccabi Haifa were keen to talk to me to replace their manager Ronny Levy, who had just been sacked for being eliminated from the Europa League qualifying stage.

I agreed to talk to Tor-Kristian Larsen, their technical director, and it was a good conversation. He invited me to Israel to meet the owners and see if we could reach an agreement. I was a little apprehensive; Maccabi Haifa are one of the most famous teams in Israel, but they had been going through a difficult period and hadn't won a league title since 2011.

I tried to educate myself about the club and the issues they had faced before I travelled to meet the president of the club, Ya'akov Shahar.

Shahar was a very wealthy man; he'd made his money in dealings with automobiles, specifically in the importing of Volvo and Toyota cars to Israel. He impressed upon me that his vision was to restore the club to the top of their game, so they were winning titles again. There was a particular sense of competition due to the strength of Maccabi Tel-Aviv, who were thriving under the guidance of Jordi Cruyff, their technical director.

My response was to consult my navigation system; I informed Shahar that I felt it might take 18 months to start to see the full value of my work, and the true direction we'd be heading in. It would give me an opportunity to work with the players I had, then in the next window, hopefully strengthen the squad. If things were going well those additions could help us challenge for the league but if it required more work, we would try and address that in the next window so we can ensure our players have time to adapt and gel.

"It doesn't matter how long it takes, as long as we get there," I was told. Fair enough.

I lived in Haifa, in a beautiful penthouse apartment with a tremendous view of the Golan Heights. The sunsets were stunning. Shahar lived an hour away along the coast in Tel-Aviv, which did sometimes make communicating and working difficult in the early days.

Our training facilities were not the best, to put it bluntly. They had static trailer units for changing in – you wouldn't expect any professional club to have to deal with that, let alone one with Champions League ambitions.

I made recommendations for upgrades, as much as I could.

There weren't even clear car parking spaces – I had to arrange that. There were flags around the facility and they were old, ripped, and tatty.

I wanted the players and staff to feel proud of where they were. The pitches were good, and the setting was fantastic, and I just felt that some little changes could make a big difference. So, we made them – and I think it contributed to a strong and positive feeling within the group. One thing I couldn't complain about was the stadium; the Sammy Ofer stadium was magnificent. It held around 30,000 of the most brilliant supporters who I struck up a good relationship with after meeting a man called Or, who was the leader of their Ultras.

We enjoyed a decent start to the season but couldn't get a consistent run of wins together. We had a player called Gili Vermouth, a talented midfielder who just didn't work hard enough. I left him out for a few games to impress the message, and the penny did drop – soon I had him back in the team and he did brilliantly for me.

I didn't have quite so much joy with Eliran Atar, who saw himself as the star of Israeli football. He always had to be different – when everyone turned up in the club car, he had to be the one who came in a Mercedes.

Yes, he had certain qualities, but there was no consistency. It wasn't like Ronaldo – where you accommodate an individual because they're so brilliant. He blew too hot and cold. In fact, I often felt he was undermining the team spirit we were working so hard to achieve, so when it was speculated that Maccabi Tel-Aviv were prepared to pay £1.2m for him, I joked to the owner that I'd be willing to drive him there myself. Not only would we be losing a problem, but we'd also be giving one to a rival. However, the owner refused to do any business with a rival.

It was the owner in fact who turned out to be the biggest headache. He was renowned for being negative, constantly. He didn't hide it – so the media lapped it up. Every day.

If we lost it was bad and if we won, we didn't win well enough. I was trying to create a closed shop, a squad with a bond, and everything I was building, he was breaking down from the outside. We had a team manager called Rafi Osmo – he'd once played for the club, and he knew Shahar very well. He was a lovely guy and great fun. He knew what I was trying to do, and he was encouraging it.

"You're going to be here for 10 years," he said one morning.

"Yeah, but if Ya'akov keeps doing what he's doing, I don't think I'll be here 10 months," I replied, almost tongue-in-cheek.

As we approached the first transfer window, I had a clearer idea of the ability level of my squad so I put them into categories of green, yellow and red. Green denoted players we could keep and build around. Yellow, we'd have to discuss, and red, we'd have to move on. There were quite a few in the yellow and red categories.

One morning, Shahar came to the training ground – he went directly to the players and told them they could go. Players in the red and yellow categories! It was a complete abandoning of the process, complete disregard of the confidence you're supposed to have between an owner and manager. You can imagine the impact that had on morale.

In February we played our local derby against Hapoel Haifa. We were playing well. Their goalkeeper, a Dutchman, Piet Velthuizen, was having a blinder. We should have been 2-0 up at least at half-time but went in at the break 1-0 down. In the 76th minute they scored a goal where it hit the post and went in off our goalkeeper's head. In the late minutes as we threw everyone forward, they countered and scored a third. A 3-0 defeat in the derby. It wasn't good.

We were in the middle of the season. Regardless of what the owner had done in telling the players, we were always going to arrive at a point where we'd need to make the changes and we needed to make the changes because some of them weren't good enough. That was proven in the results. The wolves of the media would be howling. These were the moments where you had to stay true to your long-term plan because even the bumps are part of the process.

The next morning, I tried to address the defeat with the players. It was the classic flight or fight talk. Are you lions or are you chickens? I told them this was something they'd have to address because if I wasn't there the next day, if there was another man in charge, the exact same problems would still be there.

I was called in by Assaf, the CEO, the next morning and he told me that Shahar wanted to make a change. I wouldn't be there the next day. He didn't even have the confidence, the respect, the courage to tell me face to face. I said he was making a mistake – we were right at the moment where we needed conviction in our direction. I told him what I told the players. It didn't matter. It took Maccabi Haifa until 2021 to win their next league title.

A few months after I left, I noted that Maccabi Haifa were playing a pre-season game in Holland against RKC Waalwijk, where my son Melle was playing at the time. Their new Dutch manager was Fred Rutten – so I went to see them play. Rafi and the players were pleased to see me, and I them. I even had a chat with the owner.

"Yeah, we've got a new guy in," he said, "but it takes time."

"Exactly," I told him. "I hope you're going to give it to him."

Fred was gone by November. I was somewhere else entirely. Kerala Blasters, who played in the Indian Super League, were looking for a new manager after Steve Coppell had left them to join Jamshedpur. Mikael Silvestre had some connections in the country as he'd played there prior to retirement. He was asked to reach out to me to see if I would be interested in a different job – at Delhi Dynamos, where he had played. That didn't go anywhere but Varun Tripuraneni, the CEO at Kerala, contacted me to make an offer.

We had conversations in London and I wasn't entirely sure, but over time I became a little more convinced; my son, Joppe, is an analyst and Varun seemed happy for him to be part of my set-up.

When I say I wasn't sure, I suppose I'm referring to the structure of the domestic game. There wasn't a traditional league. I didn't know if they were looking for a coach to lead the players they had or if they wanted something more comprehensive in relation to their organisation as a club in the traditional format that I was used to. Did they want a structure, a vision? I never really received a convincing answer on that, but I must admit I was swayed a little by the sporting romance within me; the club was owned by Nimmagadda Prasad and, more importantly to me, Sachin Tendulkar.

Sachin was a very, very nice man, and I loved spending time with him, but it transpired that his involvement was minimal. Varun was the most prominent member of the ownership structure in terms of the day-to-day football operations.

The squad was assembled via a draft system, and we were allowed to sign eight foreign players. I suggested bringing in four with commercial value and four we could develop and sell for a profit. Iain Hume was a Canadian forward with experience of the country. I brought Courage Pekuson, a

Ghanaian midfielder. I was able to bring in Dimitar Berbatov, and then I added two other United old boys in an unconventional way.

I was on an Emirates flight back to Manchester. I was at the bar when I felt a pat on the back; suddenly there were a few former United players, who were returning from a Legends tour. One of them was Paul Rachubka, the former goalkeeper. I mentioned that I was going to be working in India.

"Do you need a goalkeeper?" Paul asked. I was in dialogue with Shay Given but that was proving difficult due to the money he was asking for.

I started to think about the other players who were with them. Wes Brown had played but he was getting a different flight. "How did he do?" I asked. "Yeah, he's still fit," Paul said. Thankfully Wes was receptive. I'd signed my defensive spine on the plane.

It was great to lead another team who played in a wonderful venue. The Jawaharlal Nehru Stadium in Kochi had a capacity of around 80,000 – we got very good crowds. When we would arrive with the team bus 30,000 fans would be there to cheer us on outside the stadium. The Indian people were definitely very passionate about their football. For a country without a strong history of domestic football, it was clear that a concerted effort was being made to establish something.

We had a training camp in Marbella before the season. I had my staff with me – Joppe, René Skovdahl, who had been with me in Brondby and Haifa, and Giora Antman, who had been goalkeeping coach in Israel. I also brought in someone who was very good from an organisational point of view when it came to visas and contracts for the players, etc.

We were joined by a man called Deep who was effectively the team manager, Varun's conduit. I asked Deep where our training gear was – we barely had anything. I was immediately concerned and asked to make a note of every problem we faced. I talked to Mr Prasad when we were back in India and said I was concerned; we agreed we'd look at it in six games, once we were underway.

I wasn't best pleased with our start. We drew three home games, and we missed Wes, badly, as he hadn't been able to play because of an injury. Then we went to Goa.

In Kerala, there are prohibition laws on the consumption of alcohol. Those regulations were not in place in Goa. Our strength and conditioning coach, John Floros, told me on the morning of the game that he was unable to sleep because of the noise all night in the next room. Who was the occupant? Sandesh Jhingan, our captain, drinking and partying through to the early hours.

The game had barely kicked off before Berbatov was forced to come off with a knock. I was reluctant to bring Wes on because he wasn't yet ready; I wanted to see how the players coped. We took the lead – but then it fell apart.

In our pre-match analysis, we had identified Goa as a four-man team. All their play went straight through these four foreign players who linked altogether. Our plan was to break the chain. It was 2-2 at half-time. I admitted to the players that I had no clue where this game was going. We let in three goals in the first 10 minutes.

The next morning, I got hold of Jhingan. He'd clearly been drinking again. I tried to tell him about the standards you were supposed to have as a professional, the captain and international, but it fell on deaf ears.

It wasn't just me who was frustrated; we drew a game at home and Berba was so annoyed he kicked a fridge in the dressing room. He was furious with his team-mates for not doing what we'd been working on in training. He later apologised to them for his conduct, a great example – but sadly it seemed few of his colleagues wanted to follow that example.

I tried hard to make training easier for some of the players; I was simplifying it as much as I could, making it easy for them to make the right decisions. I had Berba playing as a number 10, almost deeper, so that he could dictate the play. There were drills we ran where Berba would lay chances on a plate. Easy chances. All of them would be fired over the bar or wide.

In mid-December Varun called a meeting with me. He said he would like me to dismiss two of my staff.

"What do you think my answer will be?" I asked, before quickly adding, "What's the reason?"

Of course, I knew the reason. He knew myself and our logistics team manager had been putting together the issues we had, and he wanted to get him out of the club. He threw John's name in the mix to make it look less obvious. I said there was no way they were going.

Our sixth game was at Chennaiyin. Our plan was to give the dossier to the owner the morning after the game, because after that we had a few days off for Christmas and everyone was travelling to be with their families. The game was quite eventful; Chennai went one up through a penalty in the first half, but we scored an equaliser in stoppage time by Venneeth. Afterwards we were told that Prasad was stuck in Singapore on business and wasn't going to be able to make it. We'd have to have the meeting when we returned.

In the first game after the break, it was 0-0 at half-time. The team was so erratic that I was forced to repeat my comment from earlier in the season. I didn't know what was going on. It was like throwing darts blindfolded. I didn't know if some of our players wanted to win or lose. We were 1-0 down going into injury time – we let in two more goals before scoring ourselves. It was ridiculous. I said to Skove as we walked to the dressing room: "You watch. That'll be the end."

I was called in the morning after. "The owner has decided to do something different…"

Obviously.

"Do you consider yourself a man of principles?" I asked Varun.

"Yes, of course."

"Well, I want the contracts of all of my staff to be respected if they choose to go."

They did want to go. I was still in India trying to get things sorted by the time of the next game. David James, the former goalkeeper, had succeeded me.

I sent Prasad a message to say I'd love to have a chat with him, to personally thank him. It was just a way to get to speak to him. He messaged back and said he'd call me.

When we eventually talked, I reminded him of the concerns I had, and shared the notes I made over time and which we were supposed to discuss after the sixth game. He agreed that we'd made that arrangement. I told him that Varun had informed me the meeting was cancelled because he was in Singapore.

"No," he said. "I was in Chennai. I watched the game."

He said Varun told him we were the ones who couldn't attend the meeting because of our flights home. I said Varun had either misinformed him or ill-informed him on different occasions, this being just one.

He asked me to do him a favour – write a report on my findings of my time there. I agreed to do it. I thought Prasad was a good man. He just placed his faith in a man who turned out to be incapable.

A couple of months after I returned to England, I received the devastating news that Ray Wilkins passed away. I enjoyed working with Ray in that short spell at Fulham. I went to his funeral and bumped into Steve Coppell.

"Let me guess why you left Kerala," he said. "Varun."

He wasn't wrong.

Chapter Nineteen

ROAD TO THE WORLD CUP

I HAVE always kept my sense of adventure and a desire to see different parts of the world. Life is about new experiences. I'm also a competitor by nature. I'm driven by success. It was very frustrating that the various roles after leaving United didn't work out. I do like to be a part of a long project and see it bear fruit.

Football can be as unpredictable off the pitch as it is on; you don't know what opportunities will be presented. You want to win, but as a coach, success looks different to how it does as a player – for example, playing for your country, playing or scoring at Wembley. I had dreams of going to a World Cup, to coach at the Olympic Games because, in my opinion, international football is the purest form of professional football in the game. And in my experience, club football is all about money and thus false.

I've never been the sort of guy who will ask for help or put his face out there asking for a job. After leaving Kerala, the phone wasn't ringing. But not for long, as in early February I was called by Graham Arnold. He said he was going to be taking over the Australian national team after the World Cup in Russia in 2018. Would I fancy being his assistant? I had a strong gut feeling. It wasn't easy but it was still probably a better than even chance that they could qualify for the World Cup. We also agreed to take the Olympic team as we both felt the need to create more depth for the Socceroos squad. Our job was to have them qualify for the Olympics in Japan. It gave us a great chance to see how the younger players were developing. It felt right – I had to take it.

Almost immediately after accepting, I got another message. Edwin van der Sar, who was now the chief executive at Ajax. Would I be interested in being Erik ten Hag's assistant?

"Edwin," I replied, "you are the world champion of bad timing."

I told him I'd given Graham my word. He tried to convince me. He said Ajax were on the verge of doing great things under Erik and it would be a wonderful journey. I said that I was certain he was right, and I didn't want to be rude, but wanted to pursue this opportunity with Australia. If I would've been available, I would have said yes without question – but the allure of the World Cup, a road not yet travelled, was too great and if I give someone my word, I keep it.

The 2018 World Cup didn't go very well for Australia. They'd qualified through Ange Postecoglou, who stepped down after qualifying. Bert van Marwijk took over for the tournament, but they didn't win a game and went out in the group stages. They drew with Denmark and lost to Peru and the eventual winners France. Graham had heard that the environment wasn't great in the squad. Players weren't happy. The first thing we wanted to do was to address that.

We arranged a training camp in Turkey in the September FIFA window without a fixture; we wanted to express to them what we were hoping to achieve and what we were about.

I told Graham we needed to take the end point as our starting point. When they get back on the plane to go to their clubs, what do we want them to think? We wanted them to enjoy it. We wanted them to be excited about the style of football. If we were talking about attacking football then we needed to practise what we preached; we needed to create sessions for them to express themselves, where we didn't overload them with information.

It helps that we were one of the strongest teams on the continent. We could generate some momentum in a winning run, and we did that. I told Graham he should write down his starting 11, the team he felt would start the first game if we qualified for the 2022 World Cup in Qatar. I told him to do that at every international window, and I said that I felt certain five or six of those names would be different by the time of the tournament. I was confident that the Olympic squad would have an influence; it was on a different track to the World Cup, but eventually, those tracks would come together, and it would result in the final squad for 2022.

In international management you have less contact time with the players and that means you must maximise it. You need complete clarity with your information. We achieved that by having mixed general meetings and smaller group meetings, for example, with goalkeepers, defenders, midfielders, and attackers. You tailor your video analysis for that group. The format was the same all the time, so the players knew what to expect.

Graham received an offer to coach in Korea – it was financially lucrative. He and I had been working together for two and a half years when he told me about it and asked me to come with him.

"I came here to go to the World Cup," I said. "I think we've got something special here. I feel we have an obligation to those players too."

I'm sure Graham is glad I was so determined to stay; I'm sure it influenced him too. He received a lot of unfair and unjustified criticism during those four and half years. We rode every wave of that together. We had an ambition between us – we wanted to create the greatest Socceroos team ever. We wanted an identity. We were going to play to win every game, with ambition and fire. Football is the fifth sport in Australia – rugby union, rugby league, Aussie rules, and cricket come first. Football, though, unites the nation like nothing else.

During the Olympics, COVID-19 was still affecting all of us. I was very keen to experience the Olympics as I heard so much about it. Unfortunately, because of COVID-19 it never lived up to my expectations. We brought a group of players predominantly, players from the A-league who weren't getting any game time. A few players who were stationed in Europe and Mitchell Duke, who came as our overaged player.

We were based in Sapporo in the north of Japan where we played Argentina and Spain in the air-conditioned Sapporo Dome. We beat Argentina 2-0! It was an unbelievable game, result and achievement and, in my opinion, we didn't receive the credit where it was due. A lot of those Argentinian players were playing for good clubs in South America or Europe.

Likewise, the second game against Spain. Much of that team had been part of the European Championships earlier that summer. We narrowly lost 1-0 as Spain scored late on in the game. We then had to fly to Sendai and face Egypt under tough circumstances as it was 35 degrees and 76% humidity.

We lost 2-0 and were knocked out, but Graham and I got what we needed – young players who would be able to make the step up to the Socceroos.

The qualification for the 2022 World Cup in Qatar started brightly as we won the first round of games, convincingly topping the group and scoring a lot of goals. We finished third behind Saudi Arabia and Japan in the second round of qualifiers, which meant we had to play two more play-off games to qualify. These were played in June in Qatar. This was good for us in a few ways, as we played some games there during COVID. We had won all our games there and the players got to play in the new-build World Cup stadiums.

Before our first game we played Jordan in a friendly; Arnie and I made a very bold decision to change our centre-backs, as we felt we needed more leadership and quality on the ball. This was something Arnie wasn't given enough credit for as it was a big decision. In came Bailey Wright, who played his club football for Sunderland, and Kye Rowles as Milos Degenek only arrived a day before that game so wasn't ready to play. They both did extremely well and Arnie and I felt that we shouldn't change for the first play-off game against UAE.

It was a tense game, but we beat them 2-1. It was quite convincing in the end, and both Bailey and Kye were excellent. So again, we didn't feel any need to change it for the game against Peru. Degenek, who played a lot of our qualification games, unfortunately, missed out playing because of how events unfolded and how well Bailey and Kye had played. Now it was Peru's turn.

We had already played and trained in the air-conditioned Ahmed bin Ali Stadium, so we felt that this could play to our advantage. Peru never even did a session before the game as they only arrived two days before. We knew there would be a lot of passionate Peruvian fans who were certain Peru would qualify.

Like we did during the Asia Cup in 2019, we practised penalties. I would run those penalty sessions at the end of a normal session. Graham would take all the players in the centre circle and would play a big rondo. I would have five players at a time walking up to the penalty spot and then have them take a penalty. I would look for how assured players were when taking one. How hard and accurate they would shoot and what their run-up would be like. We would do this at least three or four times so I would have a good idea who our best penalty takers were.

Then I would always have three options available. Option one, who would take the penalties and in what order if all our best penalty takers were still on the pitch. Option two, who would fill the spot if we made two or three changes and would that affect the order. Option three, if it goes beyond the first five penalties, who are number six to 10 ?

During the preparation of those play-off games, John Crawley, our goalkeeper coach, had already discussed with me that he was keen to replace Matty Ryan for Andrew Redmayne if it would come to a shoot-out as he felt that Andrew (Redders) had a better record. We agreed and discussed it with Arnie who backed the idea. We also agreed that we would not inform Matty about this, so he could keep the full focus on the game.

Perú was a different kettle of fish as they were a typical South American team, all based on slow possession and working themselves up the pitch. Our strategy was to throw something at them they wouldn't expect. A high aggressive press that didn't allow them any time on the ball. The boys did terrific. We created a number of chances but, like Peru, we didn't score.

Extra time remained goalless so we ended up with another penalty shootout.

"All over to you now," Arnie said when he walked past me. I had it all sorted. We did make a substitution just before the end with Craig Goodwin coming on for Azis Behich, as I knew Craig was a certainty, and Redders came on for Matty Ryan, who looked a bit confused when his number came up. I got everybody together in a huddle and told them: "This is why we've been practising penalties. For these moments. We are ready! Focus and just put the ball in the back of the net. Stay calm no matter what happens. Don't let your emotions get the better of you whether we or them score or miss. It's all about the final penalty! And believe me – we will be going to the World Cup."

I felt calm and relaxed, even when Martin Boyle saw the first penalty saved. It wasn't a bad penalty, just a good save. I thought that if we had to miss one it probably would be best to miss the first one as we would have time to come back as I couldn't see Peru scoring them all. Next, Peru scored. Aaron Mooy was up next. I must give a special mention to him as Aaron hadn't played a single football match since early February. Andrew Clark, our strength and conditioning guy, had given him a fitness programme and flew over to Scotland to do some work prior to these play-off games. I have to say, I always liked Aaron as a footballer. I already knew him from his time at Huddersfield and Brighton & Hove Albion when he was playing in the Premier League. Calm on the ball, good vision, and great range of passing. But what he did during those two play-off games was exceptional.

Not only did he play the full 90 minutes against UAE, but he also played the full 120-plus minutes against Peru. And now he had to step up to probably take the most important penalty in his career. I thought, when Aaron scores, we are in a good situation. He did. Peru scored also. After Goodwin blasted his pen in the right top corner, Advincula hit the post. Hrustic, Mcalren and Mabil all scored after which Alex Valera's spot-kick was stopped by Redmayne, who had been trying to off-put the Peruvian players with his antics. He would be jumping up and down the line whilst flapping his arms. It paid off in the end and Australia were going to the World Cup for the fifth consecutive time.

Mission accomplished.

What an achievement. This was another milestone in my career and one I would treasure for the rest of my life. A big part of being an assistant is to make sure that the head coach can rely on him when it mattered most. I am proud of the fact that Arnie could.

For me the World Cup in Qatar was special, it felt almost like full circle, as this was the place where my professional coaching career began. Our base camp was at Aspire, a centre of excellence where young Qatari players reside, learn, and play football. The branding company did an outstanding job as the whole building was plastered with Socceroos posters past and present. All the players' names were written on the many pillars in the building as part of the branding. The best part, without doubt, was the green and gold coffee shop where players and staff would congregate and enjoy a special coffee made by our personal barista Alexia.

We lost the opening game 4-1 against the reigning world champions France. For 30 minutes we were brilliant and got our noses in front by a good goal from Craig Goodwin after an excellent cross from Mathew Leckie. We conceded two goals before half-time through Rabiot and Giroud, who capitalised on one of our mistakes. It ended 4-1 through another header from Giroud and a header from Mbappe. In my opinion, it was never a 4-1 game.

Whilst walking through the media mixed zone, I was asked by a journalist if this scoreline was the right reflection and difference in quality and class.

"Maybe, maybe not," I replied. "I think however, that you must see this in a wider perspective."

"What do you mean?"

"First of all, do you agree that the World Cup is the highest stage for players to perform at in their careers? Look at France, England, Germany, or any other European country for that matter. They only have to play eight World Cup qualifying games and the furthest they have to travel is three and a half hours by plane. Australia play eight qualifying games in the first round, thereafter 10 in the second round and if you don't qualify directly you must play two play-off games. In all we travelled over 300,000 kilometres. How can this be a level playing field whereby some countries can qualify for the World Cup by only playing eight games and others must play 18 or even 20. The French team has a market value of over one billion euro whereas the Socceroos are between 30 to 40 million. Forget the names for a second and look at the clubs they play for. We just played against Tottenham Hotspur, Bayern, Liverpool, Bayern, Bayern, Real Madrid, Juventus, Atletico Madrid, PSG, Milan and Barcelona! Now look at us; FC Copenhagen (on the bench) Hearts, Stoke City, Hearts, Dundee United, FC St Pauli, Celtic, Middlesborough, Adelaide, Fagiano Okayama and Melbourne City. Do I have to say more?"

"Oh yeah," he said. "Never looked at it like that, but I can see where you are coming from now."

After the game I said to Arnie that the boys did us proud and reminded him that we had given World Cup debuts to Harry

Souttar, Kye Rowles, Nathanial Atkinson, Riley McGree, and Keanu Baccus. Five Olympians – which underpinned why we coached the Olympic team as well.

We didn't dwell on the defeat against France for too long as Arnie addressed the players to shift our focus directly to Tunisia. The response was magnificent and a great goal from Mitchell Duke set us up nicely for the encounter against Denmark, our last group game. I saw them beat France 2-0 prior to the World Cup in Copenhagen and was very impressed how they played. But for whatever reason, they didn't seem to get it going in their games against Tunisia (0-0) and France (2-1 loss).

We knew that if we could beat Denmark, we would be the greatest Socceroos team ever. Yes, Australia did get out of the group stage in Germany in 2006 by beating Japan 3-1 and drawing with Croatia 2-2. But if we defeated Denmark – and we did – that gave us two World Cup victories, and we both scored from open play and kept two clean sheets. Matthew Beckie's goal on the hour was one I'll remember.

Our confidence was so high that we fancied our chances against Messi's mob, Argentina. It was an incredible game and an unbelievable atmosphere. Fair dos to the Argentina supporters as they were fantastic. The white and light blue colours were everywhere and they never stopped singing. Messi scored to make it 1-0 – a simple and clinical finish after we failed to track him into the box. But we were in the game and were brave on the ball without really creating any chances in the first half. In the 57th minute Alvarez took advantage of a slip-up at the back and made it 2-0. Game over you would say – but no. We kept on going and got one back through Craig Goodwin, whose deflected shot in the 77th minute ended up past Martinez.

Aziz Behich went on a mazy run and dribbled past a few

players into the box but his shot just got blocked. It would've been the goal of the tournament for sure – something Messi would've been jealous of. In the final minutes of the game, we even threw our gentle giant Harry Souttar upfront to force an equaliser. The chance fell for young Garang Kuol but his shot got saved by Martinez. Had that gone in, I promise you, we would've had a good chance to progress to the quarter-final as we would've pushed Argentina all the way.

Argentina went on to win the World Cup. It was Messi's moment; you could see that even for a player who has won as much as him, winning in Qatar was the pinnacle. One of the greatest ever now has the medal he had seemingly coveted for most of the latter stage of his career.

Many observers saw the moment as the opportune time to declare Messi as the best player of all time. For me – the romantic in me always leans towards Pele. He was the crusader; everything that all the greats did after, he'd already done, and he won three World Cups.

The more acute comparison was Messi against Ronaldo, particularly in light of Cristiano's second exit from United. I always found it an unnecessary comparison which did a disservice to both of them. How fortunate have we been to see them both? How much did they need each other to inspire them to heights that seemed almost unthinkable? The conversation in general was a disservice to other greats like Di Stefano. Puskas. Cruyff. Beckenbauer. Charlton. Best. Eusebio. Maradona. Zico. Zidane. Romario. Artists, all of them. I say stick Pelé at the head of the table, and everyone else is joining him on the table, on par.

The subject of who is the greatest I've ever coached is different. For that, I have to say Cristiano, and I was glad to have played a small part in a sensational career. It was so exciting to work with a player of such enormous ability and potential. He went to Spain and Italy and was outstanding. His second exit from Old Trafford was not ideal; I just hope that over time, the relationship between Cristiano and Manchester United supporters retains its strength.

Back to Australia, naturally we were disappointed by the elimination and the nature of it. I was desperate to play Holland in the quarter-final for obvious reasons. That would have made it very special, very emotional. More than that, it would have set us apart from the other teams in Australian football history even more. Maybe it's a blessing in disguise that it happened the way that it did, because if we had, how do you follow it? We can now have an ambition to get to the last 16 again and maybe even further. We can dream. I am so proud of the journey we've taken – the sacrifices and the commitments we made to get there. Our success lies in the positive perception of the people who watched Australia play.

I have received offers to go back to working with clubs, but the truth of the matter is that I have loved my time with the Australian team. It gives me fulfilment in so many ways. International football is the purest form of professional football that currently exists.

At international level you must select the best players available, make them gel as a team and make them play to their strengths. There is no transfer market and no agent interference, etc. It's where coaching really needs to make a difference as contact time with the players is limited. As a coach, what could be better than going to the Olympics and possibly to the World Cup? I also get to travel around the world, which I absolutely love, and spend time enjoying many different cultures.

Chapter Twenty

FULL CIRCLE

IN 1993, when I was on one of my coaching courses with David Burnside in the UK, there was a small van that pulled up selling the shirts of all the different English clubs. I decided to buy one. I could have gone for any shirt from that van. There was no reason for me to favour any side, but I was drawn to a red one with laces. It was the name that stood out for me: "Manchester United."

Back then, if you said those words, you instantly thought of Bobby Charlton, George Best, Denis Law. I bought the shirt as a present for my brother Theo, who I had borrowed money from to make the video that launched my coaching career.

Life, as I've learned, can take you on some incredibly unpredictable journeys. There was no real reason for me to pick up that shirt in particular. It is one of those peculiar coincidences that eight years later the club would employ me, and I would go on to enjoy so many great moments.

Maybe I am romanticising a little; maybe there was a subconscious affinity that was always there. Arnold Muhren, the Dutch playmaker, scoring in the 1983 FA Cup final? I don't know. I do feel a deep connection to Manchester United. That much is undeniable.

Manchester is home now. From the moment we arrived there was something about the place. The club, and Les Kershaw in particular, were brilliant in helping us settle. Les connected with me with an estate agent and advised me to drive around the local area to get a feel for the place. The estate agent found a few houses for us; the last on the list was in Wilmslow. It had a beautiful garden; that was a key thing I wanted, for the kids. I told Les: "The quicker we settle, the more comfortable I'll feel working." We've been in the same place for 22 years.

United were always welcoming. During my time at the club, I was able to entertain a lot of visitors, especially from Holland, when they came over to watch a game. In a few cases I was allowed to bring them to Carrington to watch training. One day it was the veterans' football team from my local club. I tipped Sir Alex off about our team-manager Theo and what sort of character he was. Sir Alex played the game brilliantly.

"I've heard all about you Theo and I even know that your nickname is Schmidthuber," he said laughing out loud (Aron Schmidthuber was a German referee).

All the visitors that came to Carrington were very impressed with the facilities but even more with the warm hospitality they felt around the place. As long as Sir Alex knew who was coming, and when, he was fine with it. If he didn't, he could get in a real strop.

One day Eric Steele invited Tony Franken, who I later worked with for the Socceroos. Whilst the session was going on, the gaffer spotted a somehow dodgy individual observing the goalkeeper training.

"Hey," he shouted to Tony who was unaware what was going on. "What are you doing here?"

Eric was quick to the rescue and reminded the manager who Tony was and that he asked for permission a few weeks ago.

"Bloody Alzheimer's," the manager joked.

I must give a special mention to two pensioners, Mary and Milton Charnley, who also came to visit Carrington. I got to know them as they were related to Rob and Sue Charnley, who were friends of ours. Sue was a regular at Carrington. She would entertain sponsors for Epson when they would come to visit. Mary and Milton were lifelong die-hard United supporters, both in their 70s but still very much aware of what was going on with United. I spoke to Scholes and Giggs before training and asked if they could spare a minute after training and take some pictures with them. They were both brilliant. I still remember Mary saying to them: "Thanks guys for all the pleasure you gave us over all these years."

That really resonated with me, and I am sure it did with Paul and Ryan as well. United was like a family. It never loses that feeling.

As I come to the conclusion of my book, I am forced to consider the prospect of fulfilment. If it was all to end now, then I admit I do feel fulfilled. But I still have ambition, a yearning for adventure. To do something new. I never look beyond my current commitment for that because if I did, that would be unfair. I would not be giving it my full attention and we demand that from the players, so we must make sure they trust us. The truth is that there is plenty of potential with what we can achieve with Australia. The older players will have valuable experience to help the younger ones breaking through. I would love to say to the players – let's win some silverware. Let's win the Asia Cup again. Let's qualify and go one step further in the World Cup.

Our mantra has always been we expect to win every game.

This doesn't mean we would win every game, but it says everything about our intention how we would approach any opponent. This approach subconsciously instils confidence and belief in our players and that was evident during the World cup in Qatar.

If you were to really push me, then I could put some options on the table about things I haven't done. As a coach I've worked with amateur and professional players from a young age through to senior level. Almost everything that you could find in the game, I've enjoyed some experience in. I have coached girls, but I haven't coached a professional women's team. I haven't coached with my country at an international tournament. Having experienced what the 2022 World Cup meant to Australians, I can only imagine what it would feel like to be involved with Holland. The truth of the matter is that I really had no right to have that conviction to become a professional football coach; it was based on nothing but my own bloody-mindedness. My dad wasn't a professional – so what else instilled it within me? It's something I've been thinking about as I come to the end of writing this.

I know that the period between 2006 and 2013 will probably represent the most successful time of my career. I'm not only comfortable with that, I'm also happy with it, I'm grateful for it, and I would go back to my first day at United in 2001 and speak of the responsibility and privilege of implementing my ideas on their precious youth system; that 12-year span was surely one of the best of my career in football. To move forward, to work with the individuals and the reserve team. It was equally as exciting to see the success of the youth development programme, to witness how those young players came on. From that time, to then be part of the most successful period in the history of Manchester United. To be given such trust from the greatest manager in the world. It has been a privilege.

I can remember vividly the hundreds of times I would sit next to him at a game.

The full-time whistle went.

Manchester United had won.

He'd tap me on my knee. "Well done."

The satisfaction from that was all I needed. Our little team; Mick, Tony, Steve, Eric, Simon. We all had our input. We all contributed. It was a close-knit circle, and the proof of our successful working relationship was found in the performances and results on the pitch; the results of the biggest club in the country. I was, and remain, proud, to be a part of that.

We were such an exciting team to watch. I watch those games back sometimes – the speed, flexibility and unpredictability in our play was outstanding. Breathtaking. The goals are consequences of possession and rhythm or pace, power, penetration, and unpredictability. The pride I feel recalling the thousands of sessions we had at Carrington helping this group of sensational footballers maximise their potential is very special. We were Manchester United. We did what we wanted.

Could it be done again? Could the journey I went on at United be replicated? With the investment of time and support I do not see a reason why it couldn't. If I was given the same opportunity, I am certain I could yield a similar result. I'd do most of the things the same but add the 'Football starts at home' program to encourage the parents as it gives the young player a stronger entry level.

The biggest truth in football is that the players who have the ability to dominate a 1v1 are the ones who make the biggest difference in the game. It's not easy. You must invest countless hours. I saw Marcus Rashford score a great goal against Arsenal where he went past a player and scored from long range. It was straight from the Cliff or Littleton Road. He didn't even have to think about it.

The way I view fulfilment is through my experiences and achievements. Doing something you love doing every day. Working with great people and sharing those incredible achievements and experiences with family and friends. But without doubt, the greatest fulfilment of all is my own family. I still remember the day that I confronted my wife – then girlfriend – Marieke, by saying: "I am going to Qatar to coach football and I would love you to come with me." Without any hesitation she said: "Yes, I am coming with you." It was the start of an incredible journey, not the least as we had to get married as you could not live as boy and girlfriend in Qatar.

We have three amazing kids who funnily enough have all ended up with jobs in football. Our eldest son Joppe is the lead analyst and coach at Stockport County. He is definitely a chip off the old block as he is very passionate about coaching. He has a great understanding of the game, and he is a very promising coach.

Our daughter Pien is a sports presenter, reporter and football commentator currently working for *Sky*, *BBC Sport*, and *Radio 5 Live*. It was a great experience for us both to be involved in the World Cup in Qatar.

Melle, our youngest son, is playing for Vitesse, Arnhem. He was on Manchester United's Academy books from the age of six until 15 after which he moved to Preston. Two years later, he moved to second division team RKC Waalwijk in Holland with whom he won promotion to the Eredivisie in 2019. It was one of the craziest games I ever witnessed. After a 0-0 draw at home, they managed a 4-5 win away against Go Ahead Eagles.

Football – bloody hell! But those are the sort of experiences and achievements that will stay with you forever.

What they all have in common is that they all strive for perfection. Joppe and Pien's preparation for games is meticulous, whilst Melle has this composure and calmness on the ball that makes him stand out whenever he plays. Without doubt they are all destined to do bigger and better things. It's also great to see how they feed and support each other. But above all they're great human beings, something Marieke and I are very proud of.

Since the 3rd of February 2023, we are the proud grandparents of our first grandchild Frenkie. Joppe and his partner Elle grew up together and they would often play footie in the back of our garden. Elle in her own right was a great footballer and would run rings around Joppe, Melle and other boys. In her youth she was a very promising player for Manchester United girls. Now, so many years later they make a great couple and proud parents.

My intention when writing this book was to share the experiences of my journey in coaching and in life thus far. To give readers a good idea of how my journey in coaching started as a 16-year-old and how it developed from Beugen to Manchester to Sydney with many stopovers in between.

I wanted to give the readers an insight into all the ingredients that contribute to success; to understand the culture and identity of Manchester United, the leadership and man-management of Sir Alex Ferguson, the unique corporation between all staff, player development, training principles and match day preparation.

The experience of being the best is something I find difficult to articulate. I can remember the first time I tried to lift the

Champions League trophy; I was surprised by how heavy it was. The Premier League trophy was even heavier. But they're two stunning, beautiful trophies to lift and the privilege of being able to do so is something I'm so proud of. The definition of success changes according to perception and expectation. What Graham and I achieved with Australia at the World Cup, relative to what people expected, was arguably even better than some of the teams who went further than us in the tournament. There's always more to be achieved; but it comes in different forms.

I enjoy working with Graham very much, though I accept that I will forever be linked with Sir Alex first and foremost when my name is ever mentioned publicly. I am grateful for that. I can't tell you my greatest individual memory of him; there are too many moments to mention, enough to fill another book. I will try and leave you with an idea of the feeling I get when I think about our time working together; I smile, thinking of the fact that each day had some laughter in it. He is a tremendously funny person with a cutting sense of humour. Most of all, I admired his ability to create an environment, at the club with the highest pressure in football, that was always completely free of it.

To take what he inherited and to build three great teams, over three different eras – it has never been done to such a high standard. Those teams played magnificent football, different kinds of football, and they were all multi-skilled and capable of holding their own against any opponent. I observed the last six years of his career and worked closely with him; I marvel at how he was able to delegate so skillfully and still maintain complete control at the same time, liberating us to feel complete freedom.

He is the greatest manager in the history of the game, of that

I have no doubt. It is probably an inevitability that no matter what happens from this moment on, when people say my name, they'll mention Manchester United, and they'll mention Sir Alex Ferguson. That is an enormous privilege.

Acknowledgements

WHEN writing this autobiography, I found myself turning my attention to the people who have made a significant difference and contribution to my life, particularly my life in football. Big or small, they all add up. Unfortunately there are too many to name them all. I thank you all, you know who you are, for what you've done for me, with all my heart, to make my life in football so special.

I would like to express my special thanks to the people who have been at the forefront of my journey as both a person and a coach. To my parents, Albert and Lies, who brought me into this world in 1964. My brothers, sisters and close family who have always supported me on this journey. My close friends in Holland, England, and other parts of the world, who have always shown a keen interest and helped me along the way. I would like to thank Wiel Coerver, the inspiration for me to start coaching at the age of 16.

He truly shaped my football philosophy and showed me the importance of skill development at grassroots and beyond. A special thanks goes to the great Dave Mackay, Dave Richardson and Les Kershaw who were very instrumental in bringing me to Manchester United. Thanks to John and Matthew Peters for permission to use their images in this book.

Many thanks to all the MU players I worked with during my time at the club. It was an absolute privilege to work alongside a group with such incredible talent, commitment and hunger for success. True legends of Manchester United and the game.

It's really difficult for me to describe the gratitude I feel towards Sir Alex Ferguson. He truly is the person that shaped my life in football and I loved every minute of it. I thank him for bringing me to Manchester United and the opportunities he has given me along the way. The joy and laughter we shared and the trust I received in trying to be the best I could be.

As my coaching journey continues, I would also like to give a special thanks to Graham (Arnie, as everyone calls him) Arnold, the current national team coach of the Socceroos. Thanks for trusting me in being your assistant and right-hand man and giving me the opportunity to fulfil one of my lifelong ambitions to go to the World Cup and be part of the greatest Socceroos team ever. I truly enjoyed working with Arnie. A fantastic person who bleeds gold and green, but above all, a very good coach and manager. I look forward to creating more memories and history together.

Last but not least, my biggest thanks goes out to my family. I can't tell you how proud I am of my kids Joppe, Pien, and Melle who continue to pursue their own careers in football. Thanks for the joy you've given me over so many years.

Needless to say, all these experiences and achievements come with a price and spending time away from my family was a sacrifice I had to make. I love travelling, still do! My life in football has given me the opportunity to travel to all continents in the world. Seeing beautiful countries, cities and stadiums. Meeting great people and making new friends. But there is no better feeling than going home to my family and grandchild Frenkie. And Max, my loyal golden retriever who is always happy to see me when coming back home. Thank you Joppe, Pien, and Melle for making all those travels worthwhile and I wish you all the very best on your own journeys in life and football.

There is only one more person to thank and show my gratitude towards, which is my wife Marieke. From the very first moment until this day I have felt your unconditional love and support. You have been the cornerstone and rock of our family. Thanks for making my life so meaningful and thanks for all those wonderful moments we shared together.

Love you, Always x
Love, Learn, Live, Laugh, Legacy.
My life in football.